"In taking us straight to the heart of [the] ... us magnificently. We so need to get [...] Scriptures get into us. The fact that P[...] such submission to Biblical revelation means that we a[...] helped to be shaped by the Bible's teaching."

– Terry Virgo

"Phil makes the deep truths of Scripture alive and accessible. If you want to grow in your understanding of each book of the Bible, then buy these books and let them change your life!"

– PJ Smyth – GodFirst Church, Johannesburg, South Africa

"Most commentaries are dull. These are alive. Most commentaries are for scholars. These are for you!"

– Canon Michael Green

"These notes are amazingly good. Lots of content and depth of research, yet packed in a Big Breakfast that leaves the reader well fed and full. Bible notes often say too little, yet larger commentaries can be dull - missing the wood for the trees. Phil's insights are striking, original, and fresh, going straight to the heart of the text and the reader! Substantial yet succinct, they bristle with amazing insights and life applications, compelling us to read more. Bible reading will become enriched and informed with such a scintillating guide. Teachers and preachers will find nuggets of pure gold here!"

– Greg Haslam – Westminster Chapel, London, UK

"The Bible is living and dangerous. The ones who teach it best are those who bear that in mind – and let the author do the talking. Phil has written these studies with a sharp mind and a combination of creative application and reverence."

– Joel Virgo – Leader of Newday Youth Festival

"Phil Moore's new commentaries are outstanding: biblical and passionate, clear and well-illustrated, simple and profound. God's Word comes to life as you read them, and the wonder of God shines through every page."

– Andrew Wilson – Author of Incomparable and GodStories

"Want to understand the Bible better? Don't have the time or energy to read complicated commentaries? The book you have in your hand could be the answer. Allow Phil Moore to explain and then apply God's message to your life. Think of this book as the Bible's message distilled for everyone."

– Adrian Warnock – Christian blogger

"Phil Moore presents Scripture in a dynamic, accessible and relevant way. The bite-size chunks – set in context and grounded in contemporary life – really make the make the Word become flesh and dwell among us."

– Dr David Landrum – The Bible Society

"Through a relevant, very readable, up to date storying approach, Phil Moore sets the big picture, relates God's Word to today and gives us fresh insights to increase our vision, deepen our worship, know our identity and fire our imagination. Highly recommended!"

- Geoff Knott – former CEO of Wycliffe Bible Translators UK

"What an exciting project Phil has embarked upon! These accessible and insightful books will ignite the hearts of believers, inspire the minds of preachers and help shape a new generation of men and women who are seeking to learn from God's Word."

- David Stroud – Newfrontiers and ChristChurch London

For more information about the Straight to the Heart series, please go to **www.philmoorebooks.com**.

STRAIGHT TO
THE HEART OF

Matthew

60 BITE-SIZED INSIGHTS

Phil Moore

MONARCH
BOOKS

Oxford, UK & Grand Rapids, Michigan, USA

First published in the UK in 2010 by Monarch Books
(a publishing imprint of Lion Hudson plc)
Wilkinson House, Jordan Hill Road, Oxford OX2 8DR, England
Tel: +44 (0)1865 302750 Fax: +44 (0)1865 302757
Email: monarch@lionhudson.com
www.lionhudson.com

ISBN 978 1 85424 988 3

Distributed by:
UK: Marston Book Services, PO Box 269, Abingdon, Oxon, OX14 4YN
USA: Kregel Publications, PO Box 2607, Grand Rapids, Michigan 49501

British Library Cataloguing Data
A catalogue record for this book is available from the British Library.

Printed and bound in the UK by JF Print Ltd.

This book is for my children –
Isaac, Noah, and Esther.
My greatest prayer for your young lives
is that, just like Matthew, you may know
and love Jesus more and more.

CONTENTS

ACT TWO: KINGDOM MISSION

ACT THREE: KINGDOM MESSAGE

ACT FOUR: KINGDOM COMMUNITY

ACT FIVE: KINGDOM JUDGMENT

EPILOGUE: THE PROCLAMATION OF THE KINGDOM

About the *Straight to the Heart* Series

On his eightieth birthday, Sir Winston Churchill dismissed the compliment that he was the "lion" who had defeated Nazi Germany in World War Two. He told the Houses of Parliament that *"It was a nation and race dwelling all around the globe that had the lion's heart. I had the luck to be called upon to give the roar."*

I hope that God speaks to you very powerfully through the "roar" of the books in the *Straight to the Heart* series. I hope they help you to understand the books of the Bible and the message that the Holy Spirit inspired their authors to write. I hope that they help you to hear God's voice challenging you, and that they provide you with a springboard for further journeys into each book of Scripture for yourself.

But when you hear my "roar", I want you to know that it comes from the heart of a much bigger "lion" than me. I have been shaped by a whole host of great Christian thinkers and preachers from around the world, and I want to give due credit to at least some of them here:

Terry Virgo, David Stroud, John Hosier, Adrian Holloway, Greg Haslam, Lex Loizides, and all those who lead the Newfrontiers family of churches; friends and encouragers, such as Stef Liston, Joel Virgo, Stuart Gibbs, Scott Taylor, Nick Sharp, Nick Derbridge, Phil Whittall, and Kevin and Sarah Aires; Tony Collins, Jenny Ward and Simon Cox at Monarch books; Malcolm Kayes and all the elders of The Coign Church, Woking; my fellow elders and church members here at Queens Road Church, Wimbledon;

my great friend Andrew Wilson – without your friendship, encouragement and example, this series would never have happened.

I would like to thank my parents, my brother Jonathan, and my in-laws, Clive and Sue Jackson. Dad – your example birthed in my heart the passion that brought this series into being. I didn't listen to all you said when I was a child, but I couldn't ignore the way you got up at five o'clock every morning to pray, read the Bible and worship, because of your radical love for God and for his Word. I'd like to thank my children – Isaac, Noah, and Esther – for keeping me sane when publishing deadlines were looming. But most of all, I'm grateful to my incredible wife, Ruth – my friend, encourager, corrector, and helper.

You all have the lion's heart, and you have all developed the lion's heart in me. I count it an enormous privilege to be the one who was chosen to sound the lion's roar.

So welcome to the *Straight to the Heart* series. My prayer is that you will let this roar grip your own heart too – for the glory of the great Lion of the Tribe of Judah, the Lord Jesus Christ!

Introduction:
The Revolution Has Begun

Above his head they placed the written charge
against him: "This is Jesus, the King of the Jews."

(Matthew 27:37)

Jesus of Nazareth sparked a massive revolution. A lot of people miss that fact. They are so used to the long-haired, blue-eyed, white-robed storybook Jesus that they imagine he was about as tame and domesticated as many of his churches today. But he wasn't. Jesus was a radical, dangerous revolutionary who made big waves and powerful enemies. He was not killed for preaching pithy parables, but because he claimed to be King.

Jesus chose an incendiary word to announce his Revolution. The word *kingdom* has lost its edge in our world of democratic republics and constitutional monarchies, but in the first-century Roman Empire it was explosive. That was a world where kings could execute their enemies without a trial and slaughter hundreds of babies on a whim.[1] It was a world where kings brooked no rival and where sedition was quickly silenced. It was a world where few messages were more dangerous than the claim that *"the kingdom of heaven is near"*.[2] If Jesus was King, it meant that Caesar was not. This was inflammatory talk of the highest order.

After three years, Jesus was arrested and put on trial for his life. He stood before the Jewish Sanhedrin, before Herod and before Governor Pilate, who was the Roman emperor's man in

---

[1] Matthew 2:16; 14:3–11; Luke 13:1.
[2] Matthew 3:2, 4:17 & 10:7.

Palestine. He was accused of treason because he claimed to be King, and his enemies insisted that *"anyone who claims to be a king opposes Caesar"*.[3] He was tortured and crucified under the charge that he was *"the King of the Jews"*,[4] and when he died his tomb was guarded by a group of Roman soldiers. Scoreline: the Roman emperor *one*, Jesus of Nazareth *nil*. The King of the Jews was dead and the Revolution was over.

Well, not exactly. In fact, not at all. Three days later the corpse disappeared and rumours began to spread that he had been raised back to life. What was more, his followers began to preach that his death had not only failed to prevent the revolution, it had somehow always been part of the plan through which he would bring it to pass. Within a generation, the Jewish state was dead but their King had spread his rule across the Roman Empire. Within three centuries, even the Roman emperor himself worshipped at Jesus' feet and proclaimed him King of kings. Now, 2,000 years later, he is still by far the most loved, most worshipped, most followed and most obeyed person in the world. Google his name and you will find 170 million websites to visit. Type his name into Amazon.com and you can choose from 405,000 books about him. Search in any Western town or village and you will find a church that bears his name. The end of the Revolution? No, just the beginning.

Matthew was one of Jesus' original twelve followers. He had once been an eager employee of the Roman Empire, but when he heard Jesus' message about the Kingdom of God he quickly deserted Emperor Tiberius to follow King Jesus.[5] Matthew invested his life in Jesus' Revolution, and he wants us to do the same. That is why he wrote his gospel.

---

[3] John 19:12–15.

[4] Matthew 27:11, 29, 37, 42.

[5] Matthew 9:9. Matthew was a tax collector who worked the Capernaum road on the trade route between Damascus and Egypt. He had chosen to serve the Roman occupiers of Palestine, and was a small cog in the massive Roman fiscal machine.

Matthew wrote the fullest and most systematic account of the life, death and resurrection of Jesus. He groups his material by theme rather than by strict chronology, because he wants us to respond to five central acts in the drama of King Jesus. He uses the Greek word *basileia*, or *kingdom*, fifty-six times in his twenty-eight chapters, stressing the revolutionary call of Jesus the King and of his Kingdom. He divides each of his five acts into Jesus' *words* and Jesus' *deeds*, so that we will not mistake Jesus for a mere lecturer in religious philosophy, but grasp that he is the-King-on-a-Mission and that he wants to enlist us as his willing followers. Matthew's structure is:

Chapters 1–4
Prologue: The Coming of the Kingdom

Chapters 5–9
Act One: Kingdom Lifestyle (*words* in chapters 5–7, *deeds* in chapters 8–9)

Chapters 10–12
Act Two: Kingdom Mission (*words* in chapter 10, *deeds* in chapters 11–12)

Chapters 13–17
Act Three: Kingdom Message (*words* in chapter 13, *deeds* in chapters 14–17)

Chapters 18–22
Act Four: Kingdom Community (*words* in chapter 18, *deeds* in chapters 19–22)

Chapters 23–27
Act Five: Kingdom Judgment (*words* in chapters 23–25, *deeds* in chapters 26–27)

Chapter 28
Epilogue: The Proclamation of the Kingdom

Matthew's gospel is a revolutionary pamphlet, which shook the ancient world and still shakes the world today. A few years ago, I took a sleeper train across western China as part of a backpacking holiday and fell into conversation with an old man and his son, who spoke good English. When I felt the time was right, I reached into my bag and offered them a Chinese Bible, which I had smuggled into the country. The old man caught sight of it and held it in his hands like a prized jewel. *"Where did you get this book?"* he demanded, before telling me his story. His father had been an itinerant evangelist during the great upheavals of the 1960s. One day, the communists had discovered that he was preaching the Gospel. They confiscated his Bibles, took him to a prison camp, and ordered him to recant his faith. The old man – still a bewildered young boy when the soldiers came – told me that he had never seen his father again. He and his mother had been blacklisted by the local party officials, and he had grown up in gruelling poverty because his father proclaimed that Jesus was King and therefore Mao Zedong wasn't. I shall never forget the look on that old Chinese man's face as he was reunited with a Bible after forty years apart. His face reminds me that Jesus of Nazareth is a dangerous revolutionary who demands that we give up our whole lives to follow him, and no one else.

I have written this book to take you on a tour of Matthew's gospel and to bring you face to face with Jesus as Matthew knew him. It doesn't aim to cover every verse, but I pray that its sixty short chapters will draw you deeper into God's Kingdom and the radical message of King Jesus.

Get ready for an adventure with Jesus Christ. The Revolution has begun.

Prologue:

The Coming of the Kingdom

One of Us (1:1–17)

A record of the genealogy of Jesus Christ the son of David, the son of Abraham.

(Matthew 1:1)

Celebrities on the TV series *Who Do You Think You Are?* receive expert help in tracing their family tree.[1] A wide range of people have appeared on the show, but they all have one thing in common: they all want to learn that their ancestors were good, worthy and noble. Jeremy Clarkson's face lights up when he discovers that his ancestor was the inventor of the Kilner jar. Jerry Springer says a silent prayer as he visits the place where his Jewish grandmother was gassed by the Nazis. Patsy Kensit weeps when she discovers that her granddad was a criminal who barely knew her father. People trace their family tree because they hope to find great ancestors and a fine lineage.

Matthew starts his gospel with Jesus' family tree, and it's not pretty. More than that, Matthew seems to go out of his way to demonstrate that it's not pretty. He is descended from Judah and his daughter-in-law *Tamar*, who dressed up as a prostitute to trick her backslidden father-in-law into having sex with her.[2] He is the descendant of *Rahab*, the prostitute of Jericho, who was saved when her city was destroyed because she hid two spies on the roof of her brothel and lied to protect their lives.[3] He

---

[1] The BBC series has proven so successful that the British show has been exported all around the world. Lisa Kudrow, who played Phoebe in *Friends*, presents the American version of the show on NBC.

[2] Genesis 38.

[3] Joshua 2. Rahab was saved from the ruins of Jericho in c.1406 BC and Boaz was born over 200 years later, so the Greek *ek tēs rachab* means "whose

is descended from *Ruth*, the widowed migrant-worker from the Gentile nation of Moab, whose people were so corrupt that they were excluded from the presence of God.[4] He is the descendant of *Bathsheba*, the mother of Solomon, who committed adultery with David and became his queen even while her murdered husband's grave was still fresh. Matthew emphasizes this sin by referring to her as *"Uriah's wife"*,[5] and then adds to his list *Rehoboam, Jehoram, Ahaz* and *Manasseh*, the wickedest kings of Judah. Finally, he tells us that Jesus was the son of the Virgin Mary, conceived so miraculously that even her fiancé thought that she was guilty of illicit sex before marriage.[6] When the actress Patsy Kensit discovered her own family tree, she told the BBC that *"It hit me so hard, I stopped washing my hair and wearing make-up."* She would not have coped with a sordid family tree like Jesus.

So what is Matthew's point here? He wants us to grasp that Jesus is the Son of God,[7] the promised Messiah who ushers in the Kingdom of God,[8] so what possible benefit can he derive from starting with this terrible ancestry? Actually, he does so in order to make a very important point, and unless we grasp what he is saying we will misunderstand the very nature of *"the kingdom of God"*.

Every film-maker and novelist knows that the opening scene is the crucial moment in which they either win or lose

---

ancestor was Rahab", not *"whose mother was Rahab"*.

[4] Deuteronomy 23:2–4. Ruth's story is told in the Old Testament book that bears her name.

[5] The NIV translates this as *"David was the father of Solomon, whose mother had been Uriah's wife,"* but the Greek says literally that *"David was the father of Solomon by the [wife] of Uriah."* The Law of Moses commanded that David and Bathsheba should be executed for their sin. See Leviticus 20:10 and Deuteronomy 22:22.

[6] Matthew 1:18–19.

[7] Matthew 4:3, 6; 8:29; 14:33; 26:63–64; 27:40, 43, 54.

[8] Matthew 1:1, 17; 2:4; 16:16; 22:42; 23:10; 24:5; 26:63–64. The word *Christ* is the Greek equivalent of the Hebrew word *Messiah*.

their audience's attention. Matthew knew that. God knows that. And yet God inspired Matthew to begin his gospel, and the New Testament itself, with a genealogy that reads like a *Who's Who?* of the villains of ancient Israel. He knew that it would capture the attention of Matthew's original Jewish readership, but he also wants to use them to teach us two important principles that lie at the heart of his Kingdom Revolution.

The first thing he wants us to grasp is that his Kingdom is about *God coming down to save humankind.* If that sounds obvious, remember that religion is not about this at all. Religion is always about *humankind stepping up to reach God.* Matthew reminds us in verse 23 that the Gospel of Jesus Christ is very different from religion. Isaiah prophesied that *"'The virgin will be with child and will give birth to a son, and they will call him Immanuel' – which means 'God with us'",* and Matthew makes it clear that Jesus is *God-With-Us,* God really and truly with us. He did not come down reservedly, willing to become a man in a palace, or a Jewish nobleman with impeccable family credentials. He exchanged the highest glories of heaven for the lowest depths of humanity. He humbled himself all the way, to become *God-With-Us* and to pave a way for *Us-With-God.*

Jesus' abject humanity is not incidental to the Gospel; it is essential to the Gospel. Because he became fully human (while remaining fully God), he was able to save the human race by undoing through his righteous life all that Adam lost through his sin.[9] Hebrews 2:17 tells us that Jesus **"had to** *be made like his brothers in every way"* in order to deal with sin, and Paul tells us that we will only be raised from the dead and live forever with God because Jesus has been bodily raised as our human forerunner.[10] The fact that God has stooped down to become the man Jesus is one of the reasons why he is not simply *one* way

---

[9] Luke 19:10; Romans 5:18–19; 1 Corinthians 15:45.

[10] This is what the Old Testament word *firstfruits* conveys in 1 Corinthians 15:23.

to God but the only way to God. *"For there is one God and one mediator between God and men, the man Christ Jesus."*[11]

The second thing that God wants us to grasp is that his Kingdom is about *God's grace to people who deserve nothing* but his anger and judgment. Jesus is the Seed of Abraham, the moon-worshipping Mesopotamian whom God chose to be his prophet and the ancestor of the Saviour of the World.[12] Jesus is the Son of David, the shepherd-boy God chose and anointed to found a dynasty of kings – a man who sinned but who knew how to repent.[13] Jesus is the descendant of Zerubbabel, the man who was next in line for David's throne but whose claim was now so defunct that his heir Joseph was working as a manual labourer in the building trade.[14] Matthew wants us to grasp that Jesus came to a human race steeped in sin, so that he could outweigh our sin with even more of God's grace.

So Matthew's opening words are not a dull series of names to endure, like a long list of credits before the real action begins. They are a clue, right from the outset, that God's Kingdom is different, and far better than, the one people were expecting. He was not born into a palace to rub shoulders with the rich and mighty, but into a dirty stable to rub shoulders with sinners, Gentiles, outcasts and rejects – anyone who is humble enough to cry out for a Saviour and believe that they have found him in the carpenter's boy from Galilee.

He is *God-With-Us*, the humble Saviour who dived deep into the human problem as the divine infiltrator, and who worked God's solution from the inside out.

---

[11] 1 Timothy 2:5.

[12] Genesis 12:2–3, 7; 22:18; Galatians 3:16.

[13] 1 Chronicles 17:11–14; Psalm 89:35–36; Isaiah 9:6–7; Jeremiah 23:5–6.

[14] Matthew makes it clear that Jesus was the biological descendant of Mary but not Joseph (the Greek *ex hēs egennēthē* means that he was *born of her*), yet he gives us Jesus' legal ancestry via Joseph because it was through his adoptive father that he was the perfect heir to the throne of David. He even misses out a few names in order to stylize the genealogy as 14/14/14 generations – twice the biblical number of perfection.

Holy Joe (1:18–25)

*Because Joseph her husband was a righteous man
and did not want to expose her to public disgrace, he
had in mind to divorce her quietly.*

(Matthew 1:19)

In June 2009, the American financier Bernard Madoff was
sentenced to 150 years in prison. For almost two decades, his
Madoff Securities had offered a mouth-watering 10 per cent
return on investments, but he had been uncovered as a fraudster.
Even though his company looked like one of the soundest
financial investments in the world, he was in fact running a
"Ponzi" scheme and had swindled investors of over $65 billion.[1]
One French investment manager committed suicide when he
realized that he had lost $1.4 billion in the scheme.

God had something very precious to invest, and he was very
careful where he put it. He had one precious, only-begotten Son,
Jesus, and he was about to entrust him to a couple of parents on
Planet Earth. Jesus told us that this was like God *selling all he
had"* to buy treasure buried in a field or to buy a pearl of great
price.[2] It must have been even tougher for God the Father to

---

[1] A "Ponzi" scheme is named after the 1920s' fraudster Charles Ponzi, and
pays investors from the money paid in by other investors rather than from real
profits. Such a scheme can go undetected for years and can rob investors
of billions. It is exposed when large numbers of investors try to cash in their
money.

[2] Matthew 13:44–46. Many people assume that we are the investor and that
Jesus tells us that we need to give up all we have for the Kingdom. I don't
think that this is a wrong interpretation, but since *the Lord* is the sower, the
farmer and the fisherman in the other parables in Matthew 13, the primary
interpretation must be to do with *the Lord's* investment to purchase us.

entrust his only Son to a pair of humans than it was for Moses' mother to entrust her baby to the River Nile. Therefore if we want to discover what God prizes highly in his Kingdom, our greatest clue is to consider his big investment decision.

I find it fascinating that God was not swayed by any of the things which attracted investors to Bernard Madoff. The US financier had a solid reputation, a wealthy lifestyle, an impressive track record, natural charm, and the promise of exceptional fortune. God could easily have chosen the same. He could have placed the Messiah in the home of a wealthy nobleman, like the Jewish historian Josephus who boasts in his writings about his impeccable aristocratic and priestly family. He could have placed him with the spiritual élite, in a famous Sadducee family like that of the high priest Caiaphas, or in the home of a prominent Pharisee like the great rabbi Gamaliel or his disciple Saul of Tarsus.[3] But he didn't. He chose a manual labourer called Joseph who lacked even enough influence to get a room in a hotel when his wife was in labour.[4] God also chose Joseph's teenaged sweetheart, Mary, and the two of them were so poor that they offered the Temple sacrifices that were reserved for the lowest of the low.[5] Frankly, God's choice of Joseph and Mary is surprising and bewildering, and it shows that what God values in his Kingdom is very different from what is valued in the world. He chose them because they had three things going for them – three things that God wants to find in us too.

Joseph was very *humble*. He lacked the stylish flair of the rich and famous, but anyone familiar with the Madoff affair knows that wise investors see past superficial charms. Joseph was not self-assertive but meek and gentle, showing astonishing kindness towards his fiancée Mary when he discovered that she was pregnant, and not by him. Despite his sense of betrayal, he decided to break off the engagement quietly to minimize the

---

[3] Acts 5:34; 23:6; 26:5.

[4] Luke 2:4–7.

[5] Luke 2:24 & Leviticus 12:1–8.

pain it would cause her.[6] A lesser man would have retaliated in fury, but this was the humble kind of man whom God prizes in his Kingdom.[7] He was humble before God, observing the ceremonies required by the Mosaic Law, even though he could scarcely afford to lose precious days away from his workshop.[8] God loves humility. He just loves it. There's very little of it around.

Joseph was also a man of great *faith*. He believed the angel's story when Mary told him that she was pregnant. Remember, there was no precedent for what the angel told him, and the Old Testament prophecy which Matthew quotes in verse 23 is not obviously about the mother of the Messiah. Many modern theologians dismiss the idea of the Virgin Birth as too fanciful to believe, but none of them has as much reason to doubt it as Joseph did. I am amazed at the faith of this humble, blue-collar worker from Nazareth, who dared to believe that his pregnant fiancée had truly conceived her baby through the power of the Holy Spirit. He was so full of faith that he had a celibate wedding-night and preserved Mary's virginity after their marriage until the baby was born.[9] I am also amazed at the faith of Mary, who heard from the angel that she was about to be viewed as an immoral woman with an illegitimate baby and yet replied: *"I am the Lord's servant; may it be to me as you have said."*[10]

Joseph was also a man of *instant obedience*. He saw an angel four times in his sleep in the first two chapters of Matthew, and

---

[6] Matthew 1:19 refers to him as Mary's *husband* and says he planned to *divorce* her because engagement in first-century Jewish culture was a much more binding pledge than it is for us today.

[7] Matthew 5:5, 7; 23:12. See also Isaiah 57:15; 66:2; Proverbs 3:34; James 4:6; 1 Peter 5:5–6.

[8] Luke 2:21–24, 39–52.

[9] Some Christian traditions see Mary as a "perpetual virgin" who never had sex with Joseph. I find this impossible to reconcile with the straightforward teaching of Matthew 1:25; 12:46; 13:55.

[10] Luke 1:38. Matthew tells us the nativity story from Joseph's point of view, and Luke tells it from Mary's.

each time he obeyed without delay. He married Mary at once, and woke up his family to flee as refugees to Egypt on the very night that the angel warned him about King Herod's plan.[11] He returned to Judea and then Galilee in swift response to two more angelic visions because he was a man who obeyed rather than just weighed God's Word. Joseph was not just a *"son of David"* by birth, he was a true spiritual son of David, the man whom God found to be *"after my own heart; he will do everything I want him to do."*[12]

The human parents that God chose for his Son are therefore a radical statement of what is and isn't valued in his Kingdom. He is still looking for people today who are like Joseph and Mary, and who can be trusted with his Kingdom. He is utterly unimpressed by your looks, your wealth, your charm, your education, or your breeding. But his eyes rove all over the world in search of any man or woman who is *humble, full of faith* and *swift to obey.*[13]

God is still like the man who saw beautiful treasure hidden in an unimpressive field. He is still like the merchant who sold all he had and invested it in a pearl of great price. He is still the world's greatest investor, searching for this godly character to which he can entrust his Kingdom.

Let's examine the character which is hidden under the surface of our own hearts. Do we have the same humble, faith-filled, obedient heart as Joseph? God calls us to join his revolutionary army of Holy Joes.

---

[11] Matthew 2:13–14. Joseph did not even wait until morning before obeying.
[12] Matthew 1:20 was true biologically, but was also true spiritually based on Acts 13:22.
[13] 2 Chronicles 16:9.

Unreasonable Response (2:1–23)

Where is the one who has been born king of the Jews? We saw his star in the east and have come to worship him.

(Matthew 2:2)

Matthew's second chapter contains two reasonable responses and one unreasonable response to the birth of the Jewish Messiah. Can you identify which is which?

The response of the Magi is the easiest to identify. Their response was radical, but don't let that fool you that it wasn't reasonable. Their reaction to Jesus' birth was entirely proportionate to the momentous news that God had come to earth as a human being. Matthew tells us that they were *Magi*, astrologers from Persia. These were soothsayers who used the occult to predict the future from stars and dreams, and whose order of magicians had been involved in the destruction of Jerusalem in 586 BC.[1] Everything about their background made them natural enemies of the Jewish Messiah, but they had two important factors in their favour. First, when Daniel had been chief of the Babylonian and Persian Magi many centuries earlier, he prophesied about the coming Messiah.[2] Second, God

---

[1] The Hebrew text of Jeremiah 39:3, 13 talks about the *magi* of the Babylonian Empire. This is not made clear in English translations, but it is in the French Louis Segond and other non-English translations. Despite the tradition, Matthew does not tell us that these magi were *kings*, nor that there were *three* of them. They were astrologer-priests, from whom we derive the English word *magic*.

[2] Daniel 2:48; 5:11; 6:3.

decided to speak to them in language that astrologers could understand – through a star. Their response to these two acts of grace was utterly reasonable. They left their country, went on a journey of nearly two years,[3] and worshipped the baby Jesus as the King of kings. With remarkable insight into his future ministry, they brought *gold* to speak of him being honoured as king, *frankincense* to speak of him being worshipped as God, and *myrrh* to speak of him being mourned as a martyr.[4] It was very radical for Gentile soothsayers to worship at the Messiah's feet, but it was nevertheless completely reasonable.

King Herod's response was brutal, but in its own way it was reasonable too. We tend to treat the name *"king of the Jews"* in verse 2 as if it were entirely spiritual and about as threatening as a vicar in sandals. Herod didn't. He recognized it for what it really was: a bare-faced attack on his authority. Herod had spent years scheming, double-crossing, flattering, warring and murdering to win his throne as king of the Jews, and he was intent on keeping it. He killed his wife, three of his sons, and the babies of Bethlehem because he knew that he was not the heir of David and could therefore only rule by might, not by right. He feared the prophecies of Daniel that at the height of the Roman Empire *"One-Like-a-Son-of-Man"* would come, fully God yet fully human, to renew David's fallen dynasty and kingdom.[5] While we tend to treat the word *Christ* as a mere surname for Jesus, or at best a harmless spiritual statement, Herod knew that it was a subversive political claim to rule. The Greek word *Christ* and its Hebrew equivalent *Messiah* were the words used in the Old Testament to describe Saul, David, Solomon and the other God-appointed kings of Israel, and it was one of the reasons why Herod had destroyed the Jewish genealogical records in order

---

[3] It is evident from Matthew 2:16 that the Magi spent almost two years in preparing their journey, following the star and searching for Jesus.

[4] Exodus 30:34–38; Leviticus 2:1–2; 6:15; John 19:39.

[5] Daniel 7:13–14 talks of the *one-like-a-Son-of-Man*. Daniel 9:25–26 speaks of him as the *Messiah*.

to mask the Achilles' heel to his reign.[6] Herod knew that the arrival of the *"king of the Jews"* called for his swift and decisive attention. Therefore his massacre of the Innocents was brutal, despicable, but from his point of view utterly reasonable.

If the responses of the Magi and King Herod were reasonable, the response of the Jewish religious leaders was completely *unreasonable*. The chief priests were the descendants of Aaron, the ones called to steward the Temple and its sacrifices until the Messiah *"suddenly came to his temple"*.[7] The scribes or teachers of the law were the spiritual descendants of Ezra the Scribe, and were called to steward the Old Testament Scriptures as spiritual guides to Israel.[8] Both the priests and the scribes were waiting for the Messiah, speaking about him in their messages, praying about him in their meetings, and singing about him in their worship-psalms. They were so aware of the Messianic prophecies of the Old Testament that they instantly quoted Micah 5:2 to Herod and told him that the Messiah would be born in Bethlehem. But here's the strange thing: no matter how much they praised God for his work in the past and studied his promises for the future,[9] they were not at all willing to let him work in the present. God in the past is safe like a dusty museum, and God in the future is safe like an idle daydream, but God in the present disturbed the Jewish leaders and all Jerusalem. So, rather than let him come in and challenge their status quo, they did nothing. They watched the Magi leave Jerusalem on the last leg of their marathon journey from the east, and they didn't bother to make the six-mile journey with them to Bethlehem, frightened by what they might find. The reaction of the Jewish leaders to the birth of their Messiah was utterly, utterly unreasonable.

---

[6] 1 Samuel 12:3, 5; 24:6, 24:10; 26:9, 11, 16, 23; 2 Samuel 1:14, 16; 19:21; 22:51; 23:1; Psalm 84:9.

[7] Malachi 3:1.

[8] Nehemiah 8:13.

[9] Matthew 23:29–31.

My point here is not academic, but very practical. We can all too easily become like the priests and scribes, and God loathes it when we do. The coming of the Messiah, the King of kings, is a revolution which demands our everything. If Jesus truly is the Son of God, and if he truly is the Saviour who rules over God's Kingdom, he warrants nothing less than our full devotion. C.S. Lewis puts it this way: *"Christianity is a statement which, if false, is of no importance, and if true, of infinite importance. The one thing it cannot be is moderately important."*[10]

King Herod responded zealously but foolishly, grasping the scale of the revolution but underestimating its power. Like the nation of Andorra deciding to declare war on the United States, he attempted to put the mighty Messiah to the sword. Within months of his futile act of resistance, he developed horrific gangrene in his genitals and died in agony.[11]

In contrast, the Jewish religious leaders responded with apathy, hoping to ignore God's purposes for their generation and to bring him back into line with their own limited plans and aspirations. They completely misjudged the scale of his Revolution, and fooled themselves that tradition and religious activity could substitute for radical obedience. They sowed the seed for the next generation of leaders to crucify Jesus, and for the generation after that to be massacred in the Sack of Jerusalem in 70 AD. God's revolution is an invitation to respond to his purposes. To refuse is not to preserve the status quo, but to court disaster.

Unlike Herod or the Jewish leaders, the Magi let the coming of the Messiah transform their thinking, disturb their diaries and demand their worship. They responded to him reasonably, radically and unreservedly. They left everything behind in response to King Jesus. Wise men and women still do so today.

---

[10] C.S. Lewis, *God in the Dock* (1970).

[11] This is how medical experts understand Josephus' description of Herod's final illness in *Antiquities* (17.6.5).

Israel's Messiah (2:15)

And so was fulfilled what the Lord had said through the prophet: "Out of Egypt I called my son."

(Matthew 2:15)

Matthew was a Jew who wrote his gospel primarily for Jews.[1] Unless you grasp that, you will fail to understand the depth of its message. You will certainly not understand the fullness of its teaching about how we can be saved through Jesus Christ.

Take for example the importance of *works* in our salvation. Paul tells us in his letters that we can only be saved by grace through faith,[2] but Matthew clarifies that this is only true because our faith is placed in somebody else's works. Or take the role of the *Mosaic Law* in our salvation. Paul tells us that we are justified by grace through faith and not by the Law,[3] but Matthew clarifies that this is only true because our faith is placed in someone who has fully obeyed the Law of Moses. This teaching is left largely unpreached in many Bible-believing churches – so much so that you may even be shocked at the suggestion that *works* and *Law* are important for our salvation – but it is very important teaching. Matthew devotes a lot of his attention to it, and so should we.

Matthew is at great pains in his first few chapters to demonstrate that Jesus is the True-and-Perfect-Israel. His life mirrors the history of Israel, except that he walks perfectly along

---

[1] This is why he starts with a Jewish genealogy, quotes from the Old Testament at least thirty-five times, and uses the phrase *"kingdom of heaven"* as a Hebrew way of saying *"kingdom of God"* without using the divine name.

[2] Ephesians 2:8–9; Romans 4:5–6, 16.

[3] Romans 3:20–28; 4:13–14; Galatians 2:21; 5:4–5.

the path from which they so often strayed. The very first verse of Matthew stresses that Jesus is the true seed of Abraham, the true Isaac who blesses all nations and whose offspring will be as numerous as the stars in the sky and the sand on the seashore.[4] In 2:15 he is named as the true Son of God, the one prefigured by the nation of Israel in Exodus 4:22, Jeremiah 31:9 and Hosea 11:1. Matthew even supports this with a surprising quotation from Hosea to demonstrate that Jesus' short time as a refugee in Egypt was a deliberate re-enactment of the years that Israel spent in slavery there. He survives a massacre of babies, which echoes the one inflicted on Israel by Pharaoh,[5] and he is called out of Egypt just as God called out Israel at the time of the Exodus. All the while, Matthew is emphasizing that Jesus followed in Israel's footsteps but walked perfectly wherever they failed.

In chapter 3 he is baptized in the River Jordan as Israel was baptized in the Red Sea,[6] and in chapter 4 he spends forty sinless days in the desert to parallel Israel's forty sinful years in the desert. Having finished this, he climbs up a hill to deliver the Sermon on the Mount as the New Covenant parallel to the giving of the Law on Mount Sinai. Some of this detail is exclusive to Matthew's gospel because he wants us to grasp that Jesus is the True-and-Perfect-Israel.[7]

Matthew is also careful throughout his gospel to emphasize that Jesus fully obeyed the Mosaic Law, right down to its minutest requirement. He had no time for the "extra" rules of the Pharisees or for any other rules added to it by men,[8] but he never disobeyed a single genuine command in the Law.[9] In fact,

---

[4] Genesis 12:2–3; 15:4–5; 22:16–18; 26:2–5; Galatians 3:16.

[5] Exodus 1:15–22.

[6] 1 Corinthians 10:2.

[7] Matthew even makes a link in 2:23 between Jesus coming from *Nazareth* and him being the fulfilment of the devout order of *Nazirites*, which included Samson, Samuel and John the Baptist among its number. He is probably quoting from Judges 13:5.

[8] Matthew 12:1–14; 15:1–20; 23:1–7, 23–24.

[9] Matthew 5:17–20; 8:4; 17:24–27; 18:16; 26:59–60.

he warned very clearly in 5:17, *"Do not think that I have come to abolish the Law or the Prophets; I have not come to abolish them but to **fulfil** them."* Matthew is the only gospel writer to stress that Jesus was baptized in the River Jordan because of his perfect commitment to obey the Father and *"to fulfil all righteousness"*.[10] He wants us to grasp that Jesus is the perfect and unblemished Keeper-of-the-Mosaic-Law.

Matthew preached salvation by grace through faith, just like the other apostles. He wants to clarify, though, for his Jewish readers, that this does not mean that the Old Covenant is *ignored* with the coming of the New, but that it is *honoured* and *fulfilled* in Jesus the Messiah. We are not saved because God has decided to look upon Jesus' life, death and resurrection *instead* of the righteous requirements of the Mosaic Law. We are saved because Jesus fulfilled those requirements to the full, and because God counts his righteous obedience as if it were our own. As Paul writes in Romans 5:19, *"For just as through the disobedience of the one man the many were made sinners, so also through the obedience of the one man the many will be made righteous."* This is borne out by the teaching of the Old Testament, which tells us that we will be saved because *"**his** reward is with him, and **his** recompense accompanies him"*, and by the New where Jesus gives us the option of receiving *"**my** reward"* or else *"I will give to everyone according to what he has done."*[11]Ultimately we are all saved or condemned by *works* and the *Law*. We are either condemned through our own failure to live up to them, or we are saved through our faith in Jesus who lived up to them for us.

This was very important for first-century Jews to hear, but it is also important for us to grasp too. It will save us from many of the errors we can fall into regarding the Gospel.

Many Christians remain riddled with guilt over their past

---

[10] Matthew 3:15. The other gospels do not include this comment.
[11] Isaiah 62:11; Revelation 22:12.

or present sins, struggling to believe that God can sweep their sins under the carpet and forgive them for their actions. The reason they struggle to believe it is that they know instinctively that a just God simply cannot act that way. Matthew agrees with their conclusion, but then enlarges their understanding of the Gospel. God does *not* sweep their sin under the carpet at all. He placed their evil deeds on Christ when he crushed him to death at Calvary, and he places Christ's righteous deeds on them so that all he sees through their faith is perfect Law-keeping and unblemished obedience. The Gospel is deep, wide and gloriously perfect. Ignoring the detail about how Christ has redeemed us is to make the Gospel less like the good news that it is.

Many non-Christians struggle at the point of conversion, because they have also failed to grasp the depth of the Gospel. My wife and I met with a non-Christian friend last night who had heard the Lord speaking to her and was on the brink of conversion. She spoke her mind freely and asked, *"How can I become a Christian when I have slept with so many guys that I can't even remember their names?"* Later in the conversation she wondered *"How can I commit my life to Jesus when I don't think I could ever keep up the Christian life?"* The message that she and many other non-Christians need to hear is the Gospel of Jesus' righteous life. God can forgive her every sin and lead her by the hand every day of her new Christian life, because at the end of the evening when she prayed and asked for forgiveness she was not simply saved by grace through faith.

She was saved by grace through faith in the righteous works and perfect Law-keeping of the man Christ Jesus. Now that's what I call *Good News*.

Unconditional Surrender (3:1–12)

John's clothes were made of camel's hair, and he had a leather belt round his waist. His food was locusts and wild honey.

(Matthew 3:4)

General Ulysses S. Grant was so determined that the American Civil War should end with the complete and utter subjugation of the Confederate South that the newspapers joked that his initials, *"U.S."*, should stand for *"Unconditional Surrender"*. Several decades later, President Franklin D. Roosevelt led the Allies in a declaration that they too would accept nothing less than the *"unconditional surrender"* of Germany and Japan to end World War Two.[1] Grant and Roosevelt were agreed on one thing: there could be no meaningful future for rebellious people until they had thoroughly renounced their failed ambition to rule.

Perhaps this explains why the God of glory often chooses to reveal himself in deeply unimpressive ways. It explains why he chose a long-haired, strangely dressed, locust-eating and desert-dwelling spokesman to announce the coming of his Messiah. He could scarcely have picked a messenger less likely to appeal to the Jewish religious aristocracy than John the Baptist.[2] Perhaps this also explains why John's message was not a promise that

---

[1] Roosevelt agreed to this with Churchill and Stalin at their Casablanca Conference in 1943.

[2] Elijah actually set a good precedent for prophets wearing camel-hair clothes (2 Kings 1:8), but it was offensive to the well-attired Pharisees and Sadducees. They preferred expensive *"flowing robes"* (Mark 12:38).

God could improve people's lives, but a command to *"Repent, for the Kingdom of Heaven is near!"* and a threat that the Messiah was about to come with a *"winnowing fork"* and *"unquenchable fire"*. God does not seek to win followers by offering them a better kind of life, but by telling them that he is King, that they are rebels, and that they have just moments to lay down their weapons before he restores order to his realm. John's message is not what we tend to hear in most pulpits today. It sounds more like the ultimatum issued by a hostage negotiator just before his SWAT team storms a grounded aircraft and kills a group of hijackers.

It also explains why Jesus the Messiah came as he did. First-century Palestine was a nation ruled by the rich, the powerful, the well-connected and the well-educated. Jesus was none of those things. He was from the despised northern region of Galilee,[3] the supposedly illegitimate son of a poor widow,[4] who had been born in a stable, nursed as a refugee, and trained as a manual labourer. Those who knew him despised him,[5] and those who observed him were offended by his over-familiarity with traitors, drunkards and prostitutes: the lowest dregs of Jewish society.[6]

John's ministry was to prepare people for the coming of Jesus by calling them to humble themselves under God's hand as fully as God had humbled himself in Jesus. He told them that their hearts were cluttered and unready for the Messiah, and he set about clearing their hearts of their stubborn pride so that

---

[3] It is called *"Galilee of the Gentiles"* in 4:15 because it was an international trade route and more ethnically mixed than any part of Palestine except for Samaria. The Jews despised Galilee, and John 1:44–46 tells us that even the rest of Galilee looked down on Nazareth.

[4] It would be utterly remiss of the gospels not to mention Joseph at all after Jesus was twelve, unless he had died before Jesus began his ministry.

[5] Matthew 13:54–58; Isaiah 53:1–3.

[6] Matthew 9:10–13; 11:19.

they were ready for him when he came.[7] He attacked them for placing their confidence in their Jewish ancestry, calling them the *"offspring of vipers"* and telling them that God could just as easily make stones into the *"offspring of Abraham"* as make their stony hearts like Abraham's humble heart.[8] Then he asked them to do something which was calculated to gall a Jew like nothing else: he called them to be *baptized*. This was the ceremony which a Gentile administered to himself (along with circumcision and a special sacrifice) if he wanted to become a Jew; John used it to tell the Jews that they needed to be baptized into the People of God too, because their national identity was not enough to save them. What was more, they could not even do this to themselves in private, but needed to come to him in public and admit their need for forgiveness, salvation, and a new start in God.

Unsurprisingly, many people refused to submit to this. It didn't matter. God does not play a numbers game with his Kingdom. He wants your unilateral surrender or nothing at all. That's why we find Jesus in 8:18–22, faced with two people who want to follow him, telling them both to go away because they want him *plus* their house and *plus* their parents. Jesus would rather have a few followers who give him their all than a whole host of pretend followers who follow him with strings attached. That's why he came as a Galilean carpenter, heralded by a hairy hermit, preaching a Gospel of surrender and demanding that people be baptized.

This has very important ramifications for you if you are a Christian. If your experience of Christianity does not match up to what you expected, this passage may tell you why. Jesus demands our unconditional surrender because he can only

---

[7] The same Greek phrase that Isaiah uses in verse 3 is used by Paul in 1 Thessalonians 3:11 to describe his hope to clear an easy route for him to come to Thessalonica.

[8] Matthew tells us that John made this attack on the Pharisees and Sadducees, but the parallel passage in Luke 3:7–10 tells us that he also extended the attack to the rest of the crowd too.

build his Kingdom in our lives if they have been cleared of the old to make way for the new. You may need to take John the Baptist's advice in verse 8 and examine your life for *"fruit in keeping with repentance"*. Do you see in your heart a steady sense of humble brokenness before the Lord your Master? Is your life significantly different from that of a non-Christian who goes to church and plays at religion? Jesus tells us in 7:13–14 that *"small is the gate and narrow the road that leads to life, and only a few find it"*. If the Christianity you accepted is anything less than this Kingdom Revolution, you may not have accepted Christianity at all.

It also has massive ramifications for the way we present the Gospel to non-Christians. This passage warns us that twisting and embellishing the Gospel to win more Christian converts is not merely evil,[9] it is counter-productive. It wins false converts to a false Christ, and is powerless to offer new life because it has failed to deal with the old. Preach the Gospel of the Kingdom.[10] It's the only true Gospel there is.

This Gospel is offensive to the proud, but it is the message God has always used to attract the humble and draw them to himself. It failed to win the Pharisees and Sadducees, but it attracted the poor people of Israel in their droves to be baptized in the Jordan. It failed to win those who were buoyed by their religious accomplishments, but it drew the tax collectors, prostitutes, and "sinners" of Israel to salvation.[11] Not to *passivity*, where their will simply died and was buried in the waters of the Jordan, but to *Kingdom life* as they emerged from the waters to a new start as active subjects of God's Kingdom.

The Gospel, and baptism itself, speaks of humility, repentance, and unilateral surrender. Don't try to come to Jesus any other way, because he has stated his terms: *"If anyone*

---

[9] Paul uses a technical word in Galatians 1:8–9 to curse those who do so with being *cut off from the People of God*.

[10] Matthew 9:35; 13:19; 24:14.

[11] Matthew 21:31–32.

would come after me, he must deny himself and take up his cross and follow me. For whoever wants to save his life will lose it, but whoever loses his life for me will find it."[12]

[12] Matthew 16:24–25.

*He will save his people from their sins... He will
baptize you with the Holy Spirit... He will clear his
threshing floor.*

(Matthew 1:21; 3:11–12)

We need to take a theology lesson from the singer Meat Loaf. His
lyrics are full of tongue-in-cheek irony, and one of his greatest
is *"I want you, I need you, but there ain't no way I'm ever gonna
love you. Now don't be sad, 'cause two out of three ain't bad"*.[1]
It's a parody of the Elvis Presley title "I Want You, I Need You, I
Love You", and he uses this scaled-down version of the promise
to point out something very obvious: when it comes to romance,
love is essential. Two out of three is bad.

Matthew teaches us the same principle as Meat Loaf when
he talks about the mission of Jesus Christ. He begins his gospel
with three clear statements about Jesus' mission, and he calls
us to embrace this three-dimensional view of why he came to
Planet Earth. If we miss one of them, we will only follow a two-
dimensional shadow of the real Jesus, and when it comes to
following Jesus, two out of three is very bad indeed.

The first aspect of Jesus' mission is perhaps the most
obvious. Matthew quotes the words that the angel spoke to
Joseph in 1:21, which commanded him that *"you are to give him
the name Jesus, because he will save his people from their sins"*.
Jesus was the Greek form of the Hebrew name *Joshua* and a very

---

[1] Another wonderfully ironic Meat Loaf title is "I'd Lie for You (And That's the
Truth)".

common boy's name of the day, but Matthew wants us to grasp a deeper meaning behind the name. Jesus would be a new and better Joshua, not stepping into the River Jordan to part it en route to conquering the Canaanites, but stepping into it to be baptized en route to conquering Satan and his demons.[2] Moses renamed his servant *Joshua*, and Joseph named his baby *Jesus*, because it meant *Yahweh-Saves* or *Yahweh-to-the-Rescue*.[3] This was the first dimension of Jesus' mission. He would live how we should live and die how we should die, so that God could forgive and justify all those who are part of *"his people"*.[4]

John the Baptist proclaimed the second aspect of Jesus' mission in 3:11, telling us that Jesus *"will baptize you with the Holy Spirit and with fire"*. Now that's very interesting. Some people talk as if the Gospel is all about forgiveness, but John tells us that it isn't. Forgiveness is not the goal of the Gospel; it is merely the *means* by which we receive the Gospel. The Christian life is no more about being forgiven than my house is about the hallway. It's the entry point, and everyone must pass through it en route to the other rooms of the house, but it's not the destination. Forgiveness is what brings us into deep relationship with God and with his People, so that we can dwell with Christ in heaven, and Christ can dwell in us on earth. Paul tells us that being filled with the Holy Spirit is at the very heart of the Gospel, since Jesus died *"so that by faith we might receive the promise of the Spirit"*.[5] If we treat forgiveness as the purpose of the Gospel and forget that Jesus wants to fill us with his Spirit, we will never grow into mature Christians.

Matthew stresses the third aspect of Jesus' mission in the following verse, 3:12, telling us that *"His winnowing fork is in his hand, and he will clear his threshing-floor, gathering his*

---

[2] Matthew 8:29; 25:41.

[3] Numbers 13:16.

[4] The Greek word used for *people* in 1:21 is *laos*, which was used to refer specifically to the *People of God*.

[5] Galatians 3:14.

wheat into the barn and burning up the chaff with unquenchable fire". Jesus came to expose each person as wheat destined for the barn of heaven, or as *chaff* destined for the unquenchable fire of hell.[6] Many people told him this was unfashionable and that he must try to be more inclusive, but he was undeterred. He warned them, *"Do not suppose that I have come to bring peace to the earth... I have come to turn 'a man against his father, a daughter against her mother, a daughter-in-law against her mother-in-law!"*[7] Before the arrival of the Messiah, the Pharisees and the Jewish nation looked devout, while the tax collectors, prostitutes and Gentile nations did not. Jesus came to expose people for what they really are, and to warn them of stern judgment unless they repent. If we fail to grasp this or either of the other two dimensions of Jesus' ministry, then two out of three is very bad.

If we stress Jesus-the-Saviour and Jesus-the-Judge but neglect Jesus-the-Baptizer-with-the-Holy-Spirit, we reduce the Gospel to *formalism*. Ironically, most Christians who do so pride themselves on being *Bible-believing* and *Gospel-centred*, even though they have cut the heart out of the Gospel. They preach forgiveness and salvation from hell, but they have removed what makes the Gospel such Good News. They tell unbelievers that they can be forgiven for sins they don't know they have committed, and saved from a hell they don't know exists, and they wonder why they fail to respond. The reason is very simple: the unbelievers see their lives. Their two-dimensional gospel offers great hope for the next life but very little for the present. They have castrated the real, three-dimensional Gospel by removing the intimate life which comes from being filled with the Holy Spirit.

If we stress Jesus-the-Judge and Jesus-the-Baptizer-with-

---

[6] Matthew 18:8; 25:41; Mark 9:43, 48.

[7] Matthew 10:34–35. The final prophecies in the Old Testament particularly focused on this aspect of the Messiah's great mission; see Malachi 3:1–4; 3:16–4:6.

the-Holy-Spirit but neglect Jesus-the-Saviour, we stumble into *legalism*. When God works powerfully to revive a church, this is a particular danger for the next generation. They know that hell is real, and they know about the Holy Spirit, but they forget that their parents received the Gospel by grace through faith, not by their own prayers or exertions. If they are not careful, they sink into good works and judgmentalism, which is ironically the very thing that their parents hated and rejected in the excitement of revival.

If we stress Jesus-the-Saviour and Jesus-the-Baptizer-with-the-Holy-Spirit, but neglect Jesus-the-Judge, we reduce Christianity to mere *sentimentalism*. We may show great zeal for God and great thirst to experience God. We may even travel the world in pursuit of revival or the latest "outpouring", but we will never become mature disciples. We have failed to lay one of the main foundations of Christian discipleship, which Jesus tells us is to *"be afraid of the One who can destroy both soul and body in hell"*.[8] Christ-followers do not fear losing their salvation, but they do fear the Lord with a holy and healthy fear.[9] It helps keep them from sinning and makes the sinners around them want to follow Jesus too.[10] Fear is infectious, and when unbelievers see that we truly fear our God they start to fear him too.

Matthew emphasizes these three strands to Jesus' mission at the start of his gospel because he wants to teach us to follow the real Jesus and to proclaim his three-dimensional message to the world he died to save. We need to learn from the great theologian Meat Loaf and to make sure that we do not neglect any part of Jesus' mission. Otherwise we will learn that two out of three *is* bad.

---

[8] Matthew 10:28.
[9] Ecclesiastes 12:13; 2 Corinthians 5:11; 1 Peter 2:17; Revelation 14:7.
[10] Exodus 20:20.

Unhurried Faith (3:13–17)

Jesus replied, "Let it be so now; it is proper for us to do this to fulfil all righteousness."

(Matthew 3:15)

God is never in a hurry. Christians, on the other hand, often are. One survey in 2007 found that 40 per cent of Christians *"rush from task to task"*, and that almost two thirds feel that *"the busyness of life gets in the way of developing my relationship with God"*.[1] The God they worship is very patient, and he wants us to be patient too.[2] Perhaps that's one of the reasons why Matthew tells us next to nothing about the life of Jesus from age two to age thirty.[3] It's a salutary reminder that God's timing is perfect and that time spent waiting is not time wasted.

Jesus spent a lot of time waiting in Nazareth. Isaiah 49:2–3 had prophesied concerning the Messiah that *"[God] made my mouth like a sharpened sword, in the shadow of his hand he hid me; he made me into a polished arrow and concealed me in his quiver. He said to me, 'You are my servant, Israel, in whom I will display my splendour.'"* Therefore Jesus waited patiently for twenty-eight years, letting his Father prepare him like an arrow and choose the right time to take him out and shoot.

They were twenty-eight years of *obscurity*. Jesus went so

---

[1] "The Obstacles to Growth Survey" was conducted by a US business school in 2007 and interviewed 20,000 Christians from 139 different countries. Church leaders were no less busy than those they lead.

[2] God's patience is the subject of 2 Peter 3:9; Romans 2:4; 1 Timothy 1:16. Our need to be patient like him is the subject of 1 Corinthians 13:4; Galatians 5:22; Ephesians 4:2; Colossians 3:12; James 5:7–8.

[3] Matthew 2:16 and Luke 3:23 tell us that Jesus was aged two and thirty in Matthew 2 and 3 respectively.

incognito that when he finally stepped onto the world stage even his mother and his brothers thought that he had gone mad.[4] John the Baptist was a close relative, but even he did not realize that Jesus was the Messiah until he baptized him in water.[5] He was a child, a teenager, and – when Joseph died – the head of an active household of children. He learned to budget, to discipline his younger brothers and sisters, and to manage his mother's various requests for help.[6] He was a hard-working carpenter, embracing the simple dignity of holding down a job, perhaps meditating as he worked with the nails which would one day pin him to a wooden cross.[7] He watched as almost all his boyhood friends got married, and he knew the shame of being a single, childless thirty-something. He lived with all the same day-to-day temptations as us, and yet he never sinned.[8]

They were twenty-eight years of *polishing*, as he perfectly obeyed his Father's will for his life. John the Baptist did not know that Jesus was the Messiah, but he knew that he had no need of a baptism of repentance. He had watched Jesus for three whole decades and recognized that sinless Jesus should baptize him and not the other way round. Jesus had been perfectly righteous for thirty years, which is why he insisted that he be baptized *"to fulfil all righteousness"*. Jesus lived a perfect life in obscurity so that he could die our perfect death in full view.

They were twenty-eight years of *sharpening*, as he spent time with his Father and received training for public ministry.

---

[4] Mark 3:21.

[5] Luke 1:5–44. John was called to prepare Israel for the Messiah, but he confessed in John 1:29–34 that he did not know exactly who the Messiah was until he witnessed the great events of Jesus' baptism.

[6] Matthew 13:55–56 and Mark 6:3. See John 2:4 for Jesus dealing with a request from his mother.

[7] Work is a good thing, which existed in Eden (Genesis 2:15) and which will exist in the age to come (Luke 19:17, 19). The Christian life is not a call to *"tune in and drop out"*, but a call to enjoy work as a gift from God (Ecclesiastes 3:13; Colossians 3:24–25; 2 Thessalonians 3:10).

[8] Hebrews 4:15.

By the age of twelve, he could dazzle the Jewish teachers with his knowledge of the Old Testament, and he had learned to call God his Father, something no ordinary Jew dared to do.[9] By the time of his baptism, he was so full of Scripture that he could despatch Satan with three well-chosen verses and teach the people more powerfully than any of their rabbis.[10] The very essence of the prophecy in Isaiah 49 is that God takes time to prepare his servants. God spent ten times as long preparing Jesus in the secret place as he did releasing him in the public place.

They were twenty-eight years of *waiting* and of *watching* for his Father's perfect timing. An archer chooses the time to put an arrow to his bow, and Jesus waited for his Father to choose the right time to remove him from his quiver.[11] At last it came, quite late in John's ministry, when Jesus felt free to come to the River Jordan and be baptized. As he did so, God announced to the world that *"This is my Son whom I love; with him I am well pleased"*.[12] God honours the man who waits, and he launched Jesus' ministry with an unprecedented vindication of his identity, his authenticity, and his acceptance. In a world where the Roman emperors claimed to rule as gods, the real God endorsed his true King in a manner beyond their wildest dreams. He then anointed him powerfully with the Holy Spirit so that he could begin his ministry in earnest.

We are not very good at waiting like Jesus. We would rather plan, strategize, act, and follow up – anything other than *wait*. Jesus serves as our example so that we can be free from striving, from impatience, and ultimately from fruitlessness. Because Jesus was willing to wait, he was trained and ready by

---

[9] Luke 2:40–52; John 5:18.

[10] Matthew 4:4, 7, 10; 7:28–29.

[11] John 2:5; 5:19; 7:3–6.

[12] Interestingly, Mark and Luke both tell us that God addressed these words to *Jesus* rather than to the crowd. This reminds us that the four gospel writers often summarize speech rather than quote it word for word.

the time he took his stand. Because he was willing to wait, he received power from the Holy Spirit and went on to massive fruitfulness. We need the same patience and the same anointing. The servants of Christ cannot prosper unless they walk the way of Christ.

If you feel disappointed that you have borne little fruit in your life, this should encourage you. God may well still have you in his quiver, polishing and sharpening you ready for your moment in time. Moses felt like you for the first eighty years of his life, little knowing that they were preparing him for fruitful service in old age. Now is the time for you to study Scripture, to devote hours to prayer and worship, and to make sure that you are filled more and more with the Holy Spirit. Christian waiting is never passive. It means fixing our eyes on the Lord, devoting ourselves to him, and being poised to act the moment he puts us to his bow.

If your heart breaks for your church or your nation, and you are crying out to God to revive you and to restore you to fruitfulness, this should encourage you too. God works with churches and nations as he works with individuals. He may be sharpening you, polishing you, and refining you in the private place, ready to bless you once more in the public place.

The book of Isaiah holds this promise for those who follow the patient Messiah: *"In repentance and rest is your salvation, in quietness and trust is your strength."*[13]

---

[13] Isaiah 30:15.

Predictable Foe (4:1–11)

Then Jesus was led by the Spirit into the desert to be tempted by the devil.

(Matthew 4:1)

I am not very good at computer games. Maybe I lack hand–eye co-ordination. Maybe I just don't have the patience required to learn to predict the computer's every move in a game. But I spent an afternoon last week with my cousin and discovered something very surprising. When I am with him, I become brilliant at computer games. In fact, I got the high score. What caused this sudden turnaround in my gaming abilities? It's very simple, really. My cousin was sitting next to me, telling me exactly what the computer was about to do next, and warning me what I had to do to outsmart it. Computer games are predictable, and with an experienced guide like my cousin, anyone can win them. Even an amateur like me.

Satan is predictable too. He has been the sworn enemy of the human race from the very beginning, and his weapons are hackneyed and overused. He is merely a fallen creature, and he lacks the innovative mind of the Creator. That's why the Holy Spirit led Jesus into the desert to be tempted for forty days, not just for him to be the true Israel and to *"learn obedience from what he suffered"*,[1] but also for him to become the example you need to overcome your predictable foe.[2] Sitting next to my cousin, you could beat a computer game. Sitting next to Jesus, you can beat temptation.

---

[1] Hebrews 5:8. Writer W.H. Griffith Thomas comments that *"Innocence is life untested, while virtue is innocence tested and triumphant."*

[2] Hebrews 2:18; 4:15–16.

The Devil is predictable in his *goals*. What he lacks in innovation, he makes up for in imitation, and he has established a kingdom of his own to mimic the Kingdom of God.[3] Its values oppose the pure values of God's Kingdom, and he always tempts us to adopt his corrupted values instead of the values of the Kingdom of Heaven.

Consider his three attacks on Jesus: all attempts to persuade him to desert God's Kingdom path for an easier, human path. First, he tempts him to rely on his own strength instead of God's, to which Jesus firmly responds that he will depend on his Father alone. Second, he urges him to manipulate God into action, but Jesus insists that he will obey God's plan and his timing. Third, he promises him the nations of the earth if he will purchase them through worshipping him, which provokes Jesus' pledge that he will serve God and worship him alone.

Matthew is showing us here that there are three broad avenues along which Satan always drives his trucks of temptation. God's Kingdom call is the revolutionary path of humility, where we *depend* on him, *obey* him, and *serve* him alone. Satan's call is for self-rule, self-sufficiency, and self-promotion. Temptation is the clash of two kingdoms vying for our hearts. If we know the values of each kingdom, Satan's goals are quite transparent.

The Devil is predictable in his *methods*. The name *Devil* comes from the Greek word for *deceiver*, and Jesus warns us in John 8:44 that *"When he lies, he speaks his native language"*. He is too subtle to rely on out-and-out untruths; he is the master of exaggeration and misrepresentation. He is quite happy to take Jesus to the Temple and quote Scripture at him, because Satan often twists Bible verses for his own ends.[4] He uses half-truths, like his claim to have authority over the nations of the

---

[3] Matthew 12:26; Luke 11:18.

[4] Satan quotes from Psalm 91 in the Greek Septuagint with word-for-word accuracy. In contrast, Jesus changes the words of one of his quotations for effect. This warns us not just to focus on the precise words of Scripture, but also on the right spirit and meaning behind those words.

earth, and he packages them to sound like whole truth.[5] He sows doubts in our mind, asking *"If you are..."* or *"Did God really say...?"*,[6] and his smooth voice sounds so practical, plausible and pleasurable that it's easy to be fooled. By God's grace, Jesus sits next to us, predicting Satan's next move and showing us how to take evasive action. He tells us to remember our new identity in Christ; God had already answered Satan's doubting questions in 3:17 before he even asked them. He tells us to remember the true message of Scripture and to quote its powerful words whenever we are tempted. We are sanctified as the Holy Spirit works in us through the Word of God,[7] and he shows us that even Satan will call off his attack when stabbed enough times with the sharp edge of truth.

The Devil is predictable in his *timing*. He does not tempt Jesus at the start of his forty-day fast, but at the end when he is at his weakest. He chooses food to tempt his hunger, the Temple crowds to tempt his loneliness, and the splendour of the nations to tempt his poverty. He knows the vulnerable places in your own heart, and he knows the perfect time to exploit them. If it is sexual loneliness, he waits for you to watch TV or surf the Internet late at night. If it is discontentment, he lies dormant until you read a magazine about the fastest cars, the swankiest houses, and all that your money could buy. If it is poor self-image, he waits until your mind wanders to the married man in your office who makes you laugh and feel good about yourself, and who understands you so much better than anyone else. Temptation is not your friend; it is Satan's slow-burning fuse to demolish your life. Listen to Jesus and don't be a sitting target.

I am very glad that Jesus fought his battle in the desert and won. He encourages me that temptation is normal, because he

---

[5] John 12:31 confirms that Satan became *"the ruler of the world"* when Adam sinned in Eden and forfeited his God-given authority, but John 13:3 makes it clear that God remains the ultimate ruler of the world.

[6] Genesis 3:1.

[7] 2 Thessalonians 2:13; Ephesians 5:26; John 17:17.

was *"tempted in every way, just as we are – yet was without sin"*.[8] He encourages me that temptation is not invincible, since he overcame and *"because he himself suffered when he was tempted, he is able to help those who are being tempted"*.[9] Since he was led by the Spirit's initiative into the desert, he also encourages me that God can use my trials of temptation to refine me, to draw me to himself, and to entrust me with more of God's Kingdom. Temptations need not be our place of defeat. They can become our springboards to victory.

The passage from Deuteronomy 8, which Jesus quotes in verse 4, is still God's message to his tempted people:

> *The Lord your God led you all the way in the desert these forty years, to humble you and to test you in order to know what was in your heart, whether or not you would keep his commands. He humbled you... to teach you that man does not live on bread alone but on every word that comes from the mouth of the Lord... Know then in your heart that as a man disciplines his son, so the Lord your God disciplines you.*[10]

Satan hates God's Kingdom, but God is strong enough to help you resist temptation and use it as a way to deepen his Kingdom Revolution in your heart. Jesus has gone before you and he has won. He now sits next to you and offers to lead you in victory over your predictable foe.

---

[8] Hebrews 4:15. Matthew tells us in v. 1 that the *Holy Spirit*, not the Devil, led him into the desert.

[9] Hebrews 2:18. See also Hebrews 4:15–16.

[10] Deuteronomy 8:2–5.

Follow Me (4:17–25)

"Come, follow me," Jesus said, "and I will make
you fishers of men." At once they left their nets and
followed him.

(Matthew 4:19–20)

Jesus knew he was going to die. Soon. By the time he returned
from his forty days in the desert, his time was already running
out. He had only two-and-a-half years left before his crucifixion,
just thirty months in which to recruit and train the twelve men
who would lead his Church across the world. It must have
seemed a daunting task even to him, which is why the twelve he
chose are so surprising.

Jesus could have chosen anyone, and he spent a whole night
praying over his shortlist.[1] The result was the unimpressive Dirty
Dozen listed in 10:2–4, which included several fishermen, a tax
collector[2] and a religious terrorist.[3] Jesus chose Peter, the volatile
disciple who could speak for God one moment and for Satan the
next, and whose confident boasting would crumble before a
servant-girl.[4] He chose James and John, the angry disciples who

---

[1] Luke 6:12–13.

[2] Since Mark 2:14 tells us that Matthew's father was called *Alphaeus*, it looks
as though the disciple called James son of Alphaeus was actually Matthew's
brother.

[3] Luke 6:15 tells us that the Greek word *Kananitēs* does not mark Simon as a
Canaanite, but as a *Zealot* (from the Hebrew word *qana'*, which means *to be
zealous*). This radical Jewish sect longed for a Roman-slaughtering Messiah,
and launched armed rebellions in Acts 5:37; 21:38. They largely rejected Jesus,
and were wiped out by the Roman legions at Masada in AD 73.

[4] Matthew 16:17, 23; 26:69–72.

tried to call down fire to destroy those who rejected him.[5] He chose eleven despised Galileans, such as Thomas the doubter and Nathanael the cynic.[6] In fact, the only respectable Judean was Judas Iscariot – hardly an advert for respectability.[7]

The twelve disciples show us that no one is too *weak* to follow Jesus, but only too strong. Jesus told Paul that *"my power is made perfect in weakness"*, and God told Gideon that he will not work through people who think they are strong.[8] He didn't recruit an educated and impressive group of rabbis, but a motley crew of Galileans who knew that without Jesus they had nothing. These were men who would say to Jesus, *"Lord, to whom shall we go? You have the words of eternal life"*,[9] and this is just the kind of person that Jesus loves to use. They were men of weakness and humility, the fertile harvest-ground for God's Kingdom.

The twelve disciples show us that no one is too *talentless* to follow Jesus, because the Great Teacher is able to find potential in any of his pupils. Jesus looked at angry John and violent Simon, and preferred to re-channel their misplaced passion than choose an orthodox but passionless teacher of the law. He looked at cynical Nathanael and unstable Peter, and saw a hatred of hypocrisy and a rock-hard faith, which he could harness for his Church.[10] He saw four fishermen who failed to catch fish and promised them that *he* would make them successful fishers of men. He saw them fixing their nets and knew that he could use

---

[5] Mark 3:17 tells us their nickname was *Sons-of-Thunder*, and Luke 9:54–56 shows their bad temper in action.

[6] John 1:45–46; 20:24–29. Matthew calls Nathanael by his other name, *Bartholomew*.

[7] *Iskariōtēs* is a Greek transliteration of the Hebrew *Ish-Kerioth*, or *Man-from-Kerioth*, a town in Judea.

[8] Judges 7:1–7; 2 Corinthians 12:9. Few things dishonour God more than Christians who dismiss their own potential and church leaders who bemoan the quality of their congregation.

[9] John 6:68.

[10] John 1:42, 47; Matthew 16:18.

them to fix up broken human beings and throw back them into the fish-laden waters of the world.[11] The reason Jesus is able to choose the very weak is that he himself is so very strong.

We make a mistake if we think Jesus could have chosen anyone at all to be part of his Twelve. The one thing that these men had in common was that they were all *willing* to follow Jesus anywhere and at any cost. Peter was married, but he did not consult his wife before following Jesus. James and John had commitments to their father, but they left him at Jesus' call. Matthew was employed by Rome, but he left a table stacked with money to fall in behind the King of Israel.[12] Jesus chose the weak, but demanded that their commitment be strong. If anyone offered less than this, he refused to lower his demands.[13] He would transform earthly zeroes into spiritual heroes, but only if they left everything to follow him.

Jesus is still looking for disciples, and he calls you to follow him too. To *follow* him. Not to "pray a prayer", although a prayer of conversion is important. Not to declare yourself a "Christian", although public confession of faith is important too. He calls you to *follow* him – to turn your back on your old life and to pay the price to go wherever he leads you.

He calls you to *spend time with him*. Mark and John both emphasize that the disciples' primary calling was simply to be with him, to watch him and to listen to what he said.[14] Luke tells us that the reason that *"unschooled, ordinary men"* like these were able to shake the world was that *"these men had been with Jesus"*.[15] So whatever it may mean for you in concrete terms to leave nets or a tax collector's booth, it will definitely

---

[11] The Greek word *katartizō* is used in v. 21 to describe James and John *fixing* their nets, and also in Ephesians 4:11–12 to describe apostles, prophets, evangelists, and pastor-teachers *fixing* up those in the Church.

[12] Matthew 8:14; 9:9.

[13] Matthew 8:19–22; 19:16–22.

[14] Mark 3:14; John 1:39.

[15] Acts 4:13.

mean carving out huge chunks of time just to pray, worship, and read God's Word. "Disciple" simply means "pupil", and pupils spend time with their teacher and listen to what he says. For me, it meant getting rid of my TV for a few years until I could own one and still choose Jesus over channel-hopping. It meant committing not to go away at weekends so that I could give myself to the brothers and sisters in my church and our shared journey of faith with Jesus. For you, it may be different, but God doesn't give us more hours in the day once we start following him. Something has to leave your life so that time with Jesus can enter it.

He calls you to *seek first his Kingdom*. This means that your past plans, hopes and dreams are dead. He may resurrect them one day in a sanctified form, but first they must die. He wants to reorientate your life towards his Kingdom agenda, and this is going to affect your diary, your finances, your home, and your family. Some people give away all they have for sake of the Kingdom; others keep hold of it but set it to work for the sake of the Kingdom. No life is left unscathed by the Kingdom.

He calls you to live a new life by the *values of his Kingdom*. Dying to your old life is only part of becoming a disciple, even though it is often preached as the whole event. Dying is only the precursor to rising to a new life in Christ. The invitation to "receive Jesus" lets us focus on what *he* will do next, but he calls us to "follow him", with the spotlight on what *we* will do next. Following Jesus means a lot more than going to church meetings and accepting his *don'ts*. It means embarking upon his radical walk of discipleship and embracing his world-shattering series of *dos*. It is a call to walk with a different set of values. It is a call to let his Kingdom Revolution begin in us.

That's why Matthew takes us straight on from here into Act One and Jesus' teaching about Kingdom Lifestyle.

Act One:

Kingdom Lifestyle

Kingdom Character (5:1–16)

In the same way, let your light shine before men,
that they may see your good deeds and praise your
Father in heaven.

(Matthew 5:16)

I was converted by reading the Sermon on the Mount. Actually, let me be more precise. I was converted by reading the Sermon on the Mount and by seeing people who tried to live by it. I was an arrogant, self-serving, self-centred hypocrite, but this sermon in Matthew 5–7 brought me to my knees. I caught a glimpse of God's Kingdom way of life, and I was captivated by its beauty. It was so different, so shocking, so frightening, and yet so compelling, that I gave up everything to follow him. I spent the first three weeks of my Christian life reading this sermon every day and asking God to help me live it. It crippled me, healed me, and empowered me in a thousand different ways.

Mine was a world which prized strength and despised weakness. Jesus replied that *"Blessed are those who are spiritual beggars, for theirs in the kingdom of heaven"*. That word *ptōchos* means *"reduced to beggary"*, like a homeless person on the street corner who holds out an empty cup, and I both hated and loved it. I had spent too long pretending I was rich, and I knew it was time to admit I was bankrupt, destitute, and in desperate need of help. I started pleading with God like a beggar, and I started to receive his Kingdom.

Mine was a world of go-getters, of success, and self-promotion. Jesus replied that *"Blessed are the meek, for they will inherit the earth"*. I sneered at the naïvety of what I called *"doormat Christianity"*, yet I was sick of my own ambitious attempts to make the world revolve around me. It was accepting this verse, as much as any other verse in Scripture, which marked my Christian conversion.

Mine was a world of fear, where everything I wore, everything I listened to, everything I said, and everything I believed was the echo of what my friends told me was "cool". I wanted people to like me, and I would pay any price to make sure they did. But Jesus replied, *"Blessed are those who are persecuted because of their righteousness... great is your reward in heaven, for in the same way they persecuted the prophets who were before you"*. I saw in these "Beatitudes" a call to march to the beat of a different drum, and to pull down my false god of popularity to follow the real God.[1] It made me face up to my fears and, in my small way, do what Peter did when he left his nets.

I was drawn to respond because I did *mourn* over my sinful life, I did *hunger* and *thirst* for something better, and I knew that only God's *mercy* would ever satisfy me. I longed to be truly *happy*, as only God can make people happy, and I was deeply disillusioned with the fleeting thrills of life without him.

I'm telling you my story because we need to remember that the Sermon on the Mount is not just a beautiful collection of sayings, but the revolutionary manifesto of Jesus' Kingdom. It's a call for the unbelieving crowd to follow Jesus and live his way instead of the world's. It is a call for his disciples to act as subjects of the Kingdom of God.[2] It converted me from churchgoing to Christ-following, and it continues to convict and convert today. Like the Law of Mount Sinai, which commanded

---

[1] All nine verses in 5:3–11 begin with the Greek word *makarios*, which means *"Blessed is…"* or *"Happy is…"* The Latin word for "blessed" is *beatus*, and so many people call these verses the *Beatitudes*.

[2] Matthew tells us Jesus preached the Sermon on the Mount both to the *disciples* (5:1–2) and to the *crowds* (7:28).

the Israelites to be different from the nations around them,[3] the major theme of Jesus' New Covenant Sermon on the Mount is also *"do not be like them"* (6:8). It spells out the new lifestyle of those who follow Jesus, and tells those who profess to follow him yet live like the world that they are "unsalty salt", which is only fit to be *"thrown out and trampled by men"*. It is a call for us to lay down our lives and to walk a different road.

I'm also telling you my story because we need to remember that Jesus' strategy for convincing non-Christians that the Gospel is true depends on each of us living out this teaching. I know that many books and courses on evangelism tell you that if only you can learn a certain technique you will convert all your friends, but we both know it isn't true. There is one principal thing, far above everything else, which wins people to Christ, and that is the lives of people who have already been won to Christ. Jesus tells us that if we live his Kingdom way instead of the world's way, we will become *salt* scattered throughout the world and *light* which shines in their darkness. Both salt and light are effective because they are different, and people respond to the Gospel because they see the difference of God's Kingdom in our lives. The Sermon on the Mount is not a call to *blend in* but to *stick out*, to embrace God's Revolution in our own lives, and in doing so spark a revolution in the lives all around us.

My children love to feed our Venus flytrap, which means I used to spend a lot of time hunting for insects to put in its jaws. Then I got smart and made a great discovery. If I wait until it gets dark, then turn on the lights and open the windows, the insects come to me. I can wear myself out chasing them, or I can simply switch the light on and start attracting them. Jesus tells us that the same is true with evangelism. I would never have been convinced by any Gospel presentation, because I was so hard-hearted that I actually believed I already *was* a Christian.

---

[3] Leviticus 18:1–4. Matthew places this sermon directly after Jesus' equivalent of Egypt, the Red Sea, and the desert. Matthew expects us to grasp that Jesus turned this mount into a "New Covenant Sinai".

I was only converted because of what Jesus describes here: I saw a radical people who believed a radical message and were willing to be attractively different as Kingdom revolutionaries.

Mahatma Gandhi, the Hindu founder of the modern state of India, was once asked by a Christian missionary why he often quoted the words of the Sermon on the Mount yet refused to follow Christ. He replied, *"I don't reject Christ. I love Christ. It's just that so many of you Christians are so unlike Christ. If Christians would really live according to the teachings of Christ, as found in the Bible, all of India would be Christian today."* That is simply the teaching of verse 16, where Jesus promises that if we live this way people will *"see your good deeds and praise your Father in heaven"*.

The Sermon on the Mount is one of the most loved passages of Scripture, but it is also one of the least obeyed. Let's rise up as subjects of God's Kingdom to be light in the midst of the darkness. Let's be those whose lives preach the Gospel and attract people to Jesus Christ.

Kingdom Obedience (5:17–48)

Unless your righteousness surpasses that of the Pharisees and the teachers of the law, you will certainly not enter the kingdom of heaven.

(Matthew 5:20)

The Pharisees were deeply religious people. Christians tend to look down on them,[1] but they were actually the heroes of first-century Palestine. Their name means *"separatists"*, and they were sincere Jews who longed to revive their nation from the sins of the Gentiles. They took hold of the synagogues and used them to preach obedience to the Mosaic Law, modernizing and categorizing it into 248 commands, 365 prohibitions, and 1,521 amendments. They won the hearts of the common people and were much more popular than the élite group of Sadducees who ran the Temple. They were the greatest teachers of the law and they won many converts to radical Judaism. In short, they did everything humanly possible to bring Israel back to God.

That was the problem. Everything *humanly* possible. Jesus' Sermon on the Mount is a description of what is *divinely* possible. The Pharisees had their list of statutes to judge anyone who committed adultery, who called a person *"Raca"*,[2] or who

---

[1] In fact, not unlike the way the Pharisee in Luke 18:11–12 looked down on people too. *"Do not judge, or you too will be judged."*

[2] *Raca* is the Greek transliteration of the Aramaic word *reqa'*, which means *"you worthless one!"* The Greek word for *fool* here is a word which the Old Testament uses to describe people who reject God. Jesus uses it to describe the Pharisees in 23:17, so his point here is that we must never wish anyone to be damned.

inflicted grievous bodily harm. They had a list of rules to govern oath-taking, litigation, divorce, and Temple offerings. They had instructions for alms-giving, litigation, fasting, and loving fellow-Jews.[3] Most of these were well-meaning, but they had fallen for the oldest trick in the book. Fallen humans cannot sanctify themselves from the *outside in* through religion or *"rules taught by men"*.[4] We can only break free from sin in the same way that we are forgiven from sin – by the gracious work of God from the *inside out*.

In the TV series *Prison Break*, Lincoln Burrows is sent to jail for a crime he did not commit. He is placed in Fox River State Penitentiary, a maximum security prison, which is so secure that no one has ever managed to escape. When Lincoln's brother Michael decides to help him break out, he immediately sees that there is only one way he could ever do so. He becomes a prisoner himself at Fox River, and reveals to his shocked brother that he has tattooed on his body a map of the prison and the details of an infallible escape plan. Michael has broken *in* so that he can break his brother *out*.

That's what Jesus did when he became a man to save us from the penalty of sin. It's what the Holy Spirit does when he comes and dwells inside each believer to set them free from the power of sin. The Pharisees had assumed that the Temple sacrifices merely wiped the slate clean for them to try harder for God. Jesus revealed that his death on the cross offers not only freedom from the guilt of sin, but also freedom from the imprisoning power of sin. That's why he tells us in verse 20 that our righteousness must exceed that of the Pharisees and the teachers of the law. Anyone who can't do that, can't have received the Holy Spirit, and anyone who fails to receive the

---

[3] Verse 43 shows us the blindness of outside-in righteousness. The Pharisees had unwittingly changed the command of Leviticus 19:18 from *"love your neighbour as yourself"* to *"love your neighbour and hate your enemy"*.

[4] Matthew 15:9.

Holy Spirit cannot truly be in the Kingdom.[5] As God promised through the prophet Ezekiel: *"I will put my Spirit in you and move you to follow my decrees".*[6]

Jesus therefore endorses the righteous demands of God's Law and tells us that by the Spirit's power he will enable those who are in his Kingdom to live out what it truly commands.[7] He will not merely save us from murdering, but even from harbouring angry thoughts towards another person in our hearts. He will not merely save us from committing adultery, but also from lust, fantasy, and pornography.[8] He highlights the relational issues behind litigation, divorce,[9] and Temple sacrifices, and he calls us to obey the principles behind the Law through the enabling power of the Holy Spirit. He calls us to truthfulness instead of using oaths as get-out clauses,[10] to forgiveness instead of revenge,[11] and to sincerity instead of religious posturing. Most of all, he calls us to love even our enemies as much as ourselves, since God loves the wicked and

[5] I'm not arguing here that people who fail to receive the Pentecostal "baptism in the Spirit" are not real Christians. I'm simply echoing Paul's statement in Romans 8:9 that all genuine believers do receive the Spirit in some way at conversion. See 1 Corinthians 6:19; 12:12–13; Galatians 3:2–3; Ephesians 1:13–14.

[6] See Ezekiel 36:26–27.

[7] When Paul tells us in Colossians 2:14, 17 that Jesus has *erased* the written law, he means that it is incorporated and exceeded by Jesus' Spirit-empowered Law of Love in Matthew 22:37–39.

[8] Jesus does not use the word *masturbation* in vv. 29–30, but he seems to imply it and include it in his promise.

[9] We will look in more detail at Jesus' teaching on divorce in the chapter entitled "Back to the Beginning".

[10] Matthew 23:16–22 tells us that many Pharisees used their rules about oath-taking as a smokescreen for lies. Jesus' point here is not that we must never take an oath (such as in court), but that we should be so honest that we do not have to.

[11] This teaching in Exodus 21:24, Leviticus 24:20 and Deuteronomy 19:21 was given to *limit* the penalty for a crime, but the Pharisees had made it an excuse to exact maximum revenge. Jesus wants us to leave room for God to avenge us instead of trying to play God ourselves. See Romans 12:17–21.

will enable us to love them too. Other religious leaders have taught their followers to stop doing to others what they would not want done to themselves, but only Jesus can expect his Holy Spirit-empowered followers more positively to *"do to others what you would have them do to you".*[12]

The Pharisees treated the Mosaic Law as a series of commands, and they congratulated themselves on their ability to keep them. Jesus sneers at their pride and argues that their human efforts have simply turned them into pompous religious bigots. The Law of Sinai promised that God would sanctify his People,[13] and we must read the Sermon on the Mount in the same light too. Sadly, many Christians see these three chapters as a set of idealistic suggestions, pointing to a utopia which is beyond our reach. The truth is that they are a set of promises that Jesus will work this Kingdom obedience in the hearts of all those who leave everything to follow him. None of us will become completely sinless in this life, but by his grace we can all *sin less*. Much less.

This is the glorious Christian Gospel – a God who not only saves by grace through faith, but who also sanctifies us that way too. It's the Gospel that Peter preached on the day of Pentecost when he promised: *"Repent and be baptized, every one of you, in the name of Jesus Christ for the forgiveness of your sins. And you will receive the gift of the Holy Spirit."*[14]

---

[12] Matthew 7:12. The Apocryphal book of Tobit, the Greek Stoic philosophers, and the Chinese philosopher Confucius all taught the former, negative command. Only Jesus taught the latter, positive one.

[13] Exodus 31:13; Leviticus 20:8; 21:15, 23; 22:9; 32.

[14] Acts 2:38.

Kingdom Intimacy (6:1–18)

This, then, is how you should pray: "Our Father in heaven…"

(Matthew 6:9)

The first word that each of my children ever spoke was *"Dadda"*. It's a very easy word to say. The first word that most first-century Jewish children learned to say was the equivalent Aramaic word *"Abba"*,[1] but they never dared use such an intimate word for *God*. The Jews tried to stone Jesus when he did so in John 5:18, so there was something unprecedented about his teaching on the intimate fellowship he promised to give his followers with Yahweh. Jesus insisted that God was his *Abba*, and that his followers must call him *Abba* too.[2] This truth is at the heart of his Kingdom Revolution.

The Jews were happy with the concept that Yahweh was the Father of their nation Israel, but Jesus turned national theory into personal reality.[3] The whole of the Old Testament refers only fourteen times to God as Israel's Father; Jesus refers to God as Father seventeen times in the Sermon on the Mount alone. Because he is the Son of God, and we are saved by being reckoned in Christ,[4] he makes us into sons of God alongside him.[5] The Jewish leaders were furious at the suggestion that

---

[1] The Aramaic word *Abba* was actually a cross between *"Daddy"* and *"Dad"*, since grown-up Jewish children would still call their father by this name.

[2] Mark 14:36; Romans 8:15; Galatians 4:6.

[3] The Lord taught this in Old Testament passages such as Exodus 4:22; Deuteronomy 14:1; Jeremiah 31:9, 20; Hosea 11:1.

[4] Galatians 3:26–27.

[5] John 1:12; Romans 8:21; Philippians 2:15; 1 John 3:1, 2, 10; 5:2, 19. Although most verses speak of the *"sons of God"*, note that 2 Corinthians 6:18 speaks of

the Lord God Almighty could ever become our *Abba*, but the Gospel is the message that in Christ he has.

That's why John the Baptist and Jesus were so cutting in their response to the Jewish hope that their race made them *"children of Abraham"*. They were determined to lift their eyes towards the bigger prize set before them through the Gospel, and they called them *"the offspring of vipers"* and *"children of the devil"* to make their message heard.[6] Jesus teaches in the Sermon on the Mount that this truth is at the heart of Kingdom life. We do not strive for God's attention like the *pagans* of 6:7, or play-act at prayer like the religious *hypocrites* of 6:5. We relate to God as *Abba*, with a revolutionary kind of intimacy.

Because God is our Father, we live to *please him* and not our peers. The Pharisees found little genuine experience of God in their man-made religion, so they turned it into a self-glorifying spectacle for the crowds. They prayed publicly on the street corners to impress those who passed by, like Christians today who pray fancy prayers in public to impress the rest of their congregation. God sees into our hearts, and he hates any such pretence. Prayer is not a sideshow for the crowds, nor a way to manipulate God through long-winded speeches. Jesus tells us to fix our eyes on no one but our Father, and to approach him as his children to enjoy his presence and receive his certain answer. We should pray in secret, fast in secret, and give in secret because we live for an audience of One.[7] If we do so, Jesus tells us six times in 7:7–11 that we will definitely receive, and we can be sure of this because God is our Father. The hypocrites and pagans get nothing, but the sons and daughters of God get the desires of their hearts.

Because God is our Father, we have *joyful access* into his

the *"sons and daughters of God"*.

[6] Matthew 3:7, 9; 12:34; 23:33; John 8:37–44.

[7] This command to serve God in secret does not contradict the command to let our light shine in 5:14–16. One passage tells us not to be cowards, while the other tells us not to be show-offs.

presence. One of the most precious promises of Scripture is that our first words in prayer should be *"Our Father"*. How often are we tempted to come snivelling into God's presence with confession for sin and protestations that we are useless? We can even convince ourselves that this is humility. Jesus corrects us and tells us that the Father is dishonoured by such fawning. This may be appropriate for our first prayer of repentance, but not for our day-to-day relationship with our Father.[8] What would it reflect upon a man if you saw his children grovelling before him each morning? You would think he was the nastiest father alive! I love the way my children bound into my study each morning for a cuddle, not for confession! God loves it too, which is why the Psalmist tells us to *"Enter his gates with thanksgiving and his courts with praise"*.[9] Old English stately homes have a front door for friends and a back door for servants. Jesus tells us that we must not use the back door with our heavenly Father. It's the front door and the red carpet from now on.

Because God is our Father, we *make time* for him. The amazing truth of the Gospel is that God should make time for us, not that we should deign to make time for him, but many of us struggle in the busyness of life to find time to pray. The Bible encourages us to pray throughout the day,[10] but Jesus also tells us in verse 6 that we should build a routine of spending set times in a set place with our Father. We can snack on bite-sized prayer all day, but we need leisurely feasts if we are to grow up healthy and strong in the Lord. That's why Jesus spent long periods in solitary prayer, and it's why he urges us to follow his lead.[11] He gives us a structure in 6:9–13 to help us in our prayers, moving

[8] This was appropriate for a tax collector coming to salvation in Luke 18:13, but the father stops his son from saying it in Luke 15:18–24.

[9] Psalm 100:4.

[10] 1 Thessalonians 5:17; Ephesians 6:18; Luke 18:1.

[11] Jesus withdrew to pray for nine hours in Matthew 14:23–25 and for a whole night in Luke 6:12. This is our goal, but we can start by copying his little-and-often practice of finding time for secluded prayer in Mark 1:35 and Luke 5:16 and 9:18.

from praise to requests to confession and prayers for help.[12] He promises that if we devote ourselves to secret prayer like this with our Father, he will certainly reward us. Sometimes the joy we find in God's presence will be enough in itself, but we will also find everything else we need besides.[13]

At the heart of God's Kingdom lifestyle lies this intimate fellowship with God Almighty, who has become our *Abba*, our *Dad*. Let's pray, let's fast, and let's give because we have been adopted as his children. As we do so, praying *"your kingdom come, your will be done"*, as directed in verse 10, we will find that our listening Father answers our prayers. We will find that the Kingdom of God advances through us.

[12] Luke 11:2 tells us that there is nothing wrong with reciting this as "the Lord's Prayer", but Matthew 6:9 tells us that he gives it us as a model of *how* to pray, not as something to pray by rote like the pagans.
[13] Psalm 73:25–28; Lamentations 3:24–26.

Kingdom Priorities (6:19–34)

But seek first his kingdom and his righteousness, and all these things will be given to you as well.

(Matthew 6:33)

One of Matt Redman's worship songs asks God to *"Send revival, start with me"*. It's a very good prayer to pray. If he had based his song on the Sermon on the Mount, he might even have prayed, *"Send your Revolution, start with me".* No sooner has Jesus told us in 6:10 to pray for his Kingdom to come on the earth, than he tells us to begin by welcoming it in our own lives. God's Kingdom comes when we accept him as the only true King, renouncing every pretender to his throne, and he calls us to start with that Great Pretender, *Money*.

We are not used to seeing Money as a false god, so Jesus helps by personifying it as *Mammon.*[1] Jesus does not deny that money makes an excellent servant, but warns that it also makes for a terrible master. A campfire is good but a house-fire can be fatal; money is good but Master Mammon is deadly. Therefore Jesus warns us that *"No one can serve two masters... You cannot serve both God and Mammon."* Disciples of Jesus welcome God's Kingdom into their lives when they evict the squatter Mammon from his unrighteous throne.

Many Christians are blind to the god Mammon. We are better at sound doctrine than sound lifestyle. The early Christians were so generous that *"there were no needy persons among them"*, and they could be commended that *"you joyfully*

---

[1] Many English translations simply talk about *Money* in verse 24, but Jesus actually uses the word *Mammon*, which was *Wealth* in Aramaic. He also talks about the false god Mammon again in Luke 6:9, 11, 13.

accepted the confiscation of your property, because you knew that you yourselves had better and lasting possessions".[2] We still admire their radical obedience, but few of us are very good at copying it. The Danish philosopher Søren Kierkegaard put it this way:

> The matter is quite simple. The Bible is very easy to understand. But we Christians are a bunch of scheming swindlers. We pretend to be unable to understand it because we know very well that the minute we understand, we are obliged to act accordingly... My God, you will say, if I do that my whole life will be ruined. How would I ever get on in the world?[3]

Jesus calls us to let his Kingdom "ruin" our lives, so that he can free us from the stranglehold of Mammon.

Mammon calls us to be *short-sighted*, but Jesus restores our long-distance vision. Mammon wants us to focus on the things of this world, and to forget that they rust, decay, and get stolen. It wants to dazzle us with the myopic glitter of earthly treasures, but Jesus calls us to throw them away for the sake of heaven's true treasure. There is no baggage allowance for those who pass from this world to the next, but Jesus tells we can store up treasure in heaven as we spend and are spent for the sake of his Kingdom.

Mammon calls us to be *greedy*, but Jesus tells us to give generously. The Hebrew phrase *bad-eyed* describes a coveter or a hoarder, and *good-eyed* describes a content and generous person.[4] Jesus urges us to be good-eyed, because how we look at possessions infects or disinfects the whole of our lives. Mammon

---

[2] Acts 4:32–37; Hebrews 10:34.

[3] Søren Kierkegaard in *Provocations: Spiritual Writings of Kierkegaard*, edited by Charles Moore, (1999).

[4] *Evil-eyed* means *envious* in Matthew 20:15; Proverbs 23:6; Deuteronomy 15:9; 28:54. Similarly, *good-eyed* means *content* in Proverbs 22:9.

fools the world that a little more will satisfy, but Jesus warns that greed simply corrupts a person from the inside out.[5] This is what he means in 13:22 when he talks about the *"deceitfulness of wealth"*, and so he tells us to give our money freely so that we can escape from the tyranny of greed. Each act of giving is a violent attack upon Mammon, and Jesus promises to teach us contentment as we press home our attack, even if at times we are poor.[6]

Mammon calls us to *worry*, but Jesus tells us to trust. Mammon lusts to replace God as our source of security, which is why the opposite of loving money is to rely on God's promise that *"Never will I leave you; never will I forsake you... The Lord is my helper; I will not be afraid"*.[7] Mammon is a terrible master, because his unstable provision goes up and down like the stock exchange, and he reneges on his credit notes whenever we need them most. What worries us masters us, and so Mammon hopes to enslave the world with his chains of worry. Worry saps our energy and yields nothing in return, but Jesus gives us an even greater reason not to worry. He tells us in verse 30 that it is the opposite of faith, a great insult to the generous and all-powerful Lord God Almighty. He provides for the birds and the flowers, and we can certainly trust him to provide for his own children.

Jesus sets a radical creed for his servants to follow in a Mammon-worshipping world: *"Seek first his Kingdom and his righteousness, and all these things will be given to you as well."* Cash is not king; Jesus is, and those who follow him set their money to work for his Kingdom. We work hard, we live simply, and we give generously, so that we can help the needy and promote the Gospel message around the world. In the ten minutes it has taken you to read this chapter, 210 people died of hunger and almost 1,000 people died and went to hell. As

---

[5] Proverbs 14:30.

[6] Philippians 4:11–12, 19; 1 Timothy 6:6–10.

[7] Hebrews 13:5–6.

followers of Jesus, we take these matters seriously. The fourth-century bishop, Basil of Caesarea, taught that

> *When someone strips a man of his clothes, we call him a thief. And one who might clothe the naked and does not – should not he be given the same name? The bread in your cupboard belongs to the hungry; the coat in your wardrobe belongs to the naked... the money in your vaults belongs to the destitute.*[8]

It's a costly way of life, but no more costly that the way of Jesus who *"was rich, yet for your sakes he became poor"*.[9]

In 1984, the US Supreme Court upheld that it was constitutional for the words *"In God We Trust"* to appear on all American money, despite the separation of Church and State, because such words had *"lost through rote repetition any significant religious content"*.[10] The children of God's Kingdom remember what it really means to trust in him and not in Mammon. They live in a manner that puzzles the money-obsessed culture around them, with a radical lifestyle which causes people to sit up and take their message seriously. The answer to our prayers that God's Kingdom will come on the earth is linked to the way that we let it come in ourselves. That's the Kingdom lifestyle which convinces the world.

Lord, send your Revolution, start with me.

---

[8] Basil of Caesarea, *Homily on "I will pull down my barns"*.
[9] 2 Corinthians 8:9. Luke 3:11; Matthew 25:40 also tell us that this is simply normal Christianity.
[10] Lynch v. Donnelly 465 US 668 (1984).

Kingdom Vigilance (7:1–5)

For in the same way as you judge others, you will be judged, and with the measure you use, it will be measured to you.

(Matthew 7:2)

One of the scariest concepts in the Arnold Schwarzenegger Terminator movies is that the evil Terminator machines can morph themselves to look exactly like their victim's loved ones and friends. In their determination to shed blood, they take the form of a mother, a daughter, a policeman, and a wife, in order to get close to those that they want to destroy.[1] Jesus' teaching in the Sermon on the Mount warns us that this is not just science fiction. Satan wants to terminate us, and he has the perfect machine with which to do it. His Terminator machine is pride, and it has a million different disguises.

Pride is a coy and canny fighter. It has to be. Those who have given their lives over to Jesus Christ are well aware that they must now walk his path of humility. So Satan finds charming disguises for his Terminator machine, and hopes to sneak up on us undetected.

Take for example *success and failure*. Most of us are ready for the attack of pride when it comes in the wake of achievement. We are ready to grapple with its temptation towards self-congratulation and praise. What we often miss is the more subtle attack of pride which comes in the wake of disappointment and defeat. John Piper puts it this way:

---

[1] For the benefit of geeks, I am referring to the T-1000 machine in *Terminator 2* (1991) and to the T-X machine in *Terminator 3* (2003).

Boasting is the response of pride to success. Self-pity is the response of pride to suffering... Boasting is the voice of pride in the heart of the strong. Self-pity is the voice of pride in the heart of the weak... Boasting sounds self-sufficient. Self-pity sounds self-sacrificing. The reason self-pity does not look like pride is that it appears to be needy. But the need arises from a wounded ego... The need self-pity feels does not come from a sense of unworthiness, but from a sense of unrecognized worthiness. It is the response of unapplauded pride.[2]

Satan really believes Jesus' promises that through meekness and poverty of spirit we will inherit the Kingdom of Heaven.[3] Therefore he is hell-bent on terminating our potential through pride and will use any disguise he can to penetrate our defences.

Take the *disagreements* which are part and parcel of normal everyday life. However much we agree with Elton John that *"Sorry seems to be the hardest word"*, most of us understand Jesus' teaching in Matthew 5:23–26 – that God is not interested in receiving our prayers and our worship until we have apologized to those we have wronged. We resist stubborn pride when we know we are in the wrong, but we are easily hoodwinked when we think we are in the right. Our culture is so infected with proud self-assertion of "rights" that this attack very often slips past unnoticed. So Jesus carries on in 6:14–15 with a stern warning about how we must behave when we are the ones offended and we are the ones who deserve an apology. He tells us very straightforwardly that *"If you forgive men when they sin against you, your heavenly Father will also forgive you. But if you do not forgive men their sins, your Father will not forgive you your sins."* Only the humble can bow the knee in repentance towards God

---

[2] John Piper, *Desiring God: Meditations of a Christian Hedonist* (1986).
[3] Matthew 5:3, 7.

and receive forgiveness for their sins, and it is impossible for us to be humble towards God at the same time as being proud towards each other.

Or take the spirit of *judgmentalism*, which Jesus addresses in Matthew 7:1–5. As Christians, we tend to be very good at spotting wickedness in others, and on one level this is to be commended. Much of chapter 6 is an exhortation to do exactly that when we see pagans or Pharisees at their worship. It's also what Jesus commands us to do in 7:6 when *"dogs"* and *"pigs"* want us to take them into our confidence.[4] Jesus wants us to be discerning and to confront one another over our sins and misdemeanours, which is why he instructs us in 18:15–17 about how we should do so.

But when pride dresses up in discernment's ill-fitting clothes, what is good quickly turns into the sin of judgmentalism. The discerning Christian acts as a *witness* to his brother, warning him as a peer to watch out lest he fall.[5] The judgmental Christian wants to play *judge* over his brother, and that is a role which belongs to God alone. Satan's primeval sin was to attempt to mount an angelic coup to usurp God's rightful place on the throne of heaven. When we judge others, we forget that we are human ourselves and that God is the only true Judge. No wonder the Welsh revivalist Daniel Rowlands taught that *"We most resemble the Devil when we are proud, and we most resemble Christ when we are humble."* Jesus uses humour to convict us of the preposterousness of this pride. Imagine a sinful and forgiven Christian passing judgment on his brother for smoking or drinking or gossiping or even for being proud – while all the

---

[4] Jesus was actually making a deliberate attack in this verse on the judgmentalism of the Pharisees. They called Gentiles *dogs* and shunned them like a bacon sandwich. Jesus tells them that their pride is in danger of terminating them, making them into the real *dogs* and *pigs* who are excluded from God's Kingdom.

[5] Jesus reminds us three times in 7:3–5 that the people we are judging are *brothers* and therefore our peers.

while acting like Satan did when he made his unholy bid to sit on God's judgment-throne! It is as ludicrous as a man with a rafter in his eye who thinks he can help others get a speck of dust out of their own!

Jesus wants us to help others, but not at the expense of being terminated ourselves. With frightening justice, he warns us that God will use the same measure to judge us as we use with others. If we are merciful, he will be merciful. If we are gracious, he will be gracious. But if we are proud, he will come with a fiery reminder that he is Judge and we are not – end of story.

So we need to be vigilant for Satan's Terminator machine of pride and to be ready for its many different faces. The Devil knows that *"God opposes the proud but gives grace to the humble"*,[6] and pride's many subtle disguises are his last-ditch attempt to destroy the work of God's Kingdom in our lives. Pride once destroyed Satan, and now he hopes it will destroy you too. He will not succeed if you listen to Jesus and learn to spot it before it attacks. He will not succeed if you stay humble and vigilant. What is at stake is your share in God's Kingdom Revolution, and by his grace it can never be terminated.

---

[6] Proverbs 3:34; James 4:6; 1 Peter 5:5.

Kingdom Decision
(7:13–27)

*Many will say to me on that day, "Lord, Lord…" Then
I will tell them plainly, "I never knew you. Away from
me, you evildoers!"*

(Matthew 7:22–23)

Last month I threw someone out of a wedding. They had
been walking past the church where the reception was taking
place and decided to crash it for the free food and drink. I was
helping at the wedding and gave them a quick introduction to
the teaching of Matthew 22:11–14. When it comes to wedding
receptions, it's who you know that matters. If your name's not
down, you're not coming in.

In the Kingdom of Heaven, it's the same. John tends to use
the phrase *"eternal life"* in his gospel to express what Matthew
refers to as the *"kingdom of heaven"*, and he tells us in John 17:3
that *"this is eternal life: that they may **know** you, the only true God,
and Jesus Christ, whom you have sent"*. The Kingdom of Heaven
is about *knowing* God and *knowing* Jesus his Son. It's not about
adopting a series of rules or signing up to a religious manifesto.
It's so centred on knowing Jesus that he ends his Sermon on the
Mount with a chilling warning about the Day of Judgment. On
that day, he will turn to many who thought that they were good
Christians and tell them: *"I never knew you. Away from me, you
evildoers!"* They embraced the trappings of God's Kingdom, but
they never knew the King.

Like all good preachers, Jesus ends his sermon with a call
for decision. It is much easier to admire Jesus than to follow

him, and so he tells us plainly in these last fifteen verses what following him truly means.

It is not something we can do in addition to our other priorities. If you were travelling from London to New York and I wanted to sit next to you for the journey, I could not do so by travelling to Madrid. If I want to sit next to you, I have to be where you are. The same is true if we want to follow Jesus: we need to give up everything to be where he is and to walk the road that he is walking. Jesus contrasts this narrow road with the broad road taken by so many, which is broad enough to accommodate all their beliefs and baggage, their plans and priorities. Jesus explains that this is a very different road to the one he calls us to follow, and that many are unwittingly en route to destruction in hell.[1] He illustrates this in 8:21–22 by refusing to allow someone to follow him and be devoted to his parents,[2] and in 9:16–17 by warning that *new wine* cannot be squeezed into old wineskins. Jesus invites us to pass through the narrow door of salvation, which is too tight to admit any hand-luggage. Babies are born naked, and believers are born again naked, ready to be clothed by their new Father. Unless we enter by the narrow gate, we can never walk with Jesus on the narrow road.

Nor is following Jesus just a matter of outward religion. Many people wear Christian clothes and look like they are part of the People of God, but Jesus warns that he can see beneath their clothing. They sit in church, they live moral lives, and they are easily offended when their relationship with God is questioned. Nevertheless, Jesus tells us that they are *"wolves in sheep's clothing"*, wearing the clothes of Christianity but without its substance. Their faith is a system of *"rules taught*

---

[1] Although the Greek word *apōleia* simply means *destruction*, it is often used in the New Testament to refer specifically to destruction in hell. See, for example, Philippians 1:28; 2 Peter 3:7; Acts 8:20.

[2] Jewish corpses were buried within hours of death. The man is not so much asking to go to his father's funeral, as to wait for his father to need a funeral! Jesus replies that no one can follow him *and* their parents.

by men",[3] devoid of a heart filled with the Holy Spirit. That's why Jesus advises that "by their fruit you will recognize them", because only Holy-Spirit sap can produce true Holy-Spirit fruit.[4] They may impress enough to win leadership positions within the Church, but sooner or later their fruit will give them away. Jesus warns them to repent and truly follow him, or they will be *"thrown into the fire"* of hell.

Even pursuing successful Christian ministry is not the same thing as following Jesus. He speaks his chilling verdict that *"I never knew you"* to people who prophesied, drove out demons, and performed miracles in his name. These were not simply pew-warming idlers. They were active participators, performing miracles beyond those of many true believers. Yet they did not *know* Jesus, and that's what truly matters. Judas Iscariot drove out demons and healed the sick alongside the other disciples, but he still went to his destruction because his heart resisted Jesus.[5] Experiencing God's power is quite different from knowing God's Son.

Even agreeing with Jesus' teaching in the Sermon on the Mount does not make a person a true follower of Jesus. Although Scripture describes Christians as *believers*, it is at pains to clarify that true belief always results in action. Jesus says that those who truly believe in him will not just hear his teaching but *"put it into practice"* and *"do the will of my Father who is in heaven"*. No one can be saved through their obedience, but nor can anyone be saved without obedience, for the faith that saves always produces *"fruit in keeping with repentance"*.[6] Christians are saved by grace through faith, but there is no such thing as an "invisible conversion". When a person puts their faith in Jesus Christ, they start living differently. It's as simple as that.

---

[3] Matthew 15:7–9.

[4] Paul describes this fruit in Galatians 5:22–23 as love, joy, peace, patience, kindness, goodness, meekness, faithfulness and self-control.

[5] Matthew 10:1, 8; Luke 9:1–6; 10:17.

[6] Matthew 3:8. See also James 2:14–26.

The dictionary defines *inoculation* as *"giving a weak form of a disease to a person or animal as a protection against that disease"*. Jesus wants you to be thoroughly infected by his Kingdom Revolution, and so he ends his Sermon with a warning against Satan's many inoculations. He warns us not to be satisfied by pretend-following, by nominal Christianity, by lifeless ministry, or by lethargic spectatorship. All of these look like Christianity, but they are merely a weak form which inoculates against the genuine article.

Jesus saves spiritual beggars who mourn over their sin and thirst to be made righteous. He saves those who lay down everything to know and follow him as King. He fills such people with his Holy Spirit and grants them the fullness of his Kingdom, from the inside out. He enables them to call God their *Abba Father* and seek first his Kingdom, passing grace and forgiveness to those they meet along the way.

Jesus calls us to resist inoculation and to receive the Christian "disease" in all its intensity. He calls us to be ordinary carriers of his contagious Kingdom.

Slumdog Millionaires
(8:1 – 9:38)

The men were amazed and asked, "What kind of man is this? Even the winds and the waves obey him!"

(Matthew 8:27)

One of the most successful films of 2009 was *Slumdog Millionaire.* Jamal, the hero, is a boy from the Mumbai slums who finds himself in the hot seat on the TV show *Who Wants to Be a Millionaire?* Through a series of coincidences from his life in the slums, he is able to answer each successive question on his way to becoming the Slumdog Millionaire of the title. He finds that his life of pain and poverty in the slums has uniquely equipped him to see the right answers – answers which no privileged or affluent contestant could ever know.

Matthew chapters 8 and 9 are a first-century version of *Slumdog Millionaire.* This is the second part of Act One, the action which illustrates the teaching of chapters 5 to 7,[1] and Matthew uses it to list a succession of outcasts who see Jesus for who he is, while members of the in-crowd just can't see it. At first glance, the outcasts look as if God has dealt them a terrible hand in life, but Matthew – who was actually one of the outcasts himself – defies our expectations. He shows us that it is only *because* these people were outcasts that they were prepared to see Jesus for who he really is.

First there is a leper, disfigured by his crippling disease and

---

[1] The five acts are chapters 5–9, 10–12, 13–17, 18–22, and 23–27. Each of them moves from "teaching" to "action" with the stock phrase, *"when Jesus had finished saying these things"* (7:28; 11:1; 13:53; 19:1; 26:1).

excluded from Jewish society. Even lepers could find comfort in one another, but this one is completely alone. He is a solitary figure, a walking tragedy, the epitome of human suffering, and yet the trouble in his life has humbled his heart ready to receive Jesus. He freely admits that he is dirty, he worships Jesus as his Lord,[2] and he confesses by faith that Jesus can make him clean. Jesus responds straight away to his humility, and he heals him with a touch and a simple command, before sending him to the Temple to offer a sacrifice to God.

Next comes a Roman centurion of the occupying army, one of the servants of wicked Herod and equally wicked Emperor Tiberius. He was a Gentile and may have worked at the same army base as the soldiers who would later crucify Jesus. Nevertheless, he had one thing in his favour. His life in the Roman army had taught him how authority works, and had given him faith that Jesus could heal his servant with just a word. His background prepared him for his encounter with Jesus, and he left having been granted the healing he requested.

Next is a whole crowd of sick and demonized people, who all humble themselves to receive help from Jesus their Messiah. The first of them is Peter's mother-in-law, struck down by a terrible fever and unaware that it was the preparation-ground through which God would help her reach out to Jesus. Then her son-in-law gets into a boat with his fellow disciples and they sail out into a storm which is so deadly that even a hardened fisherman like Peter thinks he is about to die. The Twelve were already following Jesus before the storm, but the horrors of near-drowning lead them out to a greater prayer of faith: *"Lord, save us! We are perishing!"*[3]

---

[2] Matthew uses the word *proskuneō* to tell us that the leper *worshipped* Jesus and notes that he addressed Jesus as *kurios*, the word used in the Greek Old Testament for *the Lord*. It is not inaccurate to translate them with the secular words *knelt* and *master*, but it does not fully capture what Matthew is saying.

[3] The verb *apollumi* is the main word used in the New Testament for *perishing* in hell (e.g. John 3:16), so Matthew has a deliberate double meaning in their

With breathless speed, Matthew hurries on to tell us about two tormented demoniacs, about a paralysed man, and his own salvation testimony as a guilt-ridden tax collector. He carries on with an unclean woman who suffered from a non-stop period, a man whose daughter had just died, two blind men, and yet another demonized man. All of these people were desperate in their own way, and each of them was humble enough to receive Jesus as he passed them by. They were all Slumdog Millionaires, prepared by the tragedies of their life to grasp that Jesus was the Messiah and to lay hold of him by faith.

The rich and religious had received no such preparation, and Matthew peppers his account of outcast-faith with contrasting examples of in-crowd-unbelief. There is a teacher of the law in 8:19, wanting to follow Jesus but strangled to death by his love of possessions. There are the prosperous citizens of Gadara in 8:34, who ask Jesus to go away rather than risk him inflicting any more damage to their property. There are the Jewish religious leaders of 9:3 and 9:34, so engrossed in their own pious interpretations of the Old Testament Scriptures that they fail to spot the Messiah about whom those Scriptures spoke. God longed to save them along with the outcasts, but few of them were humble enough to receive him. When the Pharisee Jairus was humbled by the death of his daughter he quickly came to Jesus to raise her from the dead,[4] but without such a crisis his fellow religious leaders simply accused Jesus of blasphemy and of being in league with the Devil. Even Jairus' friends, spectators of tragedy but not actual participators themselves, simply laughed at Jesus and dismissed him in 9:24.

The pivotal theme of Matthew 8 and 9 is the disciples' question in 8:27: *"What kind of man is this?!"* That is the question which Matthew wants each one of us to answer as we read these

---

choice of words.

[4] Matthew simply calls him a *ruler*, but Mark 5:22 tells us that he was a *synagogue ruler* and therefore almost certainly part of the Pharisee sect. Mark also tells us his name was Jairus.

two chapters. He has given us Jesus' background in chapters 1 to 4 and Jesus' teaching in chapters 5 to 7, but now he wants us to respond with faith and commitment on our part.

I remember once sharing the Gospel with a woman who asked me with tears in her eyes, *"How can I believe in God when good things happen to such bad people, and bad things happen to such good people?"* Matthew turns that question back on its head. Good things happened to the members of the Jewish in-crowd, but they were actually the worst things that could ever have happened to them. Those "good things" made them so attached to their possessions, their parents, their religious rules, and their systematic theology that they were blind to see the Messiah when he came. Bad things happened to the outcasts, but they were actually the best things that could have happened to them. They were Slumdog Millionaires, prepared by the terrible experiences of their lives to recognize and reach out to the Messiah when he came. God used suffering to plough up the hard ground of their hearts so that they were ready to receive the seed of the Gospel.

These two chapters illustrate Jesus' teaching in 5:3 that *"Blessed are the spiritual beggars, for theirs is the kingdom of heaven."* They alert us to the great danger of being prosperous and honoured with the in-crowd, and to the great advantage of being humbled to our knees with the outcasts.

Whether God has blessed you with tragedy in your life, or whether you have lived the life of the rich and religious, Matthew calls you to respond to the disciples' question and to place your own faith in Jesus the Messiah. He calls you to join the ranks of God's Slumdog Millionaires.

Deliverance from Rome (8:5–13)

When Jesus heard this, he was astonished and said to those following him, "I tell you the truth, I have not found anyone in Israel with such great faith."

(Matthew 8:10)

Nobody knew how to disappoint the public quite like Jesus of Nazareth. He was the Messiah, the king of the Jews, the one everyone expected to throw off the Roman occupation and establish the kingdom of Israel through a series of conquests. He was to be like the great freedom fighter Judas Maccabaeus, only far, far better. But Jesus had other ideas. He had *God's* ideas.

Not everybody saw this at first. When Jesus called Simon the Zealot and the rest of the twelve disciples, they still had high hopes that Jesus might be the sword-wielding hero they had been waiting for. Even after his resurrection, they still asked him hopefully, *"Lord, are you at this time going to restore the kingdom to Israel?"*[1] Their first clue that something was wrong came in the Sermon on the Mount, when Jesus made passing reference to the much-resented law that a Roman soldier could force any Jewish male to carry his equipment for one mile.[2] They waited for his dangerously seditious call to resist. Surely this could be the Rosa-Parks battleground, the place where the Messiah would rally his followers to oppose Roman rule? Jesus' suggestion that they carry the equipment for two miles, not one,

---

[1] Acts 1:6.

[2] Jesus mentions the practice in Matthew 5:41, and Matthew gives us an example of it in 27:32.

was baffling to say the least. He baffled them still further with his teaching in 22:15–22 that they must pay Caesar's taxes in full. Jesus preached a revolution – there was no doubt about that – but it was a far cry from the revolution his public were waiting for. They found it downright offensive.

The Kingdom that Jesus preached had a bigger *enemy* than his public expected. He didn't fight the Romans, for he knew that their emperor and his governors were appointed and sustained by God himself.[3] He stood before Governor Pilate and warned him that *"you would have no power over me if it were not given to you from above"*, and told him that *"my kingdom is not of this world... my kingdom is from another place"*.[4] He had not come to defeat Rome, but Satan.[5] He had not come to kill the Romans, but to save them.

The Kingdom that Jesus preached had bigger *goals* than his public expected too. They wanted the liberation of 8,000 square miles of Palestinian real estate, but Jesus brought a Kingdom which would fill the whole earth.[6] They hoped the Messiah would put Israel at the head of an empire which would last for hundreds of years, but Jesus brought a Kingdom which would last forever.[7] They wanted him to destroy the nations before them, but he wanted to save the nations alongside them.[8]

The Kingdom that Jesus preached had a far greater *currency* than his public expected. They thought it would be established with swords, spears, and slaughter, but he established it with humility, faith, and submission. Not on horseback, but on a donkey. Not crowned with gold, but with thorns. Not with rings on his fingers, but with nails through his hands and his feet.

---

[3] See Romans 13:1–2, which Paul wrote to Christians in the imperial capital during the reign of the wicked Emperor Nero.

[4] John 18:36; 19:11.

[5] 1 John 3:8.

[6] Matthew 5:5; Daniel 2:35.

[7] 2 Samuel 7:16; Isaiah 9:6–7; Daniel 2:44; 2 Peter 1:11.

[8] Revelation 7:9–10; Ephesians 2:11–22.

He was the hope of Israel, but he was not what Israel hoped for. When he launched his attack on Satan and his demons, the Jews asked him to leave, or accused him of being in league with Satan himself.[9] When he offered salvation or healing, they accused him of blasphemy and plotted to kill him.[10] When he came to them in humility, they either laughed at him, ridiculed him, or tried to force him to conform to their agenda.[11]

But the Gentiles were not clouded by such preconceptions, and many of them welcomed him with open arms. Here in chapter 8, one of the Roman centurions who oversaw the occupying army accepted Jesus' teaching, believed it with simple faith, and laid hold of the Jewish Messiah. He accepted Jesus as the one who fought Satan and sickness, whose Gospel reached even to the Gentiles, and whose humble façade concealed an authority which exceeded even that of Caesar's highly disciplined legions. In short, he let Jesus be *God's* Messiah, bringing *God's* Revolution in *God's* way, and Jesus loved it. Amazed at this Gentile's faith, Jesus turned to the crowds and warned them what would happen unless they did the same. He told the Jews that they were *"sons of the kingdom"* – he left no room for foolish "replacement theology" which treats the Jews just like any other race[12] – but then warned that many of them would be thrown into hell while Gentiles joined the patriarchs in heaven. Being a Jew wouldn't save anyone, and Jewish preconceptions might even become a *hindrance* to salvation. It was time for them to humble themselves as John the Baptist had taught them. God's Kingdom Revolution was greater than they thought, and they mustn't let their earth-bound hopes obscure its glory.

It is surprising at first that Matthew, who wrote primarily for the Jews, should fill his gospel with so many references to Jesus saving the Gentiles instead of them. After quoting these

---

[9] Matthew 8:34; 9:34.

[10] Matthew 9:3; 12:14.

[11] Matthew 9:24; 13:54–58; John 6:14–15.

[12] Romans 1:16; 2:9–10.

unpalatable words in chapter 8, he goes on to quote prophecies from Isaiah and the Psalms that the Messiah would be rejected by the Jews and would save the Gentiles.[13] He also showcases the faith of a Canaanite woman over the stubborn dogmatism of the Jews and emphasizes that the Gospel call belongs to *"all nations"*.[14] Yet we should not really be surprised. He is simply pursuing the strategy that Paul outlines in Romans 11:11–14, trying to make his Jewish readers so jealous that the Gentiles are accepting their Messiah that they humble themselves and receive him too. He is telling them that God has already chosen the nature of his Kingdom, and that if they refuse to embrace it the other nations will.

This is a very relevant message for you, whether you are as Jewish as Abraham or as Gentile as Pilate. Matthew's message is for Jews, but its application is much broader. Christians in every generation have been tempted to reshape Jesus of Nazareth to fit their own desires and expectations, and Matthew warns that Jesus is not for changing. Liberation theology, which downsizes God's Kingdom enemy, prosperity theology, which twists God's Kingdom goals, and self-assertive theology, which ignores God's Kingdom methods, are all swept off the table.

Jesus is *God's* Messiah who fights *God's* enemy for *God's* goals and with *God's* methods. The Revolution which he starts is a revolution led by *God's* agenda. If we will not accept him as he is, he will simply find other would-be revolutionaries. God's Kingdom has come. We need to repent and fall into line with *his* programme.

---

[13] Isaiah 42:1–4 quoted in Matthew 12:17–21, and Psalm 118:22–23 quoted in Matthew 21:41–43.
[14] Matthew 15:1–28; 28:18–20.

Authority (8:16–17)

This was to fulfil what was spoken through the prophet Isaiah: "He took up our infirmities and carried our diseases."

(Matthew 8:17)

If *"X"* marks the spot where treasure is buried, every Christian should put a large *"X"* in their Bible next to Matthew 8:17. It is the verse which explains how Jesus snatched authority away from Satan, and which gives us certain faith to press home his Kingdom victory. If you want to heal the sick, drive out demons, plant a church, or simply see a lost friend saved, you need to stop at this verse and start digging. You won't be disappointed.

Jesus wielded unsurpassed authority. That's the constant cry of praise as Jesus heals sickness and drives out demons in chapters 8 and 9.[1] In that context, as Jesus drives out demons *"with a word"* and heals all those who are sick, Matthew explains how he was able to do so. He quotes from Isaiah 53 and the Messianic prophecy that *"He took up our infirmities and carried our diseases"*. This is the ground where our treasure is buried, so let's roll up our sleeves and go digging together.

Matthew tells us that Jesus healed people because he is King. The primary reason he was able to drive out sickness, Satan, demons, and death was not that he was God (although he was) or that he had God's power (although he did). It was because he possessed a legal authority which simply could not be resisted. That's why Matthew quotes here from one of the most famous Messianic prophecies in the Old Testament

---

[1] Matthew 7:29; 8:9; 9:6; 9:8; 10:1.

and firmly links Jesus' healing ministry to his Kingly authority. Jesus did the same when he told his enemies that *"if I drive out demons by the Spirit of God, then the kingdom of God has come upon you"*, and when he quietened John the Baptist's doubts that he might not truly be the coming King by pointing out that *"the blind receive sight, the lame walk, those who have leprosy are cured, the deaf hear, the dead are raised, and the good news is preached to the poor"*.[2] We need to understand that healing and deliverance are not just acts of divine compassion, but the natural consequence of the fact that Jesus is King and Satan is not.[3] They are not just *proof* of the Gospel of the Kingdom. They are part of the Gospel itself.[4]

Next, Matthew tells us that Jesus gained this authority through his death on the cross. Isaiah 53 is probably the clearest Old Testament prophecy about the atoning death of Jesus, and Matthew quotes it for a reason. He wants us to grasp that healing is not just the fruit of God's character and his desire to save, but is something that has been won through a definitive legal transaction. Sickness was an aspect of God's just curse upon sin,[5] but our standing changed when Jesus *"became a curse"* for us on the cross and died with the victory-cry *"It is finished!"* on his lips. When the man Jesus died at Calvary, he undid the God-given authority which Satan stole from Adam in the Garden of Eden.[6] He disarmed him and stripped him of

---

[2] Matthew 11:5; 12:28.

[3] The Bible does not teach that physical sickness is *always* linked to demonic activity, but Peter teaches in Acts 10:38 that sickness is a work of the Devil. Since Matthew 9:32–33 and Luke 13:11–16 both treat a mute and a woman with backache as victims of spiritual as well as medical problems, we should take this seriously.

[4] Matthew links healing to *"the Gospel of the Kingdom"* in 4:23 and 9:35. Paul even writes in Romans 15:19 that preaching and performing miracles is an integral part of fully proclaiming the Gospel of Christ.

[5] Deuteronomy 28:21–22, 59–61; Romans 5:12.

[6] Galatians 3:13; John 19:30. It did not matter that Jesus had not yet physically died in chapter 8, since he was *"slain from the creation of the world"* (Revelation

every weapon that could resist the advance of God's Kingdom.[7] We see his demons in 8:29 and 31, literally grovelling on their knees before King Jesus. Because of the Gospel, they know that they are doomed.

Finally, Matthew tells us that Jesus dealt with the curse of sickness on the cross *in the same way* that he dealt with our sin. This was much more obvious to his original Jewish readers than it is to us, because they were familiar with the Old Testament in Hebrew and Greek, but if we slow down and dig deeper we can see what they saw:

> *He was despised and rejected by men; a man of pains [mak'ob], and acquainted with sickness [holiy]; he was despised like one from whom men hide their faces, and we esteemed him not. Surely he has carried [nasa'] our sicknesses [holiy] and borne [sabal] our pains [mak'ob]... He will bear [sabal] their iniquities... He carried [nasa'] the sin of many.*

Can you see now why Matthew chose Isaiah 53 out of all the chapters of the Old Testament to give an explanation for Jesus' healing ministry? It's a passage which uses two Hebrew words – *mak'ob* and *holiy* – which almost always refer to physical, rather than spiritual, pain and sickness. In case we miss this point, Matthew discards his usual practice of quoting from the Greek Septuagint because that translation spiritualized the passage to mean, *"he bears our sins and is pained for us"*. Instead, he goes back to the Hebrew Old Testament and retranslates it more accurately as *"he took our sicknesses and carried our diseases"*.[8]

13:8) and was therefore able to heal in the same way that he forgave the paralysed man of his sin in 9:1–8.

[7] Colossians 2:15. Jesus disarmed Satan of *all* his weapons at the cross, including sickness.

[8] Unlike the Greek Septuagint, Matthew chooses the words *astheneiai* and *nosoi*, which refer specifically to physical *sicknesses* and *diseases*. Matthew normally quotes from the Septuagint, so this is deliberate.

Jewish readers who went back to the passage in Isaiah would also notice that the words *nasa'* and *sabal* (which both mean *"to carry"*) are used to refer to the way that he carried both our sin *and* our sickness. Neither Matthew nor Isaiah wants us to make a distinction between the way Jesus bore our sin and the way he bore our sickness. Jesus was able to heal sickness and drive out demons because he was about to die on the cross to carry both our sins *and* the curse which lay on humankind through sin. Jesus is our Saviour, both from sin and from sickness, because he can justly free us from the curse of human sin.[9]

Some people object to this link between Jesus' healing ministry and his cross because he ministered this way before his crucifixion. This ignores the teaching of Revelation 13:8 that Jesus was *"slain from the creation of the world"*. He could both heal through the cross before he went to Calvary in the same way that he could forgive through the cross in 9:2.

If we ignore what Matthew 8:17 teaches us about the link between Jesus' cross and his authority over sickness and demons, we are left trusting only in God's compassionate character for such miracles today.[10] This gives us reason to *hope* for success against these symptoms of Satan's rule, but no sure ground for genuine *faith* that Christ has given us authority to command such miracles in his name. However, if we grasp that these things come through Jesus' death and resurrection, and that he has received all power and authority as a definitive legal mandate through his own blood, we have confidence to *rebuke* sickness like Jesus, *dispense* healing like Jesus, and *expel* demons like Jesus. It is only when we grasp the scope of Jesus'

---

[9] This explains why Matthew uses the Greek verb *sōzō*, to save, in 9:21–22 to describe Jesus' healing ministry. He did not see a distinction between *saving* and *healing*. They are both part of one great salvation package.

[10] Matthew stresses the important of Jesus' compassion in 9:36, but only after he has emphasized in the previous verse that Jesus acted on this compassion as part of the good news that he is King.

victory at Calvary that we are able to insist that Satan flee and that he take his vile work with him.

The Devil does not want you to understand Matthew 8:17. He is like an outgunned general who frightens his enemy into calling off their attack by the clever use of mock gun emplacements. We need to unearth this treasure and to let its beauty draw our gaze. It helps us to see him as he really is – a toothless foe relying on guile alone to hold on to his crumbling kingdom. Satan trembles at the thought that you might see him as he truly is through the message which is buried in Matthew 8:17. Settle in your heart that his kingdom has no authority left before the Kingdom of Jesus Christ, and then you can push forward in the spiritual battle and plunder his usurped territory for the Kingdom of God.

Son of Man (9:1–8)

"But so that you may know that the Son of Man has authority on earth to forgive sins..." Then he said to the paralytic, "Get up, take your mat and go home."

(Matthew 9:6)

Revolutionaries always have to watch their back. The Emperor Tiberius killed a tenth of the Roman nobility in the latter years of his reign, consumed with paranoid fear for his throne. He would not have thought twice about eliminating a Jewish carpenter who claimed to have founded a rival Kingdom. So Jesus used a code name, a title which meant much to his followers but little to anyone else. It was very clever.

Jesus called himself *"the Son of Man"* thirty-one times in Matthew's gospel alone. It was by far his favourite way of describing himself – both innocuous and incendiary at one and the same time. To ignorant onlookers, it was a normal Jewish way of referring to a *human*.[1] But to those in the know, it was the most dangerous claim a Roman subject ever could make: it meant that Jesus was King and the Emperor Tiberius was not.

Six hundred years earlier and six hundred miles away, the prophet Daniel had seen a vision in Babylon of the next four empires in world history. The Babylonians, the Persians, the Macedonians, and the Romans all passed before him in vivid array. Then suddenly, when the Roman Empire was at its height, he saw a new king with a different kind of empire. He tells us in Daniel 7:13–14 that

---

[1] God uses it ninety-three times in the book of Ezekiel to refer to the prophet's humanity and several times in the rest of the Bible to refer to human beings in general (Numbers 23:19; Job 25:6; Psalm 8:4; Mark 3:28).

I looked, and there before me was one like a son of man,
coming with the clouds of heaven. He approached the
Ancient of Days and was led into his presence. He was
given authority, glory and sovereign power; all peoples,
nations and men of every language worshipped him.
His dominion is an everlasting dominion that will not
pass away, and his kingdom is one that will never be
destroyed.

This figure *"like a son of man"* was the coming Messiah, who would establish God's universal and eternal Kingdom on the earth. When Jesus chose the name *"Son of Man"* to use as his calling card, he chose something missable yet momentous.

Little by little, Jesus revealed the meaning behind the name *"Son of Man"*. He linked it to wielding *authority* to heal and forgive, to end world history, and to judge humankind.[2] His claims became more and more outlandish for anyone other than God, until the startling dénouement as he stood on trial before the Sanhedrin in 26:63–64. When asked to *"tell us if you are the Christ, the Son of God"*, he replied *"Yes, it is as you say, but I say to all of you: In the future you will see the Son of Man sitting at the right hand of the Mighty One and coming on the clouds of heaven"*. Andrew Wilson comments that:

> *It doesn't sound as if Jesus is downgrading [from Son of God to Son of Man], does it? It doesn't sound like they are asking if he is fully God, and he is saying, "Yes, but I am also fully man." It sounds like he is upgrading, dramatically. It sounds like a schoolboy who has just been secretly cast as the lead part in a Hollywood blockbuster – when the bullies ask him, "Did you come top of the class in Drama?" he replies, "You said it;*

---

[2] See Matthew 9:6; 16:27; 19:28; 24:30; 25:31; 26:64. These verses make no sense whatsoever except as a direct claim to be the Messiah, Daniel's great King of kings, who would receive the worship of the nations.

but from now on you will see me as Harry Potter, on billboards and film screens all over the country."[3]

No wonder they screamed that they had all the proof they needed for their blasphemy charge. Little by little, Jesus revealed what *"the Son of Man"* meant. When he did so, it got him killed.

Even so, this code name is still surprisingly effective. In 2003, Dan Brown published his best-selling novel, *The Da Vinci Code*, with its strident claim that the Early Church foisted divinity upon Jesus long after his death, by *"a relatively close vote"*.[4] Educated Westerners snapped up over 60 million copies of the novel and largely imbibed its theology. More seriously, 1.5 billion Muslims claim Jesus as their prophet but react angrily to the idea that he might have claimed to be God. I have even heard Jews – ignorant of their own Scriptures – use the title *"Son of Man"* as a proof that he claimed to be nothing more than human. Jesus continues his Revolution, and sometimes he still prefers to travel incognito.[5]

But to those who have eyes to see, Jesus reveals his divinity everywhere. He does so through the authority of his teaching, claiming that *"you have heard that it was said... but I tell you"*[6] and amazing the crowds with his teaching *"because he taught as one who had authority, and not as their teachers of the law"*.[7] He reveals it through his miracles, and supremely through his resurrection. But here in Matthew 9:1–8, he

---

[3] Andrew Wilson, *Incomparable* (2007).

[4] Dan Brown's novel *The Da Vinci Code*, and especially pp. 316–318. *The Rough Guide* produced a travel guide in 2004 to the monuments in the book, and concluded that *"It is a mishmash of historical nonsense... Dan Brown is effectively saying that the institution of the Church is built on a lie. But the lie is Dan Brown's and it is deliberate."*

[5] See Matthew 7:6; 11:25–26; 13:10–17.

[6] Matthew 5:21–22, 27–28, 31–32, 33–34, 38–39, 43–44.

[7] Matthew 7:28–29.

does so with such clarity that even the thick-skinned scribes understand he is claiming to be God. Jesus sees that the primary need of the paralysed man is forgiveness, not healing, and he declares over him that *"Your sins are forgiven"*. The scribes are furious: *"Who is this fellow who speaks blasphemy? Who can forgive sins but God alone?"*[8] They grasp what still eludes most Muslims and Jews – and Dan Brown – as Jesus heals the man to prove that *"the Son of Man has authority to forgive sins"*. They grasped that the *"Son of Man"* was a code name to conceal Jesus' claim to be God in human flesh.

C.S. Lewis puts it very succinctly:

> *One part of the claim tends to slip past us unnoticed because we have heard it so often that we no longer see what it amounts to. I mean the claim to forgive sins: any sins. Now unless the speaker is God, this is really so preposterous as to be comic. We can all understand how a man forgives offences against himself. You tread on my toe and I forgive you, you steal my money and I forgive you. But what should we make of a man, himself unrobbed and untrodden on, who announced that he forgave you for treading on other men's toes and stealing other men's money?... Yet this is what Jesus did... He unhesitatingly behaved as if he was the party chiefly concerned, the person chiefly offended in all offences. This makes sense only if he really was the God whose laws are broken and whose love is wounded in every sin... You can shut him up for a fool, you can spit at him and kill him as a demon or you can fall at his feet and call him Lord and God. But let us not come with any patronising nonsense about his being a great*

---

[8] This is Luke's expanded version of Matthew 9:3 in Luke 5:21.

human teacher. He has not left that open to us. He did not intend to.[9]

Jesus is the Son of Man. Look beneath the code.

[9] C.S. Lewis, *Mere Christianity* (1952).

Friend of Sinners (9:10–13)

When the Pharisees saw this, they asked his disciples, "Why does your teacher eat with tax collectors and 'sinners'?"

(Matthew 9:11)

Jesus spent lots of time with prostitutes, tax collectors, drunkards, and "sinners". Frankly, that's a bit surprising for the one that the Old Testament promised would *"love righteousness and hate wickedness"*.[1] It certainly shocked the Pharisees. What's more, these "sinners" loved him and wanted to be with him. Normally, creatures of the dark shrink away from the light, but Jesus drew them to him like moths to a flame. Sadly, that isn't always the case with his followers. Too many Christians repulse "sinners".

A worker on the streets of Chicago tells the following story:

A prostitute came to see me in wretched straits, homeless, sick, unable to buy food for her two-year-old daughter. Through sobs and tears, she told me she had been renting out her daughter – two years old! – to men interested in kinky sex. She made more renting out her daughter for an hour than she could earn on her own in a night. She had to do it, she said, to support her own drug habit. I could hardly bear hearing her sordid story... At last I asked if she had ever thought of going to a church for help. I will never forget the look of pure, naïve shock that crossed

---

[1] Psalm 45:7, quoted as a reference to Jesus in Hebrews 1:9.

*her face. "Church!" she cried. "Why would I ever go there?
I was already feeling terrible about myself. They'd just
make me feel worse."*[2]

When I first read that story, I cried. My city is full of prostitutes, binge drinkers, thieves, and brawlers, but not many of them turn up at church meetings. I wonder if people look at my church and think the same thing – the house of salvation, too heavily disguised for those who need it most. What was it about Jesus that made him the *"friend of sinners"* and won the hearts of the lost and the hurting? I'm convinced that it was above all else his understanding of the Gospel.

The Pharisees put their faith in *separatism*. They longed to be righteous, so they avoided unrighteous company and devoted themselves to prayer, fasting, and almsgiving. They meant well, but their "gospel" was simply self-righteous rule-keeping. The more they pursued righteousness, the more they hated sinners, and the less they became like God himself. In contrast, Jesus pursued the Gospel of *love*, the love which leaves ninety-nine "righteous sheep" behind to go and find the one "lost sheep".[3] He sat among "sinners" because God's loving grace triumphs over judgment through the Gospel, and comes to seek and save those who are lost. When my wife was a little girl, she fell into a slurry pit on a dairy farm and started to drown in a tank filled with cow dung. Her dad was in earshot and immediately waded in after her and pulled her to safety. Love is like that. It gets involved and dirtied and soiled by the mess of broken lives, because the Gospel is for "sinners", not for those who are too proud to feel any need of a Saviour.

The priests put their faith in *cleanness* and went to extraordinary lengths to ensure that they touched nothing that would make them ceremonially unclean. They hoped to impress

---

[2] This story is taken from Philip Yancey's book *What's So Amazing About Grace?* (1997).

[3] Luke 15:3–7.

God with their purity, so much so that a priest ignored a dying man in the Parable of the Good Samaritan rather than risk being contaminated by his bleeding wounds.[4] Jesus behaved the opposite way as he *touched* those in need. In chapters 8 and 9 alone, he touches a leper, a woman with a fever, a menstruating woman, a corpse, and two blind beggars.[5] He even offered to enter a Gentile's home, something he knew would make him ceremonially unclean.[6] While the priests worried about being infected, Jesus knew that through the Gospel infection now works the other way around. He did not fear unclean company, for one touch from him would be enough to make the unclean whole.

I have conducted a little survey in many different churches across the UK. I simply ask people to write down the names of all the non-Christians with whom they spend at least an hour a week. For those who follow the *"friend of sinners"*, we're not doing very well. Few Christians can honestly name more than five such non-Christian friends, and among church leaders the figure is even lower. I don't believe that this is a minor side-issue. I believe it exposes a flawed understanding of the Gospel itself.

We can reduce the Gospel to a call for *separatism*, so that Christianity becomes the loveless pursuit of morality. One of my closest Christian friends recently complained to me that he hates his job because he is forced to share an office all day with smutty and blaspheming colleagues. I know what he means, but you don't have to wear a *WWJD* bracelet to recognize that as Pharisee- and priest-thinking. We can also reduce the Gospel to an introspective call to church meetings and Christian friendship cliques, so that we are too busy to share life with the "sinners" Jesus sends us to save.

Jesus quotes Hosea 6:6 to rebuke the Pharisees with a warning that God wants his People to *love mercy* more

---

[4] Luke 10:25–37.

[5] Matthew 8:3, 15; 9:20, 25 & 29.

[6] Matthew 8:7; John 18:28; Acts 10:28.

than moralism or busyness. He calls them to admit that they themselves are "sinners" and to exchange their false gospel for the true Gospel of grace. This Gospel by which we were saved is also the Gospel through which we save others. It's the Gospel that stops us from being Pharisees or priests, and which makes us true followers of Jesus, the *"friend of sinners"*.

I recently told a story in one of my Sunday sermons, which involved a friend who is a convicted paedophile. Afterwards, two Christians approached me with concerned looks on their faces, eager for reassurance that I had never brought him to their church. There is a Pharisee and a priest lurking in all of us, but if we keep our eyes on the Gospel we will drive them out.

Only then will the "sinners" in our towns and cities start to believe that the Gospel offers real hope for their lives. Only then, when they see our conviction that the Gospel is for them, will they start to believe it too. Only then will they dare to believe that Jesus Christ is the *"friend of sinners"*.

Faith (9:18–31)

She said to herself, "If I only touch his cloak, I will
be healed." Jesus turned and saw her. "Take heart,
daughter," he said, "your faith has healed you." And
the woman was healed from that moment.

(Matthew 9:21–22)

Many Protestants find it hard to understand what happens at
Lourdes. Few dare to insist that every healing is counterfeit,
but most struggle doctrinally that God should heal pilgrims at a
shrine to the Virgin Mary. Many Roman Catholics, for their part,
fail to understand how some Protestants can deny modern-
day miracles altogether. They can't fathom how any follower
of Jesus can so readily dismiss a core part of his ministry. Both
Protestants and Catholics are offended when God entrusts
healing ministry to men of low character, whose lifestyle brings
such miracles into disrepute.

The truth is we all have questions about God's healing.
Good questions. Questions that God wants to answer. And one
of the places he does so is here in Matthew's gospel.

Matthew doesn't tell us her name. For twelve long years
she had suffered from non-stop menstrual flow. That would be
horrible enough in any culture, but in Jewish society it was more
than a medical nightmare; it was a complete social catastrophe.
The Mosaic Law declared that any menstruating woman
was ceremonially unclean, and that anyone she touched was
unclean until morning.[1] For twelve years this woman had been

---

[1] Leviticus 15:19–31 and Numbers 19:20 tell us she risked being cut off from
Israel for daring to go out in public.

barred from the Temple and banned from the crowded streets of Jerusalem, but she flouted the law in a desperate bid to find Jesus. She had spent all her money on doctors, but her bleeding had only gone from bad to worse.[2] Jesus was her last hope, her only hope, and she would brave the crowds to find him.

Matthew doesn't tell us explicitly *why* she had faith to receive healing. He tells us that she touched the *"edge of his garment"* because she was convinced that through this she would be healed, but he doesn't tell us *why* she believed this so strongly. Jesus hadn't healed that way before, and there was no Old Testament prophecy to indicate he would do so in the future. Nevertheless, she was convinced that if she could only touch the *kraspeda* of Jesus' cloak – the same word is used in 23:5 to refer to the *tassels* of a rabbi's prayer shawl[3] – she would be healed by the power which would flow from his tassels. The only Old Testament verse which made any such promise was Malachi 4:2, the fifth-from-last verse of the Old Testament, which promised that *"the sun of righteousness will rise with healing in its wings".*[4] It appears the woman concluded that since Jesus was the Messiah, the "sun of righteousness", it therefore followed that she would be healed if only she touched one of the tassels on the corner of his cloak.

She had remarkable faith but terrible theology. Malachi did not mean this at all. He called the Messiah the *"sun of righteousness"* because he would bring light to creation by dying like the setting sun and rising again like the breaking of dawn. The Messiah's *wings* were his *sunrays*, not the tassels on his robe. No one could seriously argue from Malachi 4:2 that the

---

[2] Mark 5:26.

[3] The Greek Septuagint also uses the word *kraspeda* to refer to the *tassels* worn by Jews in Numbers 15:38.

[4] This verse is best known today as a line in the third verse of Charles Wesley's Christmas carol, "Hark, the Herald Angels Sing". The Greek Septuagint does not use the word *kraspeda*, but the same word which Numbers 15:38 uses for the corners where the *kraspeda* were attached.

Messiah would heal people when they touched his tassels, but the woman read it that way and believed what she read. She acted in faith, and God healed her as she did. Jesus wasn't angry at her unclean touch, and nor did he respond with a lecture on the true meaning of Malachi 4. He simply saw her faith, expressed his delight, received her as a daughter, and spoke the words she longed to hear: *"Your faith has healed you"*.

This passage is powerfully moving, but it is also highly instructive. It answers our questions about Lourdes, televangelists, and why God sometimes doesn't heal. It tells us that God prizes flawed steps of faith above orthodox unbelief. No one prized systematic theology like the Pharisees, yet they were shut out of God's blessing in 9:3 and 34 because their studies left no room for faith. The mourners at Jairus' house had been well taught at the synagogue he led, yet their Scripture knowledge didn't stop them laughing at Jesus and being thrown out in 9:24–25 because of their unbelief. Meanwhile, Jesus heals a centurion's servant in 8:13 because *"It will be done just as you believed it would"*; he looks at a paralysed man's friends in 9:2 and healed him *"when Jesus saw their faith"*; and he heals two blind men in 9:29 by telling them that *"According to your faith will it be done to you"*. In fact, despite the bleeding woman's muddled theology, we find that Jesus later allowed a whole town to touch the tassels of his cloak in 14:36, and healed them through their faith in what had happened to her. Matthew wants us to know that Jesus loves raw faith – even flawed faith – and rushes to meet it with his power.

The promise *"according to your faith will it be done to you"* can be a blessing or a curse. If we believe in the power of God – even in a flawed and mistaken manner – it brings wonderful hope of healing and blessing. However, if our doctrine is much better than our faith in the power of God, it can become a terrible curse. It is very easy for a church to become like the synagogue at Nazareth, where Jesus *"did not do many miracles because of their lack of faith"*.[5] That's why Jesus repeatedly rebuked the disciples for their inexcusable lack of faith,[6] and why this incident forms part of Jesus' teaching on Kingdom lifestyle.

You may struggle with shrines and faith healers, and I know how you feel. It would be easier for me too if Jesus only chose to heal through you, me, and anyone else who shares our theology. But he doesn't, and in Mark 9:38–40 he tells us such partisan hopes are sinful. Jesus longs to find faith among his People, and because there is so little of it around he is committed to work wherever he finds it.[7] Sometimes this is in the unlikeliest of places, but Jesus really meant it when he promised that *"If you have faith and do not doubt... you will receive whatever you ask for in prayer".*[8] This promise belongs to us, but if we refuse to believe it others will believe it instead.

I wish that those with faith for miracles could be more orthodox, but that's God's issue, not ours. Our role is to be provoked by their faith and to make sure that our good doctrine produces more, and not less, faith in our own lives. God wants to heal, and he is determined to use faith wherever he finds it, so let's learn from this bleeding woman and act in faith upon what we read in Scripture. Faith is one of the hallmarks of Kingdom lifestyle, and of all who follow in the footsteps of Jesus the King.

---

[5] Matthew 13:58.

[6] Matthew 6:30; 8:26; 14:31; 16:8; 17:20.

[7] Luke 18:8.

[8] Matthew 21:21–22.

Act Two:

Kingdom Mission

Little Christs (10:1–42)

He called his twelve disciples to him and gave them authority to drive out evil spirits and to heal every disease and sickness.

(Matthew 10:1)

Jesus' time was running out. He had only fourteen months left, fourteen months in which to prepare a Kingdom army from his ragtag collection of followers. As he looked out at the end of chapter 9 on the sick, unsaved, and unshepherded people of Israel, he knew that if his Kingdom Revolution was ever to reach the whole world he needed to multiply workers and multiply them fast.[1] Act Two of Matthew's gospel is therefore the training manual for an army of "little Christs",[2] and it begins in chapter 10 with Jesus' crash-course in Kingdom mission.

The most astonishing thing about Jesus' instruction in this chapter is that he clearly has no expectation that the power of his ministry will in any way be diluted through its multiplication. This was the first leg in a lifetime of learning for the disciples, but right from day one he told them to heal, drive out demons, and even raise the dead in exactly the same way that he did. He

---

[1] Compare Matthew 9:37 with Numbers 27:17 where Moses prayed for shepherdless Israel and was told to appoint Joshua as his successor. Matthew deliberately echoes that verse to emphasize that Jesus told his disciples to pray for shepherdless Israel, and then turned them into an army of successors like Joshua.

[2] God uses this phrase in 1 Chronicles 16:22 and Psalm 105:15, where he refers to his People as *meshiyachay*, meaning *my Messiahs* or *my Christs*. The word *Christian* simply means *"little Christ"* and was originally a term of abuse which the believers adopted as a badge of honour. See Acts 11:26; 26:28; 1 Peter 4:16.

conferred on them his own authority and power, and expected his Father to work as faithfully through his delegates as he did through himself. After all, the crowds who watched him heal rejoiced in 9:8 that God had given such authority to *men*, not just to a *man*. The last-ditch hope of Satan's doomed empire is that you and I will tone down our expectations for Kingdom mission, but Jesus insists that *"anyone who has faith in me will do what I have been doing. He will do even greater things than these".*[3]

Jesus did not expect his followers to innovate, but merely to imitate. They were to preach the same message that he did, that God's Kingdom had come and that Satan, sin, and sickness could not stand before his Messiah.[4] Like Jesus, they were to offer the Gospel promise of peace, whilst also threatening judgment upon all who rejected him.[5] As for specifics, they were simply to listen to what Jesus whispered in their ear through the Holy Spirit, and to speak this aloud to all who would hear. They were heirs to the Messianic promise of Isaiah 50:4:

> *The Sovereign Lord has given me an instructed tongue,*
> *to know the word that sustains the weary. He wakens me*
> *morning by morning, wakens my ear to listen like one*
> *being taught.*

The success of their ministry of the tongue would depend entirely upon their diligence to the ministry of the ear. So long as they lived in Kingdom intimacy, they would never run out of Kingdom messages.[6]

---

[3] John 14:12. Verse 11 makes it clear that Jesus is talking about miracles.

[4] Compare Matthew 10:7–8 with Matthew 4:17; 4:24; 9:35.

[5] The Hebrew word *shalom* which is behind v12–13 meant more than simply *peace*. It also meant *wholeness*, *healing* and *salvation*. The disciples were to warn those who rejected God's offer of salvation that they were destined for judgment in hell. See Acts 18:6 for an example.

[6] Verses 19–20 and 27. When the evangelist George Whitefield was asked the secret of his powerful preaching, he referenced v. 27, saying that *"What Christ tells us by His Spirit in our closets, let us proclaim upon the housetops".*

Jesus made no promises that Kingdom mission would be easy. He wanted them to place themselves in poverty and need in order to give those who heard their message a practical way to embrace it.[7] He wanted them to be vulnerable and defenceless, *"like sheep among wolves"*, relying on him at every moment for protection and deliverance.[8] Those who resist the King will also resist his ambassadors, and so he warned them to expect to be hated, persecuted, flogged, and even killed because they bore his name. If they suffered with him they would reign with him, but if they disowned him he would disown them too.[9] The Gospel of the Kingdom would draw the ire and fury of a rebellious world, and unless they renounced all earthly hopes and ties they would never be any heavenly good. True pupils are honoured when they are treated like their teacher, and he told them that anyone who is not prepared to walk the path of Christ's suffering for the sake of a dying world is not a Christ-follower at all.[10]

Like Jesus, they were to be the *"friends of sinners"* and dwell in the houses of those whom they sought to reach. They were to think wisely and strategically, finding one significant convert and discipling him to become a fellow missionary, and not flitting aimlessly from one superficial conversion to another. Jesus trained them, working alongside them in their various towns, and told them that they must likewise train up others.[11]

---

[7] Only those who accept the Kingdom Revolution of Matthew 6:19–34 can accept the challenge of 10:6.

[8] Verses 23 and 29–31.

[9] Verses 28 and 32–33. One of the reasons why our involvement in Kingdom mission yields great heavenly reward is simply that it tests our discipleship and makes us more able to receive them.

[10] See 2 Timothy 3:12. George Whitefield continued his advice by warning that *"Unless your hearts are free from worldly hopes and worldly fears you will never speak boldly as you ought to speak".*

[11] Matthew 11:1 tells us literally that Jesus taught and preached *"in their towns"*. Some translations assume that *their* refers to the people of Galilee, but the subject of the sentence is clearly the disciples he sent out. He coached them on the job, so that they were well prepared to lead the Seventy-Two later in Luke 10:1–24.

This first trip was to the lost sheep of Israel, but it was simply the start of a greater task, which would require a greater-sized army. The fact that verses 17 to 23 were never fulfilled on this first mission-trip was a powerful reminder to them that their adventure had scarcely begun.

Last, but by no means least, Jesus promised them that they would be successful. Contrary to what many Christians believe, the problem is not a lack of harvest, but simply a lack of workers. God, and not Satan, is *"the Lord of the harvest"*.[12] If you have ever complained that it is *"hard"* in your workplace or street or town or nation, you are in danger of falling for Satan's great lie. We are pupils of Christ the Conqueror, and we simply gather the harvest he has pre-purchased with his own blood.

Jesus has raised up a mighty Kingdom army, and he has sent it to continue his mission with the same power and authority, the same message and dangers, and the same certain fruitfulness as when he began. It's simply Act Two of discipleship for all those who follow him. It's what it means for us to be his "little Christs".

---

[12] Matthew 9:37–38.

Gehenna (10:28)

*Do not be afraid of those who kill the body but
cannot kill the soul. Rather, be afraid of the One who
can destroy both soul and body in Gehenna.*

(Matthew 10:28)

Jesus talked a lot about hell. He just did. He knew that it would
make him unpopular – the philosopher Bertrand Russell
complained that *"There is one very serious defect to my mind
in Christ's moral character, and that is that he believed in hell"*[1]
– but he did so all the same. The gospels quote him speaking
four times about *Hades*, twice about the place of *torment*, eight
times about hell's *fire*, and seven times about *gnashing of teeth*.
He talked more about hell than the whole of the Old Testament
put together, and he even pioneered a new way of describing it.
Eleven times he called it *Gehenna*.[2]

Gehenna was simply the Greek way of writing *Gey Hinnom*,
or the Hebrew name for the *Valley of Hinnom*. This deep and
narrow gorge ran along the south-western side of Jerusalem,
and was once quite a beautiful place before the kings of Judah
corrupted it. King Ahaz chose the valley as the site for his shrine
to the Ammonite god Molech, and burned his sons alive there
as sacrifices to the demon-idol. King Manasseh did the same,
and the common people followed him.[3] Part of the valley even
became known as *Topheth*, or *Drums*, because the priests of
Molech played a loud and frenzied drumbeat to drown out the

---

[1] Bertrand Russell, *Why I am not a Christian*.

[2] Matthew 5:22, 29, 30; 10:28; 18:9; 23:15, 33; Mark 9:43, 45, 47; Luke 12:5. It
is also used in James 3:6.

[3] 2 Chronicles 28:3; 33:6.

screams of the children they sacrificed.[4] Ahaz and Manasseh turned a place of beauty into the foulest place in Judah, so God promised to judge that valley. He prophesied that when the Babylonians slaughtered and exiled the wicked people of Jerusalem, the corpses would be piled up in Gehenna, and there the birds and the beasts would feed on their flesh.[5] When this was fulfilled in 586 BC, the valley became a horrific reminder that God will always judge sin.

Seventy years later, the Jews began to return from their exile in Babylon. No one wanted to live in Gehenna, and so it became the municipal rubbish tip. Cartloads of waste and offal were piled up in the valley, and fires burned day and night while writhing maggots devoured the rotting flesh. A Jew would travel the long way round Jerusalem just to steer clear of its stench. There was nowhere in Israel as disgusting as Gehenna. All this explains why Jesus, quoting from the last verse of Isaiah, chose *Gehenna* as his normal way of referring to hell. It was a blood-curdling image, which made people sit up and listen.

Jesus chose the name Gehenna to show us that hell is both *real* and *eternal*. Jews could go to Gehenna and see that it was a real flesh-and-blood place, with real stench and real heat. They could not dismiss his talk of *fire*, *maggots*, and *darkness* as mere metaphors. If they are metaphors at all, Jonathan Edwards reminds us that *"when metaphors are used in Scripture about spiritual things... they **fall short** of the literal truth"*.[6] Jesus uses the most horrific place in the whole of Israel to convince us that hell is real, terrible, and eternal. At Gehenna, the fire never stopped burning and the maggots never stopped wriggling because every new morning brought them fresh deliveries. Jesus tells us in Mark 9:48 that in hell *"their worm does not die,*

---

[4] 2 Kings 23:10; Isaiah 30:33.

[5] Jeremiah 7:30–33; 19:1–7. God told the Israelites that child-sacrifice to Molech was utterly detestable in Leviticus 18:21; 20:5 and Deuteronomy 18:10.

[6] Jonathan Edwards in his sermon "The Torments of Hell are Exceedingly Great".

and the fire is not quenched", because hell has no end and it knows no reprieve. Even though Gehenna's fires and maggots finally ended, the pain and torment of hell never will.[7]

Jesus chose the name Gehenna to show us that hell is *entirely just*. Gehenna was where God judged the demon-god Molech and avenged the blood of his child-victims. It was entirely fair, and long overdue. In the same way, Jesus tells us in Matthew 25:41 that hell was created as a place to punish the Devil and his demons for their rebellion against God – also entirely fair and long overdue. Those who sided with Molech were thrown into Gehenna, and those who side with Satan will be thrown into hell. There is nothing unfair or excessive about this; it is simply the fair response to high treason against our Creator-God. Ultimately, it is the very thing which rebels demand, as C.S. Lewis reminds us: *"There are only two kinds of people in the end: those who say to God 'Thy will be done,' and those to whom God says, in the end, 'Thy will be done.' All that are in Hell choose it."*[8] Gehenna is a reminder that God will judge justly, and that rebels will get what they ask for.

Jesus also chose the name Gehenna because he wants us to grasp his great *love* for us. Unless we look into the horrors of the valley, we will not grasp how much it cost Jesus to bear our judgment on the cross, exclaiming that *"My soul is overwhelmed with sorrow to the point of death."*[9] Unless we peer into the fires of the valley and recoil from their heat and stench, we will not understand why the Father turned his back on Jesus, and why he cried out from the cross, *"My God, my God, why have you forsaken me?!"*[10] Gehenna is a great statement of God's love, a love which stepped into the valley to pull us out on his resurrected shoulders. If we object to Jesus' teaching on hell

---

[7] Hell's fires are also called *unquenchable* or *eternal* in Matthew 3:12; 18:8; 25:41; 25:46.

[8] C.S. Lewis, *The Great Divorce* (1945).

[9] Matthew 26:38.

[10] Matthew 27:46.

because it doesn't sound loving, we have not grasped the heart of the Gospel. Hell doesn't make God less loving. It reveals the depth of his love, which went to hell and back for us.

Yet, important as this message is for unbelievers, Jesus talked most about Gehenna to his followers. He used it as a heavenly siren to awaken their souls to lay down their lives in Kingdom mission. Because hell is real, we deal radically with our own sin, because nothing must come between us and the Gospel. Because hell is real, we would rather be killed than stop preaching to the world about our Saviour Jesus. Charles Spurgeon warned that *"He is the true lover of men who faithfully warns them concerning the eternal woe that awaits the impenitent; while he who paints the miseries of hell as though they were but trifling is seeking to murder men's souls under the pretext of friendship."* In the midst of these chapters on God's Kingdom mission, this warning is terribly apt.

Jesus taught about Gehenna for the sake of his followers and for the sake of the world he would save through them. He calls us to gaze long into its torment, and to rise up to plunder the gates of hell.

Tyre, Sidon and Sodom (11:20–24)

> *And you, Capernaum... will go down to hell. If the miracles that were performed in you had been performed in Sodom, it would have remained to this day.*

(Matthew 11:23)[1]

Before Jesus' first-century followers could give themselves fully to his Kingdom mission, two great questions needed to be answered: *"Could Jews be saved through their Judaism without Christ?"* and *"Could nations which had never heard the Gospel be spared through their ignorance?"* These are still very big questions today. Just this week, I was asked both questions by a group of young Christians. If Jews could be saved without Christ, it would be foolish for the early believers to risk persecution and death for the sake of telling them about him. If the nations could be spared through their ignorance of Christ, it would be an act of cruelty for the believers to put them at risk by telling them about him. These two questions needed to be cleared up if an army of Kingdom missionaries was ever to be unleashed upon the world. They are two of the questions that Matthew addresses in the narrative of Act Two.

The first question has an easy answer, particularly if we grasp that the Greek word *genea*, which Jesus uses five times here, refers either to a *generation* or to an ethnic *race*. Matthew constructs chapters 11 and 12 with this question in mind. First,

---

[1] The NIV actually translates the Greek word *Hades* in this verse as *the depths*, but the word simply means *hell* – as in Matthew 16:18 or Luke 16:23.

Jesus tells the crowd that John the Baptist is greater than Moses, David and all of the other Old Testament heroes, because he heralded the Messiah whose Kingdom trumps the Old Covenant at its best. Next, he attacks the Jewish *genea*, or *race*, for being impossible to please.[2] They complained that John ate too little and that Jesus ate too much, and they rejected miracles which would have converted pagan Tyre and Sidon, and even proverbially wicked Sodom. Therefore Jesus quotes to them from Jeremiah 6:16, part of an old prophecy in which God called Jerusalem to listen and repent, or be destroyed.[3]

Matthew then goes on to demonstrate that Judaism without Christ is not merely powerless to save, but even acts as an obstacle to the message of salvation. The Pharisees clash so violently here with Jesus over the Sabbath that they go out and plot murder.[4] For his part, Jesus withdraws from the Jewish synagogue and heals a group of outcasts in his own alternative meeting. Matthew warns his Jewish readers with a quotation from Isaiah 42 that if they reject their Messiah he will *"proclaim justice to the nations"* and *"in his name the nations will put their hope"*. Things then go from bad to worse, as the Pharisees dismiss Jesus as a Satanist, and he replies that if they dare to dismiss the Holy Spirit's work as Satanism they will spend eternity with Satan themselves.[5] He calls them *"children of vipers"*,

---

[2] For example, this word can only refer to the Jewish *race* in Luke 17:25; 21:32, or in Acts 2:40 where Peter tells the Jews on the day of Pentecost to receive their Messiah and therefore save themselves from perishing with the rest of their *race*. Matthew uses this word *genea* five times in 11:16 and 12:39–45.

[3] The words *"you will find rest for your souls"* in Matthew 11:29 are taken from Jeremiah 6:16.

[4] Matthew wants us to see the full irony of 12:14. The Pharisees lecture Jesus about the fourth commandment, but think nothing of breaking the sixth commandment to silence him!

[5] *Beelzebub* was a Philistine god based at nearby Ekron. The Jews used his name to refer to Satan or one of his senior demons. Since none of the New Testament letters say anything about an "unforgivable sin", Jesus must be referring to the sin of treating the work of the Holy Spirit as if it were the work

not of Abraham, and tells them that unless their *"wicked and adulterous race"* responds with faith when he casts out demons, they will open themselves up through their unbelief to seven times as many demons. Then, to add insult to injury, he tells them that the Gentile queen of Sheba, as well as bloodthirsty Nineveh which destroyed the northern kingdom of Israel in 722 BC, responded to the Gospel better than them. Finally, in case anyone should still think that being part of the Jewish bloodline is cause for comfort, Matthew ends chapter 12 with Jesus saying that even his mother and brothers cannot be saved unless they submit to his call. Matthew therefore draws together a powerful narrative in chapters 11 and 12, which underlines chapter 10's call to preach the Gospel to the Jews. There is no salvation for anyone outside of Christ. Not even for the ethnic descendants of Abraham.

Now for the second question: can nations which have not heard about Jesus be spared through their ignorance? Matthew answers this in 11:20–24. He tells us that God does not merely judge people on the basis of their *sin*, but on the basis of their *sin* plus the *revelation* they have received. Tyre and Sidon were the cities which had spawned the wicked Queen Jezebel and her prophets of Baal,[6] yet they would be judged less severely than the towns of Korazin and Bethsaida in Galilee, to whom Jesus appeared as Messiah with mighty miracles. Sodom was a city which was destroyed for its pride, complacency and oppression, and whose citizens had famously once tried to homosexually gang-rape two angels.[7] God rained down fire and sulphur on the

---

of Satan. If we do this, by definition we reject the very Gospel through which God wants to forgive us.

[6] 1 Kings 16:31. God was so gracious to these cities that he removed his prophet Elijah from backslidden Israel and sent him to a widow of Sidon (1 Kings 17:9; Luke 4:25–26). Jesus briefly visited Tyre and Sidon in Matthew 15:21–28 and responded to the faith of a Gentile woman there.

[7] Genesis 19; Ezekiel 16:49–50; Jude 7.

city as a graphic demonstration that hell awaits the ungodly,[8] yet they would be judged less severely than Capernaum in Galilee because they never saw Jesus the miracle-working Messiah. The Lord God judges justly, based on both *sin* and *revelation*, and Israel should have known that through the Mosaic Law.[9]

Nevertheless, being judged *less severely* is different from not being judged at all. The fact that there are different grades of punishment in hell will offer little comfort to anyone who is barred from the gates of heaven. Tyrians, Sidonians, Sodomites, and their modern equivalents, all have eyes to see the glory of God, all have consciences to know right from wrong, and all fall short of their *own* standards, let alone God's.[10] They will not be judged for rejecting a Christ of whom they never heard, but for doing what their own consciences told them was sinful. Accepting Christ brings forgiveness from sin, but rejecting him is not the beginning of sin. *"Whoever believes in him is not condemned, but whoever does not believe stands condemned already."*[11] There is no salvation outside of Christ. Not even for the ignorant.

This is why the early Christians rose up and fell in behind King Jesus as an army of Kingdom missionaries. They laid down their lives to tell Jew and Gentile, Greek and barbarian, that Jesus is King and people of every nation must receive him or pay the price. Two thousand years later, our mission is just the same. For the sake of the 2,200 language groups which still have no access to even a single verse of the Bible in their own tongue,[12] for the sake of the many thousands of tribes which have no indigenous Christian witness – even for the sake of the millions of people

---

[8] 2 Peter 2:6.

[9] Numbers 15:22–31 makes a clear distinction between sins of *rebellion* and sins of *ignorance*. Both must be punished, but punished differently.

[10] Romans 1:18–20; 2:12–15. Also Luke 19:22.

[11] John 3:18.

[12] Wycliffe Bible Translators data in 2008. This represents nearly 200 million individuals, and a third of the world's spoken languages.

in your own nation who are ignorant of the true Gospel of Jesus Christ – rise up and fall in behind Jesus. Without him, no one can be saved.

My Yoke Is Easy (11:25–30)

*Come to me, all you who are weary and burdened,
and I will give you rest. Take my yoke upon you and
learn from me, for I am gentle and humble in heart,
and you will find rest for your souls. For my yoke is
easy and my burden is light.*

(Matthew 11:28–30)

Jesus likes to play with your mind. He likes to grab your attention
through absurd non sequiturs. A man with a rafter stuck in his
eye; another with a camel in his coffee; another camel, this time
squeezing through the eye of a needle.[1] Here's another one:
Jesus invites us to let him place his yoke on our necks so that we
can finally get ourselves some rest. It's an invitation which flies
in the face of logic. It's meant to.

There was nothing nice about a first-century yoke. It was
a heavy wooden beam used by farmers to join a pair of oxen so
that they could pull a plough or a cart together. It was a symbol
of hard labour and even oppression, which is why God used it
in the Old Testament as a symbol of slavery.[2] In fact, it was one
of the pictures he used to prophesy about his Messiah's future
work of salvation, but with a promise that he would *break* their
yoke of slavery, not invite them to wear a new one![3]

If we want to understand what Jesus means by this
invitation, we need to understand the context in which he made

---

[1] Matthew 7:3; 19:24; 23:24.
[2] Genesis 27:40; Exodus 6:6–7; Leviticus 26:13; Deuteronomy 28:48; 1 Kings
12:4; Isaiah 58:9; Jeremiah 28:14.
[3] Isaiah 9:1–7; Jeremiah 30:8–9; Ezekiel 34:23–27. The government would be
upon *his shoulders*.

it. We are in Act Two of Matthew's gospel, and so chapters 11 and 12 are the narrative which Matthew collates to illustrate Jesus' teaching in chapter 10. This whole section is a call to Kingdom mission, and an invitation to become "little Christs" in his army of Kingdom revolutionaries. When Jesus talks here about yoking us to his plough, he is not simply talking about giving us rest, but specifically about giving rest *as we minister with him*. The passage has some general things to say about resting from busyness, but that's not the main thing on Jesus' mind. Jesus wants to train us to be agents of his Kingdom who can plough up the hard ground of our world and pave the way for the Kingdom harvest of chapter 13. He wants to teach us to do so under the yoke that he gives, so that we can find the work exhilarating instead of exhausting.[4]

He wants us to minister by *his grace alone*. Anything else just wears people out and eventually they give up trying. One of the main reasons that so many in the Church are indolent and inactive for the Kingdom of God is that they were saved by grace but then tried to minister by grit. If you run a car engine without oil for a day, it will grind, burn and break. If you try to communicate the Gospel through anything other than the grace of God, your activity will go the same way. Jesus invites us to wear his yoke, because a yoke is a pulling-collar for two. It's *his* yoke and he does the pulling. That's what makes it so easy and light. We make rapid progress by the grace of God, because Jesus is the one doing almost all the work.[5]

He wants us to minister on *his terms alone*. Chapters 11 and 12 are one long account of the Pharisees refusing the terms that he offers. They find John too reclusive but Jesus too inclusive, and they would rather leave people sick and demonized than

---

[4] This is Jesus' point in John 4:34 when he declares that *"My food is to do the will of him who sent me"*.

[5] Paul saw his missionary success as the fruit of his ministering through grace, not grit. See Romans 15:15–16; 1 Corinthians 15:10; 2 Corinthians 3:4–6; 4:1; Ephesians 3:2, 7.

let him threaten their rules. In contrast, Jesus rejoices that God makes *"little children"* like his ignorant disciples lay down everything to minister on his terms.[6] If a young ox yoked to an older ox pulled in a different direction, the result would be confusion, exhaustion, and not much ploughing. The same is true of Jesus' yoke, which is why it is so heavy until we completely surrender. A friend told me last week that she is *"at a fork in the road"* concerning her marriage and is finding it terribly hard to know what to do. I reminded her that when she gave her life to Jesus she decided ahead of time not to go down one of the two roads. Christian conversion is hard and heavy, but if we truly surrender then our subsequent Christian life and ministry are easy and light.[7] *would want this sort of a little more forthrightly — these sort of statements over and*

Jesus wants us to minister by *his power alone*. He describes Christian ministry in John 15:26–27 this way: *"When the Counsellor comes, whom I will send to you from the Father... he will testify about me. And you also must testify."* He explains that all Christian ministry begins with the Father, as the mission of the Son, executed by the Holy Spirit, worked out through us. All Christian ministry belongs to the three Persons of the Trinity before it ever rests upon our shoulders. That's why Jesus tells us earlier on in the chapter that *"I am the vine; you are the branches. If a man remains in me and I in him, he will bear much fruit; apart from me you can do nothing."*[8] Human evangelistic initiatives are – forgive the irony – quite simply soul-destroying. Human co-operation with God's initiatives, however, is empowered by the Spirit and refreshes us, even as we serve.

MY YOKE IS EASY (11:25-30)

123

---

[6] Verse 25 tells us literally that *"At that time, Jesus said in reply..."* Most English translators omit those two words because they cannot see how v. 25 can be Jesus' reply to what he saw the Father doing in vv. 16 to 24. Hopefully you can.

[7] That's why Jesus warns us in Matthew 10:37–39 to count the cost before conversion because it means *"taking up our cross daily"*. If we try to negotiate with God, his yoke is heavy, but if we begin the Christian life by *dying* to ourselves, life under his yoke becomes easy.

[8] John 15:5.

What is more, this is *his* yoke because he has already modelled for us how it should work. He is able to tell us to *"learn from me, for I am gentle and humble in heart"*, meaning that if we have any doubt as to how to wear his light yoke we can simply look at how he wore it himself. He only ever ministered by God's grace, on God's terms, and by God's power. He refused to start his own initiatives, because *"the right time for me has not yet come; for you any time is right"*. He refused to do things his own way, because *"the Son can do nothing by himself; he can only do what he sees his Father doing"*. He refused to do things through his own power, waiting until the Spirit came on him at his baptism before he performed any of his miracles, so that only *"by the Spirit of God"* would he minister.[9] He bore the yoke for us in every way, so we can now bear the yoke alongside him.

Jesus walked around Palestine, spotting where God was working, going where God was leading and ministering as God empowered him. He now walks the whole earth, yoked to his "little Christs" who are willing to do the same. It's a yoke which means working and ploughing and pulling, but there's simply nothing in the world more restful or refreshing. There's simply nothing lighter than the burden of Christ.

---

[9] John 5:19; 7:6; Matthew 12:28.

Sabbath (12:1–14)

For the Son of Man is Lord of the Sabbath.

(Matthew 12:8)

The Sabbath day of rest stood at the very heart of what it meant to be a Jew. It wasn't simply one of the Ten Commandments. It was one of the great national reminders that God had chosen Israel to be his holy people.[1] Sabbath-breakers were punished and even put to death.[2] Every devout Jew took the Sabbath very seriously.

So did Jesus. He observed the Sabbath faultlessly. He was only able to offer himself as the perfect sacrifice for sin because he had completely fulfilled the Mosaic Law with all its Sabbath regulations.[3] In fact, while the Pharisees filled their notebooks with commentary on the Sabbath, Jesus embodied the very spirit behind the day of rest. Therefore Matthew chooses the Sabbath, that most quintessentially Jewish part of the Mosaic Law, to highlight the difference between Jesus and the rabbis. He wants to free his fellow-Jews from the straitjacket of their religion, and to warn generations of Christians not to make the same mistakes themselves.

The Hebrew verb *shabath* means *to stop work* or *to rest*, and the essence of the Sabbath was *not working*. The first Sabbath day was at the end of creation week, thousands of years before Moses ever climbed Mount Sinai. God made the whole world in six days of creative activity, and then he rested on the seventh day, not because he was tired but because he wanted

---

[1] See, for example, Exodus 31:13, 17; Ezekiel 20:12, 20.

[2] Exodus 31:14–15; 35:2; Numbers 15:32–36; Nehemiah 13:15–22.

[3] Matthew 5:17–20; 24:20; 26:59–60.

to give us a model to follow. Human beings need rest to keep on functioning well, which is why God gave us the warning-bells of tiredness and hunger and snappiness and stress. The Sabbath ring-fenced one day in every week for rest, relaxation, and looking to God.[4] But that first Sabbath day of rest was about more than just resting. Adam didn't need to rest on that first Sabbath because he was tired, but because he needed to learn an important spiritual lesson: The seventh day of creation was Adam's first day, and a reminder that he should rest by grace through faith in the finished work of God. Adam didn't work on his first day because God had already worked on his behalf, and invited him to relax in the glories of Eden.

When God formalized the Sabbath for Israel, it was the same. For six days they worked hard, and on the seventh day they rested in God. Similarly, when Joshua led the Israelites into the *"Sabbath rest"* of the Promised Land, it was to give them ready-made houses and wells and vineyards and olive groves, all as an effortless gift of grace.[5] The young man who was put to death in Numbers 15:32–36 was not executed just for gathering sticks on a Saturday, but because his actions betrayed a self-sufficient refusal to trust in his Provider God. The Sabbath was not just about resting. It was about having faith to stop working because God has worked for us.[6]

It was therefore no wonder that Jesus clashed so hard with the Pharisees. In blind irony, they had actually turned the Sabbath into a day about *working*! Their rules, regulations, and restrictions had turned the day's rest into seriously hard work! So much so, that they sucked all the life out of the Sabbath and replaced it with hypocrisy, inconsistency, and salvation through works.

---

[4] Regardless of whether or not you think the Sabbath law still applies to Christians, it would be very foolish for you to ignore this self-evident Sabbath principle.

[5] Hebrews 4:9–10; Joshua 24:11–13; Deuteronomy 6:10–12.

[6] Leviticus 25:20–22.

Take their clash with Jesus' disciples over picking and eating grain on the Sabbath. The disciples were hungry and saw the corn on their journey as God's gracious and effortless provision for their need. It was a perfect opportunity for them to *Sabbath* in his grace. The Pharisees, on the other hand, saw it as a form of harvesting and food preparation, both prohibited tasks. Or take their second clash with Jesus over his healing a man's deformity on the Sabbath.[7] Jesus saw a man in dire need of healing through the Gospel and invited him to Sabbath in God's gracious work on his behalf. The Pharisees, however, saw healing as Jesus' day-job, and something to avoid on the Sabbath if he wanted to earn the favour of God.[8]

Jesus shows them that their religion is not only inconsistent – they treat a sick and needy man worse than they even treat their own animals – but also something far, far worse: *it is not the Gospel of the Old Testament.* That was the crux of the matter, and the killer blow that Matthew wants to press home to his readers in unmistakable terms. The religion of the Pharisees – the religion which is now mainstream modern Judaism – does not merely need to *embrace* Christ but *give way* to Christ. It has become so twisted and mutated from the Gospel of grace in the Old Testament, that it even treats as lawbreakers King David and every high priest from Aaron down to Caiaphas.[9] They need to confess that their Judaism has ceased to be the Gospel, and that they need to turn to their Messiah and back to what the early Christians called simply *"the hope of Israel"*.[10]

Jesus loves the Pharisees and the Jewish nation so much that he resorts to a last-ditch, make-or-break tactic which he

---

[7] Luke 6:6 tells us that this actually happened on a different Sabbath day, but the gospel writers group the two events together to form one united challenge about trusting in the Gospel of God's grace.

[8] On a different occasion in Luke 13:14, a synagogue ruler told his congregation that *"There are six days for work. So come and be healed on those days, not on the Sabbath."*

[9] 1 Samuel 21:1–6; Numbers 28:9–10; John 7:22–24.

[10] Acts 28:20. See also Acts 24:14–15; 26:6–7.

knows will either end in surrender or murder. It is a risk worth taking for the Gospel and for the lost sheep of Israel. He turns up the contrast, declaring frankly that he is the Son of Man from Daniel's great vision, that he is the Yahweh who created the Sabbath day,[11] that he is God the Judge who alone is able to declare a person innocent, and that he is even greater than their Old Covenant Temple because he is the true Temple, the place where God dwells in human flesh.[12] He tells the self-appointed experts in the Law that they need to go back to the drawing board and re-read what Scripture actually says. If they had completed the homework assignment he set them in 9:13, they would have known that they had changed the Gospel of grace and mercy into a handbook for law and human effort. It was, and still is, an unpalatable message. It would ultimately cost Jesus his life.

Matthew warns his Jewish readers that the Gospel plus works is no Gospel at all. He issues the same warning to the Christian Church. We are all potential Pharisees, and we can all too easily forget the finished work of Christ. The true Gospel is the Gospel of the Sabbath: *"When a man works, his wages are not credited to him as a gift, but as an obligation. However, to the man who **does not work but trusts God** who justifies the wicked, his faith is credited as righteousness."*[13]

---

[11] The Greek word for *Lord* in verse 8 is *kurios*, which is the Greek equivalent of the Hebrew name *Yahweh*.

[12] Jesus also touches on this theme in John 2:18–22.

[13] Romans 4:4–5.

The Sign of Jonah
(12:38–42)

A wicked and adulterous generation asks for a
miraculous sign! But none will be given it except the
sign of the prophet Jonah. For as Jonah was three
days and three nights in the belly of a huge fish, so
the Son of Man will be three days and three nights in
the heart of the earth.

(Matthew 12:39–40)

About two months after my conversion to Christ, I had a crisis of faith. Ironically, it was because I was trying to convert my friends. I had spent the previous evening with my friend Crazy Paul, who was a brilliant engineering student and the toughest atheist I knew. I had been praying for an opportunity to share the Gospel with him, and finally I had my chance. I told him the Gospel, backed it up with my testimony, and urged him to repent and follow Jesus.

What happened next is still a blur. All I remember is that I made some foolish and very unscientific speculations about creation, and that Crazy Paul lived up to his name. He went bright red, lost his temper, and gave me both barrels on what he thought of my new-found faith. An hour later, I beat a hasty retreat from his bedsit, with my mind reeling and my faith in tatters. Since then, I've received plenty of verbal attacks for the Gospel, but nothing quite prepared me for the first one.

The following morning I sat in the Cambridge University History Library, my head still spinning from the night before. *Was I following a lie? Were the last two months of walking with God just an illusion?* Suddenly, I remembered the words Jesus spoke in Matthew 12 about "the sign of Jonah". Of course! Christianity was not just a philosophy, like Buddhism, communism, or existentialism, to be debated at leisure with my friends. It is faith in a person, and in a historical event, when Jesus of Nazareth died and three days later came back to life. Put simply, if Jesus died and rose again, then even if I couldn't argue science with Crazy Paul, the Christian faith was still true. However, if he didn't die and rise again, I should face up to my non-Christian friends, confess I was wrong, and get back to my old life of binge drinking and sin. Looking up, I saw shelf after shelf of the greatest history books money could buy, so I got up and quickly set to work. I was not going home until either I proved that Jesus didn't rise again or I became satisfied that he did.

Perhaps Jesus didn't die at all, or at the very least his body remained in the tomb? No, Matthew and friends wrote within thirty years of Jesus' death, and I found that even their enemies concurred with their story that Jesus died, was buried, and three days later his body disappeared. The Romans and Jews who guarded the tomb didn't even try to deny that this was true, but simply charged that the disciples had stolen his body.[1] As the great Oxford professor Geza Vermes writes:

> *When every argument has been considered and weighed, the only conclusion acceptable to the historian must be that the opinions of the orthodox, the liberal sympathiser and the critical agnostic alike – and even perhaps of the disciples themselves – are simply interpretations of the one disconcerting fact: namely that the women who set out to pay their last respects to Jesus found to their consternation, not a body, but an empty tomb.*[2]

---

[1] Matthew 28:11–15.

[2] Geza Vermes, *Jesus the Jew: A Historian's Reading of the Gospels* (1973).

Perhaps first-century people were simply gullible, then, and too readily assumed that a missing body meant a risen Christ? No, that was pretty unconvincing too. All the evidence suggested that first-century people were every bit as cynical as my friends and me,[3] and I could find no other example of a "resurrection myth" surrounding any of the other would-be Messiahs. N.T. Wright points out that

> *They knew better. Resurrection was not a private event. Jewish revolutionaries whose leader had been executed by the authorities, and who managed to escape arrest themselves, had two options: give up the revolution, or find another leader. Claiming that the original leader was alive again was simply not an option. Unless, of course, he was.*[4]

Perhaps the disciples made up the whole story? But then why make the empty tomb so central to their message, and confess that unless Christ rose then their Gospel was a lie?[5] Why would almost all of them lay down their lives for a claim which they knew was a scam? Even if they did, how would they possibly manage to convince the world that their preposterous story was true? Cambridge professor C.F.D. Moule points out that the growth of the Church from a handful of Galilean peasants *"rips a great hole in history, a hole the size and shape of the resurrection"*, and he asks *"what does the secular historian propose to stop it up with?"*[6] It is not enough to say that a resurrection is impossible – we need to produce an alternative theory. There is simply nothing else which fits the size of the hole.

Then perhaps it wasn't Jesus who really died? No, no one

---

[3] Cynical Jews in Matthew 28:17; Luke 24:11; John 20:25; cynical Greeks in Acts 17:32; 1 Corinthians 15:12; and a cynical Roman in Acts 26:23–24.

[4] N.T. Wright, *Who Was Jesus?* (1992).

[5] 1 Corinthians 15:1–20.

[6] C.F.D. Moule, *The Phenomenon of the New Testament* (1967).

could fool a watching mother, and even if they did it would still not explain how the corpse disappeared. Perhaps Jesus fainted and recovered later in the tomb? John Stott answered that one in no uncertain terms:

> *Are we really to believe... that after the rigours and pains of trial, mockery, flogging and crucifixion he could survive thirty-six hours in a stone sepulchre with neither warmth nor food nor medical care? That he could then rally sufficiently to perform the superhuman feat of shifting the boulder which secured the mouth of the tomb, and this without disturbing the Roman guard? That then, weak and sickly and hungry, he could appear to the disciples in such a way as to give them the impression that he had vanquished death? That he could go on to claim that he had died and risen, could send them into all the world and promise to be with them unto the end of time? That he could live somewhere in hiding for forty days, making occasional surprise appearances, and then finally disappear without explanation? Such credulity is more incredible than Thomas' unbelief.*[7]

I never converted Crazy Paul, but in some ways he converted me. He burst the delicate bubble of my early Christian excitement, and threw me hard against the ropes of study and apologetics and the stuff that sterner Christian faith is made of. He made me come of age and step into a confidence which was based on fact as well as faith, examination as well as experience.

Jesus tells us that the Queen of Sheba and the city of Nineveh were converted by lesser proof than this. He has given us compelling proof through his powerful Sign of Jonah.

---

[7] John Stott, *Basic Christianity* (1958).

Act Three:

Kingdom Message

Kingdom Secrets (13:1–52)

The disciples came to him and asked, "Why do you speak to the people in parables?" He replied, "The knowledge of the secrets of the kingdom of heaven has been given to you, but not to them."

(Matthew 13:10–11)

Memo to the Director re Steven:
Steven, the newest member of the team, can always be found hard at work in his cubicle. Steven works independently, without wasting company time talking to colleagues. He never thinks twice about assisting fellow employees, and he always finishes assignments on time. Often Steven takes extended measures to complete his work, sometimes even skipping lunch breaks. He is an unusual individual who has absolutely no vanity in spite of his strong qualifications and profound knowledge in his field. I firmly believe that Steven can be classed among our very best employees, the type which cannot be dispensed with. Consequently, I duly recommend that Steven be promoted to senior management, and a proposal will be sent away as soon as possible.

Second Memo to the Director re Steven:
Steven was looking over my shoulder as I wrote my previous memo, so please read only every alternate line (1, 3, 5, 7, etc.) for my true assessment of him.

Sometimes Jesus needed to speak in code. He did so using parables. Contrary to what most people assume, he told parables not just to illustrate truth, but also to *conceal* it.[1] As the curtain rose on Act Three of his ministry, Jesus knew that it was time to prepare his followers for the challenge of carrying his Kingdom message to the world. He needed to teach them deep Kingdom secrets, which would equip them to provoke great Kingdom growth, but he needed to do so under the noses of his enemies. The seven parables of chapter 13 are therefore like this business memo about "Steven": they are encrypted enlightenment, which requires us to read between the lines.

Jesus warns his disciples to guard at all costs the Gospel message which they proclaim. His Kingdom could only thrive in the hands of his motley bunch of followers because its power was in the message, not the messengers. It is the *seed* which grows, the *yeast* which spreads, the *mustard seed* which skyrockets, and the *net* which draws in the fish. All the workers need to do is sow, throw, mix, and wait. It's both easy and terribly difficult. Everything within us wants to tweak, change, adapt, and reconstitute the Gospel message in the hope of winning more converts to Christ. But we mustn't. However unimpressive the *"message about the kingdom"* may appear to our eyes, unless we sow what God gives us we will never reap what God promises us.

What we preach is what we get. Wheat seed produces wheat, barley seed produces barley, and a superficial or selective "gospel" message only produces superficial and partial conversions. Superficial converts respond quickly and joyfully, but in the long run they do more harm than good. When they fall away in the face of trials, they become less likely to respond to the true Gospel, and they give a whole group of friends and relatives yet another excuse to write off the Gospel. Partial conversions, where people reach out for forgiveness but hope to worship an unholy trinity of Jesus, Mammon, and the cares

[1] The word *parable* literally means *comparison*, so they do illustrate. However, Matthew 13:10–17, 34–35 tells us that their primary purpose was to *conceal* as well as *reveal*.

of this world are also very destructive to the Church. Such oxygen-starved converts dilute her radical counter-culture, and too many of them can sink a church's witness altogether. Better to preach from the outset that anyone who follows Jesus *"must deny himself and take up his cross"*, and that *"you cannot serve both God and money"*.[2] Jesus aimed for fewer, genuine converts because quality matters more than quantity; one genuine convert will go on to win thirty to a hundred times more. A few radical revolutionaries are all it takes to transform the world, one genuine convert at a time.

Consequently, Jesus warns his disciples to be ready for discouragement. Some people will point blank refuse the Gospel message. Others will make steps towards conversion, only to baulk at the cost. I remember being very discouraged in my early days of church leadership when several promising contacts decided they had heard enough. One of my mentors encouraged me that, *"Phil, you can't take the Parable of the Sower out of the Bible!"*, and those words picked me up and made me carry on. People will choose self-rule over God's Kingdom, producing the mixed-up world of the Parable of the Weeds. Even worse, some of those rebels will stay and masquerade as Christians inside the Church, like the rotten fish in the Parable of the Net.[3] Jesus warns us not to deal too harshly with them or we will lose some of the genuine catch. Instead, we must train ourselves to see the grace of God in even the most compromised of churches, and remind ourselves that one day he will return and set all things right.[4]

Most of all, despite the setbacks, Jesus repeats that we must expect him to save large numbers of people all over the earth.

---

[2] Matthew 6:24; 16:24.

[3] Jesus does not just refer to these false converts as *bad* fish in v. 48, but literally as *rotten* ones.

[4] If Paul managed to rejoice over the grace of God in 1 Corinthians 1:4, despite seeing doctrinal error, gross moral failure and mishandled spiritual gifts, we can also rejoice over the grace we see in our churches.

We can scarcely imagine how daunting it must have felt for the small group of Jewish nobodies who were tasked with taking the Gospel to the great halls of Rome and Athens, and to the dangerous borderlands of Parthia and Britannia. Jesus simply reminds them that only a few grams of yeast can work its way through more than forty litres of dough,[5] and that even if the Gospel message looks like a tiny mustard seed, it can conquer more lands than the mightiest empires of history.[6] Harvesting, baking, and fishing all take time, but they are worth the wait when each radical convert becomes a radical missionary and produces many others like himself. Jesus has already purchased the nations of the earth as treasure which cost him his life.[7] Therefore, if we announce his unadulterated Gospel, nothing will thwart his Kingdom Revolution from filling whole earth.

Jesus speaks in code in chapter 13, and reveals for our eyes only what Abraham, Moses, David, and Isaiah all longed to see.[8] This Gospel message is the hope of the world, which delivers thirty, sixty, or a hundredfold growth for each believer and each local church. Therefore do not be satisfied with anything less in your own life. So long as we are preaching the Gospel message that he has given us, Jesus promises us that *this is what the Kingdom of Heaven is like*.

---

[5] Three *sata* or *seahs* in v. 33 equates to 42 litres of flour.

[6] The reference in v. 32 to birds perching in the mustard plant's branches is a reference to Daniel 4:12 which describes the king of the Babylonian Empire, to Ezekiel 31:6 which describes the Assyrian Empire, and to Ezekiel 17:23 which speaks about the Messiah's much greater Kingdom.

[7] Since the farmer with the seed and the woman with the yeast both represent *Jesus* not us (v. 37), we should understand that the Parables of the Hidden Treasure and of the Pearl talk primarily about *Jesus'* sacrifice for the Gospel, not our own. We sacrifice all for the Gospel, but only because he did so first.

[8] Verses 16–17 are simply one of the most remarkable statements in Scripture about the New Covenant.

Why Does God Allow Suffering?
(13:24–30, 36–43)

The servants asked him, "Do you want us to go and pull them up?" "No," he answered, "because while you are pulling the weeds, you may root up the wheat with them. Let both grow together until the harvest."

(Matthew 13:28–30)

"I cried all the time." That's how Steven Spielberg recalls his months directing *Schindler's List*. German soldiers butcher helpless women and children in the Jewish ghetto; an SS officer takes target practice at the prisoners with his rifle, just for fun; trainloads of bewildered Jews arrive at the death-camp at Auschwitz. Spielberg re-creates one of the darkest moments in human history, which made one survivor, Simon Wiesenthal, conclude that *"God must have been on leave during the Holocaust."*[1]

When faced with such injustice and suffering, most people point the finger at God. Is he not strong enough to stop it? If he is, then – worse – is he not good enough to want to? This is the greatest non-Christian objection to the Gospel, so Jesus answers it in his Parable of the Weeds. He will talk later in the Parable of the Net about how he will judge evil and hypocrisy in

---

[1] This quotation comes from Joseph McBride's book *Steven Spielberg: A Biography* (1997). The film was released by Universal Pictures in 1993, grossed over $300 million, and won seven Oscars.

the Church, but here he explains why he has not yet judged the evil and suffering in the world.[2]

First, he reassures us that God is good. He hates pain and injustice far more than we do, as is obvious from the Old Testament prophets. Jesus tells us that he sowed nothing but *"good seed"* in the world. He was able to look at his finished creation and declare that it was *"very good"*.[3]

But we invited Satan's *"very bad"* seed to take root in God's perfect world. He caught the human race napping and promised to turn us into mini-gods.[4] As soon as Adam and Eve swallowed his bait, they argued and blamed one another, and within a few verses one of their sons was murdering his brother. Before the end of Genesis, their offspring had embraced deception, violence, genocide, vendettas, incest, adultery, prostitution, rape, binge drinking, idolatry, slavery, and homosexuality – a catalogue of corruption. They reeled under God's curse against sin, stricken with guilt, restlessness, loneliness, sickness, disease, infertility, and eventually death. They inflicted pain and suffering on one another, and their corrupted planet echoed back natural disasters of its own.[5] Our outrage at the evil in *Schindler's List* betrays a primal instinct that the world should not be this way, and our finger-pointing heavenwards that God alone can set things right. When we complain that God permits such suffering, we are effectively asking *"Let your Kingdom come on earth as it is in heaven"*.[6] It will indeed come, but when it does many will wish that they had never asked.

Jesus tells us that suffering persists in the world not because of God's indifference, but because of his *mercy*. A day is

---

[2] Jesus is very clear in v. 38 that the field is the *world* and not the Church.

[3] Genesis 1:31.

[4] The Greek text in v. 25 does not tell us that *"everyone"* was sleeping – including the farmer – but merely that *"men"* were sleeping. Satan caught people napping, but not the Lord (Psalm 121:3–4).

[5] Genesis 3:17–19; Isaiah 24:4–6; Romans 8:19–22.

[6] Matthew 6:10.

coming, very soon, when he will root out *"everything that causes sin and all who do evil"*, but he delays because we ourselves are part of the problem. We are not just victims of suffering, but perpetrators too. None of us is free from guilt – not even Oskar Schindler, heroic saviour of 1,100 Jews, yet at the same time a Nazi war profiteer and serial adulterer. God refuses to end the world's suffering right at this moment because to do so would be to obliterate the entire human race. In tender mercy, he delays the great Day of Judgment because he has many more "children of the Kingdom" still to call and save. He lets human suffering continue because each hour's delay saves more and more of them from the greater suffering of hell. Until the full number of his People has been saved, he restrains his harvesters because *"while you are pulling the weeds, you may root up the wheat with them"*.[7]

Holocaust victim Anne Frank wrote in her diary that *"I can feel the sufferings of millions and yet, if I look up into the heavens, I think that it will all come right"*.[8] Jesus does not dodge our questions about suffering because he knows that indeed it will. He talks plainly about the great harvest day to come, when he will return with his angels to throw every evildoer and cause of suffering into hell like weeds onto a fire. Having done so, he will gather his People into God's barn, the glorious new world where *"there will be no more death or mourning or crying or pain, for the old order of things has passed away"*.[9] Because of God's mercy, both weeds and wheat grow alongside each other

---

[7] The Greek word *zizanion* means literally *darnel*, a false wheat which looks very similar to true wheat right up until the moment that it bears fruit. God gives every opportunity for non-Christians to repent of being "children of the evil one", but has set a day of harvest when their true nature will be revealed.

[8] Anne Frank wrote this in her *Diary of a Young Girl* on 15th July 1944. She was a Jewish teenager in Nazi-occupied Holland and wrote this months before her death in the Bergen-Belsen concentration camp.

[9] Revelation 21:4. Note that John the Baptist also used this image of the Fire and the Barn in Matthew 3:12.

in our mixed-up and pain-filled world. There will be a harvest, but thank God it's not yet.

Jesus sympathizes with our questions about suffering because the very reason he came to earth was to open up his arms and embrace the worst of human suffering in his own frail body. God is good enough to care about suffering, forgiving enough to redeem those who cause suffering, and strong enough to make a way for them to be redeemed through his own suffering on the cross. He became part of the wicked human race – the Farmer stooping to become a blade of wheat – so that he could bear the punishment that we deserve. Like the victims of the Holocaust, he became a refugee at the hands of an evil dictator, he was betrayed by a trusted friend, he was unlawfully imprisoned and tortured, and he was stripped and murdered by a group of anti-Semitic foreign soldiers. He drank the cup of human suffering down to its very last dregs, enduring the full weight of Adam's curse on his crushed and broken body, and with his final breaths he cried out *"It is finished!"*[10] That cry will echo across the harvest fields on the great day of reckoning, as many are pronounced righteous through their humble faith in the blood of the Farmer. He endured our hell so that we can share his heaven, and he holds off the day of harvest because there are still more people to be saved.

Jesus does not mind us asking why God allows suffering, but he wants to move us on from complaining about suffering to joining him in doing something about it. At the end of his movie, Steven Spielberg shows us Oskar Schindler on the day the Nazis were routed. He looks at the faces of those he has saved, then looks down at his possessions and the many more who could have been purchased through his sacrifice. *"I could have done more"*, he wails, breaking down in tears. The things of this earth will look very different on harvest day.

We who have responded to the Gospel message of Jesus

---

[10] John 19:30.

Christ are all Oskar Schindlers. We are able to save sinful humans from the fire to the safety of the barn, simply by telling them the story about the Farmer who laid down his life to redeem a mighty harvest. In the face of human suffering, we cannot keep this message to ourselves.

Mincemeat (14:13–36)

Then Peter got down out of the boat, walked on the water and came towards Jesus. But when he saw the wind, he was afraid and, beginning to sink, cried out, "Lord, save me!"

(Matthew 14:29–30)

Operation Mincemeat was one of the greatest deceptions ever carried out in wartime. By the spring of 1943, the Allied armies had recaptured North Africa and were ready for the seaborne invasion of Italy, the soft underbelly of Hitler's Fortress Europe. There was just one problem: the enemy knew that Sicily would be the first objective, and they had filled the island with troops and tanks. Enter Major William Martin, "The Man Who Never Was".[1] An anonymous corpse was dressed like a Royal Marine and dropped by submarine off the coast of Spain. The bogus Major's body bore a forged letter to the commander of the British forces in North Africa, which spoke of a plan to land in Greece and Sardinia. Sure enough, the letter soon found its way to the in-trays at German High Command, and Hitler quickly gave the order to move divisions out of Sicily to prepare for the new-found threat. On 10th July 1943, the Allied forces landed on the shores of a much depleted Sicily. A jubilant telegram was sent to Winston Churchill: *"Mincemeat swallowed whole."*

The Devil has his own Operation Mincemeat, which he launches against the followers of Jesus Christ. He really believes the promises of chapter 13, and he is taking no chances. He will

---

[1] This was the title of Ewen Montagu's 1953 book in which he tells the true story of Operation Mincemeat.

do anything he can to fix our eyes on our own priorities, on our own stretched resources, and on the challenges which face us – anything, in fact, other than on Jesus himself and his power for us to succeed. He wants to divert our gaze from where it belongs and to snatch victory from defeat through our careless distraction. That's why we must notice that Matthew structures the narrative of chapters 14 to 17 as a deliberate follow-on from the teaching of chapter 13. The parables about wheat, fish, yeast, and mustard seeds lead into a series of practical lessons using bread, fish, yeast, and mustard seeds.[2] We mustn't miss this and let the Devil make mincemeat of us in the battle ahead. Victory is ours, if only we will reach out to take it, but to do so we must fix our eyes on Jesus and on nothing else.

It is so easy to fix our eyes on our own priorities. The disciples did so when they urged Jesus to "*Send the crowds away*", and later to "*Send her away*".[3] He had every reason to comply as he reeled from the news of John the Baptist's execution, grieving for his friend and deeply conscious that he would soon be next. Yet, even as the crowds hounded him and mercilessly robbed him of the time and space he craved, Jesus "*had compassion on them and healed all their sick*". If we fix our eyes on our own plans each day, we will never see the daily Kingdom victories which God has laid out for us. Jesus preached the message of the Kingdom, authenticated it with breathtaking miracles,[4] and

---

[2] Matthew refers to *yeast* in 13:33 and 16:6, 11, and to a *mustard seed* in 13:31 and 17:20, yet mentions neither of them anywhere else in his gospel. Jesus multiplies *bread* and *fish* for two vast crowds, he argues with a Canaanite woman over *bread*, and then gives Peter four drachmas in the mouth of a *fish*. All this is deliberate.

[3] Matthew 14:15; 15:23. It was a reasonable suggestion, but growth comes through *unreasonable* compassion.

[4] Mark 6:34 and Luke 9:11 tell us that Jesus both taught and healed this particular crowd. He rarely preached the Kingdom without demonstrating it, and rarely demonstrated the Kingdom without preaching it.

then stayed up all night to find his time to mourn and pray.[5] Even in the morning, as he was mobbed by yet another crowd in Gennesaret, he kept on serving their needs. Chapter-13 growth only comes through chapter-14 love and compassion. We must not get distracted by the siren-cries of self.

In any kind of Christian ministry, it is also very easy to fix our eyes on the smallness of our own resources. Jesus taught his disciples through not just one but two miracles that they must not fall for this ploy of the Devil. Satan would rather have us complain that *"We have here only five loaves and two fish"*, than have us offer our weakness to Jesus and let him turn it into strength. It was logical to step back and tell the crowd to find food for themselves, but faith must triumph over logic if we are to see Kingdom growth. Note how Jesus deliberately multiplies the bread and the fish as *the disciples* hand it to the crowd, and how he orders each of them to gather up a basketful of leftovers to help build their faith.[6] If we focus on our own slender resources, the Devil may yet snatch millions down to hell. If we fix our eyes on Jesus and preach his simple Gospel message, we can yet save their souls.

It is also very easy to fix our eyes on the adverse circumstances which so frequently assault us. When Peter fixed his eyes on the mighty face of Jesus, he stepped out of the boat and walked across the water towards him. When he looked at the wind and the waves, he began to sink and drown. Now here's the amazing thing: Jesus does not commend him for becoming the only person in history other than himself ever to walk on water. Instead, he rebukes him as *"you of little faith"*,

---

[5] The *fourth watch of the night* in v. 25 was from 3 a.m. to 6 a.m., so Jesus had been praying for nine hours since he dismissed the crowd at nightfall.

[6] Matthew tells us that each of the seven baskets of 15:37 was a *spuris*, the same-sized basket which was used to lower Paul down the Damascus city-wall in Acts 9:25. Therefore the seven basketfuls may have contained more leftovers than the twelve smaller baskets of 14:20. Jesus upgraded rather than downgraded the lesson.

and asks a disappointed question which literally means *"why did you look in two places?"* [7] We tend to admire Peter for his moment of faith, when he believed the word of Jesus above the laws of physics. Jesus, however, is appalled that he should ever do anything less. Fixing our eyes on Jesus means growth, success, and victory. Fixing them anywhere else lets the Devil make mincemeat of us.

Jesus has called us to proclaim his Gospel message each day and every day, and to back it up with a purity and power which proves that it's true. That's the way his Kingdom grows like wheat, yeast, or a mustard seed. If we will only keep our eyes fixed on him, our efforts will be utterly unstoppable.

Of course the Devil hopes to distract us with his Operation Mincemeat. Its lure is reasonable, logical, and thoroughly understandable, but it is also inexcusable. We cannot allow our busy priorities, our sense of inadequacy, or the hard winds of circumstance to turn our heads the other way. We mustn't let the Devil make mincemeat of our God-given potential. Jesus has commanded us to step out with his Kingdom message. Let's fix our eyes on him, confident that his love, his strength and his power can always bear us on to victory.

---

[7] The Greek word *distazo* has at its root the word *dis* or *twice*. Jesus does not want us to fix our eyes on two places – on him plus circumstances – but on him alone.

The God Who Offends (15:1–20)

Then the disciples came to him and asked, "Do you know that the Pharisees were offended when they heard this?"

(Matthew 15:12)

Like most humble people, Matthew is brutally honest about his own shortcomings. We might have been tempted to gloss over our stupidity, but not Matthew. Far from it. He gives us the uncensored story of the twelve disciples, with all their ups and downs, highs and lows, breathtaking insights and toe-curling errors. He encourages us through their failures, but he also has a deeper aim. He lays down their foolish questions as a trap for his readers, willing us to agree with them and then dealing us an uppercut by proxy as Jesus rebukes their blind stupidity. Jesus shaped the disciples into men he could trust with the message of his Kingdom. As we study their questions, he shapes us too.

Take, for example, this question in verse 12, which has to be a strong contender for the dumbest question in the Bible: *"Do you know that the Pharisees were offended when they heard this?"* The disciples had had enough of Jesus' confrontational manner and his willingness to pick a fight with his audience. It was time to give him a little advice. Did he not see that a more inclusive message might increase the size of his crowds? Couldn't he be a little less offensive and just a little bit more winsome? Jesus' reply is short and to the point: When they heard what? Me calling them lawbreaking hypocrites who are spiritually dirty? Me dismissing their tradition and precious food laws as the invention of men?[1] Yes, I knew that they would be offended. Can't you see that I go out of my way to offend people? It's what God's messengers are called to do.[2]

It's not that Jesus *liked* offending people. He performed a miracle in 17:27 precisely to avoid having to offend the officious Temple tax collectors. He simply knew that the Gospel message must be preached with calculated offence if it is ever to yield the full Kingdom growth that he promised in chapter 13. The attractive, winsome, seeker-friendly yet declining churches of the West are in dire need of this lesson from Jesus. The Gospel needs to be offensive. It doesn't work any other way.

The Gospel needs to offend people because of the Parable of the Net. Every congregation contains both good fish and rotten fish, and the rotten ones can spoil the whole catch. Therefore, since *"every plant that my heavenly Father has not planted will be pulled up by the roots"*, we preach such a counter-cultural message that only those truly planted by God will want to remain. We make the church a hotbed of radical discipleship, so that people either yield to God's Kingdom or withdraw in disgust. We do not help modern-day Pharisees and scribes by humouring them for fear of losing them. Left unchallenged, they will not only lose their own lives but will infect true believers and convince non-Christian onlookers that the message of the Kingdom is as dead as they are. Jesus deliberately whittled down the size of his crowds, preaching a Gospel which was so offensive that people either got saved or got out. He warned the

---

[1] These ceremonial washings were part of the Jewish oral tradition, which was only written down in about 200 AD in the Mishnah, part of the modern-day Jewish Talmud. They criticized Jesus for breaking their traditions, but he demonstrated that their traditions turned them into lawbreakers, not him. The parallel passage in Mark 7:19 explains that *"In saying this, Jesus declared all foods 'clean'."*

[2] We often think very much like the disciples. If someone accosted his audience like Jesus did the Pharisees, he would probably be dropped from our preaching rotas. If someone told a would-be convert to renounce all his idols or not come at all (see 19:16–22), he might well be branded an insensitive zealot.

crowd to avoid such hypocrites, because they were leading their nation to destruction.[3] Paradoxically, the more Jesus attacked the hypocrisy of the élite, the more the common people loved him.

The Gospel also needs to offend people because of the Parable of the Sower. It is tempting to offer people a discount on discipleship, in the hope that their commitment will deepen along the way. In the words of Pope Gregory the Great:

> *Destroy as few pagan temples as possible; only destroy their idols, sprinkle them with holy water, build altars and put relics in the buildings, so that, if the temples have been well built, you are simply changing their purpose... They should build booths out of branches round the church as they used to round pagan temples... Be assured that it is impossible to rid such deluded souls of all their misconceptions at once. You do not climb a mountain in leaps and bounds, but by taking it slowly.*[4]

It is a tempting and prevalent approach, but Jesus taught a very different way. Seed planted in rocky and thorny soil will be scorched and throttled, so we must thoroughly prepare the ground before the seed ever grows. Jesus went head-to-head with his listeners' false gods and split priorities. Knowing that good crops only grow in good soil, Jesus thoroughly ploughed his listeners' hearts to see a few people truly saved instead of a whole field of false converts.

The Gospel also needs to offend people because of the Parable of the Mustard Seed. Although it is only a millimetre in size, that seed is so potent that one first-century botanist complained that *"when it has once been sown, it is scarcely possible*

---

[3] The Greek word *laos* in v. 8 is often used in the Greek Old Testament to refer specifically to the Jewish *people*.

[4] Pope Gregory gave this advice to his missionaries to pagan England in about 600 AD.

to get the place free of it".[5] The disciples underestimated the power of the Gospel message to break stubborn hearts and to grow in the unlikeliest of places. Like Pope Gregory, they assumed that conversion means such a massive change of direction that it can only happen as a gradual process. In the Parable of the Mustard Seed, Jesus teaches that the opposite is true. Conversion *is* a massive change, but it is so massive that it can never happen by human means, whether fast or slow. It can only happen when the Father breathes his Holy Spirit into someone's heart in the miracle of rebirth. No amount of softly-softly teaching can coax the unregenerate into salvation. It can only offend the God whose message we dare to corrupt, and haemorrhage our churches.

Finally, the Gospel needs to offend people because of the Parable of the Buried Treasure. We preach the message of Jesus Christ who laid down his life on the cross, and we must not sell cheaply what he bought so dearly. He gave up his life to save the lost, and he calls them to give up their own lives to receive his salvation. The disciples were astounded by the outrageous price tag which Jesus attached to his Kingdom, but in the next chapter they would be equally astounded by the price he himself was willing to pay. The Gospel is free, but it is not cheap. It is the most expensive free gift in history.

The radical preacher from Galilee offended the Pharisees, and he will offend us too. He knew more than anyone that nothing attracts unbelievers more than the raw truth and beauty of the offensive Gospel message. The God-Who-Offends is looking for a bold army of messengers. Let's do it his way. It's the only way that works.

---

[5] Pliny the Elder wrote this in the 70s AD in chapter 19 of his *Natural History*.

When God Is Silent
(15:21–28)

A Canaanite woman from that vicinity came to him, crying out, "Lord, Son of David, have mercy on me!"... Jesus did not answer a word.

(Matthew 15:28)

One summer's day in late nineteenth-century London, a group of friends decided to visit the Metropolitan Tabernacle to hear the great Charles Haddon Spurgeon. Hailed by many as the "prince of preachers", they wanted to see the man who had built a church from 200 to 10,000, and who had equipped an army of students to plant similar churches across the United Kingdom. They were greeted at the door by a man who offered them a tour of the building. *"Would you like to see this church's heating plant?"* he asked them, and without waiting for a reply herded them down a steep flight of stairs. He slowly pushed open an unimpressive door and declared with an excited whisper: *"This is our heating plant."* The friends were startled by the roar of 700 people, fervently praying for the service which was about to begin upstairs. Amused that his trick had been successful, the man extended his hand and introduced himself. Their tour-guide was none other than Charles Spurgeon himself.

Every great work of God can be traced back to praying men and women. We all know that, but it is easier to agree with the theory than to live by the practice. Most of us find the discipline of prayer quite difficult, probably because the Devil is acutely aware of its devastating power.[1] We get frustrated when our prayers seem to go unanswered, and we are tempted to neglect the place of prayer altogether. Just last week I asked a man why he had abandoned the churchgoing of his youth, and he shot back tersely, *"I used to pray but nothing happened."* Matthew puts the story of Jesus and the Canaanite woman in the middle of Act Three because he wants to prepare us for the moments when heaven falls silent. He wants us to become like Charles Spurgeon, who declared in later life that, even if God offered him everything he wanted without the need for persevering prayer, he would refuse it point blank for the blessing of prayer itself. Spurgeon had learned to endure and even enjoy the rich training ground of unanswered prayer, and Matthew teaches us to do so too.

If God answered all our prayers straight away, we would never learn true humility. Proud people pray little, and even when they do pray they often rely on prayer *plus* self-help. Unanswered prayer humbles us and forces us to admit that God alone can be our helper. The Canaanite woman was so desperate when she found Jesus that she called him *kurios* or *Lord* and hailed him as the Messianic *Son of David*. Nevertheless, she grew humbler still when he refused her requests, grovelling at his feet, and even letting him label her a Gentile dog.[2] Spurgeon found that *"True prayer is an inventory of needs, a catalogue of necessities, an exposure of secret wounds, a revelation of hidden poverty."* The Canaanite woman grew more and more reliant on Jesus each time he rebuked her, and eventually she displayed the humble poverty which God cannot ignore.

If God answered all our prayers straight away, we would never see the fruit of true persistence. Although it is true that

---

[1] This is one of the reasons why Jesus urges us in Matthew 6:6 to devote a regular time and place to prayer, on days when we feel like it and on days when we do not.

[2] The Greek word *proskuneō* in v. 25 can actually be translated that she *worshipped* him.

Jesus normally answers prayer with a *yes*, a *no*, or a *not yet*, Matthew warns us that there will be many times in life when *"Jesus does not answer a word"*. He keeps silent, he hides himself, and he even pushes us away in order that we may lay hold of him with dogged determination. He is training us to rule with him in the age to come, and so he forces us to grapple in prayer to prepare us for that day. He commanded us in 7:7 to *"go on asking... go on seeking... go on knocking"*, because princes must learn to be kings before they can be entrusted with a throne.[3] No one will complain to God in the age to come that he took too long to answer their prayers. We will be too busy praising him that he subjected us to light and momentary frustrations in order to train us for eternal glory.[4]

We must not miss that fact that the story of the Canaanite woman is sandwiched (forgive the pun) between two miracles with bread, and comes just before a warning about the yeast of the Pharisees.[5] Matthew wants us to grasp that this woman only came to Jesus for deliverance, but learned through her persistence that her true need was far greater. While the proud Jewish leaders refused to swallow the bread of God's Kingdom message, this Gentile woman was prepared to lick up even the little breadcrumbs which fell from the Jewish table. Unanswered prayer does not necessarily mean that God refuses our request. It may simply mean that he has something far greater to give us while we wait.

If God answered our prayers straight away, we would never develop true faith. Great bodybuilders grow their muscles through long hours of lifting weights, and spiritual heroes grow strong faith through stretching it to near breaking point in God's gym of unanswered prayer. Peter rejoices in his first letter that

---

[3] The three commands in 7:7 are Greek "present imperatives", which urge a person to *go on* doing something.

[4] 2 Corinthians 4:17.

[5] The Greek text of Matthew 15:2 also refers to *bread*, even though many English translations omit the word.

trials *"come so that your faith – of greater worth than gold, which perishes even though refined by fire – may be proved genuine and may result in praise, glory and honour when Jesus Christ is revealed".*[6] It was only when the Canaanite woman had fought her way through delay and disappointment that Jesus praised her great faith and granted her request.

Whether you need *"daily bread"* to meet your basic needs,[7] or God's power to advance with the bread of his Kingdom message, Jesus promises to answer your fervent prayers. Sometimes he will appear silent and will even seem to refuse your requests for help, but he is simply teaching you humility, persistence, and faith. There, on the battlefield of unanswered prayer, he will teach you to rule with him in the age to come.

Charles Spurgeon taught that *"We cannot all argue, but we can all pray; we cannot all be leaders, but we can all be pleaders; we cannot all be mighty in rhetoric, but we can all be prevalent in prayer."* We can all take our place in God's "heating plant" and draw down miracles from heaven in our own generation.

---

[6] 1 Peter 1:6–7.
[7] Matthew 6:11.

Yeast (16:1–12)

"Be careful," Jesus said to them. "Be on your guard against the yeast of the Pharisees and Sadducees."

(Matthew 16:6)

Yeast can be a wonderful microscopic ally. Although each yeast cell is just a hundredth of the size of a grain of sand, it can leaven two hundred and fifty times its own weight in flour. If you are making bread, beer, wine, or Marmite, yeast is an indispensably powerful helper. That's why Jesus compares it to the Kingdom of Heaven in one of the parables of chapter 13. God loves to take the unremarkable and render it unstoppable.

But yeast can be a nasty little fungus too. Airborne yeast can ruin cheese or meat, ferment sugary fruit or jam, and even produce yeast infections in humans. That's why the Bible tends to use yeast as a negative picture for the spreading corruption of sin. God gave the Israelites the Feast of Unleavened Bread as a week every year to abstain from yeast and remember their covenant purity.[1] Later, he told the priests, *"Do not offer the blood of a sacrifice to me along with anything containing yeast"*,[2] and Paul picked up on this to warn against the *"yeast of wickedness"* because *"a little yeast works through the whole batch of dough"*.[3] Yeast is a powerful helper, but it is also a stealthy destroyer.

Jesus has already talked about the yeast of his Kingdom, but now he warns us that Satan has yeast of his own. He has the yeast of the Pharisees, that spirit of legalism which hopes for

---

[1] Exodus 12:15, 19. Those who failed to keep this feast were to be cut off from the People of God.

[2] Exodus 23:18; 34:25. The only exception to this was in Leviticus 7:13.

[3] 1 Corinthians 5:6–8; Galatians 5:9.

salvation through *human works*. The Pharisees, or "Separated Ones", had once been a vibrant group of synagogue-planters who carried with them a spirit of revival. Yet over the years they had suffocated Judaism with a thick blanket of rules and tradition. They had succumbed to the yeast of smug hypocrisy, strong on externals but dead on the inside.[4]

He also has the yeast of the Sadducees, the sworn enemies of the Pharisees. Named after the former high priest Zadok[5] and dominating both the Temple and the Sanhedrin, they lived by the spirit of *human reason* and placed their hope in *human compromise*.[6] Rejecting the authority of any Scripture except for the five books of Moses, they denied the existence of angels, demons, supernatural miracles, life after death, and the resurrection of the dead. They were pragmatists, cosying up to Herod and the Romans in return for political position[7] and the freedom to collect taxes in the Temple.[8] Their yeast treated Judaism as a licence to print money and an easy way to control the masses. They held office as God's priests, but denied his power.

Unless you know the geography of Palestine you will miss the important sub-plot of Act Three. Matthew is warning his Jewish readers (who knew the geography far better than us) that the yeast of the Pharisees and Sadducees is fatal. It had infected Judaism and made it a dead, worldly, formalistic shadow of its

---

[4] Jesus adds in Luke 12:1 that the yeast of the Pharisees always involves hypocrisy.

[5] The Lord singled out the priestly line of Zadok in Ezekiel 40:46; 43:19 and 44:15 to hold the high priesthood.

[6] The *Sanhedrin* was the council of seventy-one Jewish priests, elders, and scribes to which the Romans gave authority to govern internal Jewish affairs. It was led by the high priest and dominated by his Sadducee friends.

[7] So much so that Mark 8:15 calls *"the yeast of the Pharisees and Sadducees"* *"the yeast of the Pharisees and Herod"*.

[8] The former tax collector Matthew is the only gospel writer to mention the miracle of 17:24–27. He evidently still maintained a professional interest in all things related to taxation.

former self.[9] So much so, that the Gospel could thrive better in Gentile lands.

The narrative of Act Three begins with Jesus' rejection in Nazareth and John's execution at the hands of wicked Herod. The common people marvel that Jesus feeds 5,000, but the Pharisees complain that his disciples broke their rules by failing to wash their hands before eating. Jesus responds by withdrawing to Gentile Syro-Phoenicia and to a Canaanite woman whose eager faith sought out the breadcrumbs which the Jews rejected. He then turns south to the Decapolis, a league of ten Greek-speaking cities on the eastern shore of Lake Galilee, where the Gentile crowds saw his miracles and *"praised the God of Israel"*.[10] After a brief trip back to Galilee to clash again with the stubborn Pharisees and Sadducees, Jesus heads north to Caesarea Philippi in the mixed-race region of Batanaea. It is in this context that Jesus warns against *"the yeast of the Pharisees and Sadducees"*, before a final clash which shows that the Sadducees are more interested in his taxes than his teaching. Matthew sends out a warning that God will not allow the Jewish leaders to contaminate his Gospel with their hellish yeast. If they won't accept the unleavened Gospel, the Gentile dogs will.

Does it sound like ancient history, meant for someone other than you? Actually, it couldn't be more relevant to today. The yeast that infected first-century Judaism can just as easily infect the Church today unless we stay true to the Gospel of Christ. Paul warns us in Romans 11:21, when discussing God's judgment on the Jewish olive tree, *"If God did not spare the natural branches, he will not spare you either."*

Every single year, around 4,000 American and 300 British

---

[9] Mark writes for a predominantly Roman audience, so he gives more geographical detail in Mark 7:29–9:29.

[10] The people of the Decapolis had begged Jesus to leave their region in Matthew 8:28, 34 and Mark 5:20. Now their hearts have changed, and Matthew warns his Jewish readers that if they hang on to their yeasted religion then such Gentiles will be saved instead of them.

churches close their doors for good. The Western Church is in nosedive, and many Christians see it as a mighty triumph for the Devil. Jesus has another explanation in Revelation 2:5. He says that he is the only one who can close down a church, and that he does so like a surgeon who removes deadly cancer cells before they spread unchecked to the rest of the body. Where churches deny the supernatural and let twenty-first-century reason sit in judgment upon Scripture, his scalpel does its work. Where churches compromise their message and place more faith in elections than in Easter, once again he cuts and amputates. Where churches smother the Gospel of grace under the weight of smug self-righteousness, yet again he cuts deep to save the whole Body. Jesus loves his Church, and will not allow the yeast of the Pharisees and Sadducees to corrupt his Bride or her message.

In the meantime, the Devil's yeast is outpaced by the yeast of God's Kingdom. The Jewish leaders got infected, so the common Jewish outcasts received Jesus instead. The common Jews were hoodwinked, so the Gentiles received him in turn.[11] Even today, as the Western Church continues its decline, each year sees 1,150 new church plants in America and 150 more in the United Kingdom. Even as the Devil contaminates, the yeast of the true Gospel continues to grow.

Guard God's message in your life and in your church at all costs. Shun the deadly yeast of human works, human reason, and human compromise. Learn the lesson of Church history: Jesus is fiercely committed to the true Gospel of salvation.

---

[11] The New Testament does not tell us that the Church has *replaced* Israel, but that the Christian faith is the true and unyeasted continuation of Old Testament Judaism. Modern, Christless Judaism is heir to the yeast of the Pharisees, not to the pure religion of Abraham, Moses and David.

The Master-Questioner
(16:13–16)

When Jesus came to the region of Caesarea Philippi, he asked his disciples, "Who do people say the Son of Man is?"... "But what about you?" he asked. "Who do you say I am?"

(Matthew 16:13, 15)

Many Christians struggle to begin Gospel conversations with the people around them. That's tragic because Jesus has shown us how to do so. Many struggle to progress a conversation when it starts, because they don't know how to communicate the Gospel without upsetting, and even losing, their friend. They haven't understood Jesus' masterful method of evangelism. They fail to grasp the power of asking questions.

Consider the wise manner in which Jesus led the disciples to confess him as the Son of God. He doesn't preach a sermon. He doesn't give a lecture. He just asks questions. He begins with a third person question – *"Who do **people** say I am?"* – because no one minds a third person question. It's unthreatening and it casts them in the role of the expert. The disciples are full of answers, unaware that they are walking into Jesus' trap. The next question is second person and goes much deeper: *"Who do **you** say I am?"* It's a direct, challenging question but it's easy to ask because the first question paved the way.[1] Peter replies that *"You are the Christ, the Son of the living God"*, and

---

[1] As an experiment, ask a non-Christian friend: *"Why do you think most people in our country never go to church?"* then *"Is that why you never go to church?"* Two simple questions can open up a great conversation.

Jesus affirms what is right (God revealed this to you and I can build my Church on your statement) before challenging what is wrong (get behind me Satan!). Two simple questions, but a giant leap forwards for the disciples. That is the power of asking people questions.

I'm not saying that this is easy. I spent the first few years of my Christian life assuming that effective evangelism involved me dealing out my ten-minute testimony or Gospel presentation to any non-Christian who would listen. I felt really good when I did so, but I quickly noticed that it was pretty ineffective. People's eyes would glaze over, they would raise their defences, and I'd feel as though the Gospel had failed to connect with their heart. Jesus' way is refreshingly different. It's very, very effective.

Jesus was the Master-Questioner, the man who knew what was in people's hearts yet was forever asking questions. He understood the proverb that *"The purposes of a man's heart are deep waters, but a man of understanding draws them out"*.[2] From the age of twelve to the morning of his crucifixion, he asked question after question, skilfully drawing out what people believed.[3] He asked questions to clarify (Luke 10:25–27), questions to expose error and muddled thinking (Matthew 21:23–27; 22:41–46), and questions to deliver a stinging rebuke in a winsome fashion (Luke 7:39–47). He was willing to be offensive, and used questions to make sure that people felt his offence as sharply as steel. Whenever and with whomever, Jesus was always asking questions. His followers must learn to do so too.

I want to earth this with a concrete example, but please don't think I'm claiming to be an expert. I'm just faithfully imitating Jesus the Master-Questioner, through many ups and downs along the way. But I find it's really working, and I hope

---

[2] Proverbs 20:5.

[3] Luke 2:46; John 18:34.

that a practical example may help you to grasp the power of asking questions too.

My neighbour – we'll call him Ahmad – is a Muslim. As soon as he moved into the house next door, my wife and I invited him and his family round for a meal. On one of our many visits to each other's house, the conversation suddenly turned to his beliefs and mine. Drawing a deep breath, I followed the lead of the Master-Questioner:

Me: Ahmad, you're my most intelligent Muslim friend. Perhaps you can answer one of my biggest questions?[4]

Ahmad: Well, I hope I can. What is it?

Me: Why do smart Muslims like yourself put up with the imams when they clamp down on your excellent questions? Whenever I ask the really big questions, the imams get upset with me and I've even received a death threat. Doesn't this make you wonder what they've got to hide?[5]

Ahmad: What kind of questions did you ask them?

Me: Why the Qur'an and the Bible disagree over how we can be forgiven for sin.

Ahmad: That's easy. The Bible has been changed and corrupted over time.

Me: *When* was it changed and corrupted?

Ahmad: Some time before the Prophet Muhammad.

Me: Then why didn't he point that out in the Qur'an? On the contrary, he encourages Muslims to take their

161

---

[4] I'm casting him in the role of the expert, like Matthew 16:13. Everyone loves to play this role.

[5] Can you spot Matthew 16 in this question? I am asking a *third person* question, attacking the imams rather than him, and suggesting that they have hoodwinked him. This paves the way for a *second person* question.

questions to the Christians,[6] with a promise that no one can change the Word of God.[7] Doesn't that seem strange to you?

Ahmad: You're right. It must have been corrupted after the time of Muhammad.

Me: But how can that be right? Only a few miles from here, in the British Museum, there are manuscripts of the New Testament which date back to 350 AD. That's almost three centuries before Muhammad, but the texts are almost identical to the Bibles which Christians use today.

Ahmad: I don't know. You've obviously thought more about my religion than I have.[8]

Me: Have you ever read the Injil, the gospel of Jesus?

Ahmad: No. We have the Qur'an, so we don't need the other Scriptures.

Me: Hold on a minute. You told me that Jesus is a prophet, a messenger from God. Don't you think that every Muslim should read the message God gave him?

Ahmad: No, the leaders of my mosque discourage us from reading the Injil.

Me: But that's precisely my question! Aren't you suspicious of why the imams are too scared to let you read it for yourself? Don't you think it is at least possible that it may be the Qur'an which is corrupt? If so, aren't you at least a little bit worried that you and your family have misunderstood Jesus, that perhaps he did die on the cross, and that this might truly be the only way that you can be forgiven? Aren't

162

---

[6] For example, Surah 10:94 instructs Muslims that *"If you are in doubt as to what We have revealed unto you, then ask those who have been reading the Book from before you."*

[7] For example, Surahs 6:34; 10:64.

[8] This kind of confession often comes when we ask people questions. See Luke 2:47.

you even a little bit concerned that your religious devotion might not be earning you a ticket to heaven, and that perhaps you are being hoodwinked by the imams into hell?

When I got home that night, I was worried that I had blown our friendship. I had done what Jesus teaches in Matthew 16, but I was worried that I had gone a step too far. So imagine my surprise a few days later when I met Ahmad in his driveway with an elderly Pakistani gentleman. He introduced me to his father and then turned to him and announced that *"This is Phil, the nicest neighbour anyone could ever hope to have."*

Three days earlier, I had sat in Ahmad's kitchen and suggested to him that the Qur'an was corrupt, his religion was a lie, and that he and his family were probably hurtling to hell. Now he thinks I am *the nicest neighbour?!* Suddenly I grasped the power of evangelizing Jesus' way. When we ask subversive questions to undermine false ways of thinking, when we use third person questions to pave the way for second person follow-on questions, and when we listen with genuine interest to what our friends believe, I have found that we can ask the toughest questions and provoke the deepest reflection.

I cannot get over the God-given power of questions. I have become a sold-out imitator of Jesus the Master-Questioner.

Jesus is Not a Carpenter
(16:13 – 17:13)

*There he was transfigured before them. His face
shone like the sun, and his clothes became as white
as the light.*

(Matthew 17:2)

Jesus Christ is the same yesterday, today, and forever, but don't
let that fool you. If you merely worship him as the humble
carpenter from Galilee, you are not worshipping the real Jesus
at all. He's different now, very different. And that's why three
out of four gospel writers talk about his Transfiguration.[1]

Jesus came to earth in disguise. When people passed him
in the street, they hardly gave him a second glance. Isaiah tells
us: *"He had no beauty or majesty to attract us to him, nothing in
his appearance that we should desire him."*[2] His close relative
John the Baptist didn't even realize he was the Messiah until
the Father called down from heaven at his baptism.[3] His
childhood friends in Nazareth assumed he was nothing more
than a clever Jewish peasant.[4] In fact, Jesus the Son of God
became so completely human that people ignored him, mocked
him, tortured him, and murdered him without suspecting he

---

[1] John, the fourth gospel writer, did not recount the Transfiguration because
it had already been so well reported in the other three gospels. Instead, he
conveys the same message by telling us in John 17:5 that Jesus spoke to his
Father about his being restored to *"the glory I had with you before the world
began"*.

[2] Isaiah 53:2.

[3] John 1:32–34.

[4] Matthew 13:54–58.

was in any way divine. Jesus walked the earth in disguise, but his followers and Gospel messengers need to see beneath the disguise. That was the point of his Transfiguration.

Look at the description of Jesus in Matthew 17:2. His face shone like the sun and his clothes were dazzling white. Does that remind you of anything? How about John's vision of the glorified Jesus in Revelation 1? There, *"his face was like the sun shining in all its brilliance"* and his appearance was *"white like wool, as white as snow"*.[5] John had seen that face before, along with Peter and James on the Mount of Transfiguration.[6] There, for a moment, he was granted a glimpse of Jesus' true divine glory.[7] He watched him talk with Moses, the great lawgiver, and Elijah, the great prophet, who encouraged him on his path to create a new and better covenant. The three disciples heard the Father's booming voice, which echoed the same endorsement that he had spoken over the Son two years earlier at his baptism. Seeing Jesus as he really is was essential preparation for the turbulent early years of Church history. Their memory of a disguised Jesus yesterday would never be enough to sustain them as apostles and Gospel preachers. They needed to see him as he is in heaven today. So do we, if we are to follow in their footsteps.[8]

This vision of Jesus in his heavenly glory gave the disciples confidence to minister with authority after the Day of Pentecost.

---

[5] Revelation 1:12–16. Another link to Revelation and its mind-boggling oxymorons is Matthew's reference in v. 5 to a cloud *full of light* which *overshadowed* the disciples! The glorified Christ defies description.

[6] The Mount of Transfiguration may have been the 1,929-foot-high Mount Tabor near Nazareth but, in view of Jesus' travels in Act Three, it could also have been the 8,000-foot-high Mount Hermon next to Caesarea Philippi. If so, the Transfiguration took place outside of the borders of Israel as a hint towards the global mission of the Church.

[7] The Greek word used in Matthew 17:2 is *metamorphoō*, which has at its root the noun *morphē*, or *essential nature*. This is the word Paul uses in Philippians 2 to refer to Jesus being *in essential nature* God but taking *the essential nature* of a servant.

[8] The apostle Paul had his own experience of the glorified Christ for the same reason in 2 Corinthians 12:1–4.

Their revelation that Jesus is the Son of God became the rock on which he could build his Church through them.[9] It gave them faith that the gates of hell could never prevent the advance of his Kingdom, and it convinced them that if they bound and loosed things on earth he was able to enforce it from his heavenly throne.[10] It persuaded them that they no longer followed a bullied and beaten carpenter from Galilee, but the undisputed Master of the universe.

This vision of the transfigured Jesus also gave them faith to obey his commands to the letter throughout all the stormy days which lay ahead. The Father spoke the exact same words over Jesus at his Transfiguration as he had at his baptism in 3:17, but this time he had a small but important addition to make: *"Listen to him."* Up until this moment, Peter had struggled to listen and had even been rebuked as "Satan" for trying to talk Jesus out of the cross. Now, however, in the light of this vision, he would trust Jesus' wisdom and obey his strategy alone. Those who have seen Jesus in his heavenly glory reject *"the things of men"* and embrace *"the things of God"*.[11] This vision of Jesus stopped them arguing with his startling teaching in 16:21–23 and 17:12. Instead, they took up their own crosses daily, and set out as fully sold-out disciples on the revolutionary path of 16:24–26.

This vision of the glorified Jesus also gave them zeal to obey Jesus' commission when they founded the first church in the aftermath of Pentecost. Peter was so excited at the sight of Jesus in his divine majesty that he instantly tried to build three

[9] The Greek word for *Peter* is *petros*, and the word Jesus uses for this rock in Matthew 16:18 is *petra*. He does not so much build his Church on Peter as he does on the rock of Peter's confession that he is the Son of God.

[10] The promise of Matthew 16:19 is a *you singular* promise to Peter, but Jesus repeats it in 18:18 as a *you plural* promise to all his followers.

[11] This was the first time in Matthew's gospel that Jesus had taught explicitly that he would be killed by the Jewish leaders. Before the Transfiguration, Peter was infected with the rationalist yeast of the Sadducees and tried to win Jesus round to his own way of thinking. After the Transfiguration he stopped arguing.

tabernacles to recreate the past worship-centres of Israel. Jesus needed to correct him, and to tell him that the Church must be much more than a non-stop mountain-top prayer meeting.[12] The Church would break out of the introspective mould of Old Testament Israel, and would bring the Kingdom of God to the world beyond its walls. The Greek verb *akouō* can mean either to *listen* or to *obey*, and so the Father commands the three disciples to listen to Jesus and obey his Church blueprint instead of their own.[13] Straight away, Jesus leads them down the mountain to heal a demonized boy, to die on a cross, to ascend back to heaven, and to pour out his promised Holy Spirit. Now that they had seen him in his undisguised divinity, they were through with arguing and were ready to follow.

I love the gospels and I love to worship the man Christ Jesus in the glory of his humanity. But to minister with authority, faith, and zeal, we also need to see and worship him in the glory of his divinity. Unless we discover Jesus as he is today on the throne of heaven, we will merely worship him as he was yesterday, as a heavily disguised itinerant teacher and healer. Ultimately, we will worship a shadow of the true Jesus and be guilty of the sin of idolatry. Jesus Christ has ascended to heaven. The Suffering Saviour is now the unrivalled ruler of creation.

Through chapters like this one, we need to gaze deeply into the face that shines as brightly as the sun, and to know the ascended Christ in his heavenly glory. This is the Master that we must know and love. This is the vision that strengthens Jesus' followers to announce the great message of his Kingdom.

---

[12] The Greek word *skēnē* does not merely mean *tent* but literally *tabernacle*. Peter wants to stay on the mountain and recreate the glories of the Old Covenant, but Jesus wants to go down and inaugurate the New.

[13] *"Listen to him"* was Moses' command in Deuteronomy 18:15 about the great Messianic Prophet who would follow him, and Matthew uses this as a warning to his Jewish readers that true Jews will follow Jesus.

Why Doesn't God Heal?
(17:14–21)

I tell you the truth, if you have faith as small as a mustard seed, you can say to this mountain, "Move from here to there" and it will move. Nothing will be impossible for you.

(Matthew 17:21)

Once upon a time, there was an enthusiastic young evangelist. He had seen some successes in praying for the sick, and was in quite some demand on the healing circuit. He was frustrated when an epileptic boy was not healed, but he quickly gathered a team of friends to help. Nine evangelists in all, each with a proven track record of healing ministry, who prayed, commanded, shouted, bound, and loosed. Several hours later, they were hoarse, their audience were disappointed, and the boy was as epileptic as before.

I wonder what advice you might have given to that group of young zealots? Stop being so insensitive? Accept that it simply isn't God's will to heal this time around? You might have convinced them. Now imagine their surprise when Jesus came down from the Mount of Transfiguration, berated them for their lack of faith, and then healed the boy in an instant! If the nine disciples were ever tempted to assume that God was unwilling to heal, surely this was the time. Yet God *was* willing. They simply lacked what it took to lay hold of a willing God.

Healing the sick is part of the Gospel. The fact that this statement is in any way controversial shows just how far we have strayed from Matthew's teaching. He uses the words *healing* and *saving* interchangeably in 9:21, 9:22 and 14:36, and he tells us in 8:17 that the message of healing is part of the message of the cross.[1] That's why he reports this episode at the end of Act Three, because he wants us to grasp that healing is an integral part of God's Kingdom message. The fact that Jesus is King means that Satan is not, and that his weapons are powerless to resist the new King in town. Jesus proved his authority to forgive sins in 9:1–8 by demonstrating his authority to heal. He told the disciples, and us, that this is still the best way to convince the world that the Gospel is true.[2] Our experience may often be similar to that of the nine frustrated disciples, but we have to press through until experience catches up with Scripture. If we've learned nothing else in Act Three of Matthew's gospel, it's that we dare not make changes to the message God has given us.

Truthfully, I would quite like to find a "theology of sickness" in the Bible to excuse the fact that many people are not healed when I pray for them. I would like to persuade myself that God is unwilling to heal, because people can glorify him more through trusting him in their sickness. The problem is that the gospel writers constantly tell us that Jesus glorified the Father by healing people, not by leaving them sick![3] He never turned away anyone who asked him for healing. He rebuked unbelief but never presumption.

Yes, Job did glorify God in his sickness, but he was miraculously healed at the end of the book and at least one of the reasons why he was not healed sooner was that his theologically challenged friends were so busy theorizing about

---

[1] He uses the verb *sōzō* or *to save* in 9:21–22 and the verb *diasōzō* or *to save utterly* in 14:36. He also makes it clear that healing is an integral part of *"the Gospel of the Kingdom"* in 4:23 and 9:35.

[2] Paul writes in Romans 15:18–19 that the reason so many believed in his preaching was that he backed it up with miracles through the Holy Spirit. He argues that preaching anything less is an incomplete Gospel.

[3] For example, Matthew 15:31; Mark 2:12; Luke 5:26; 9:43; 18:43; 19:37; John 11:4.

why God might not want to heal him that they actually failed to pray for him![4] Yes, Epaphroditus, Trophimus, and Paul himself were not healed instantly either, but the fact that Paul was healed eventually should caution us against building theology on these few examples of failure.[5]

Francis MacNutt writes:

> *When we say that God sends sickness or asks us to endure it, we are creating for many people an image of God they must eventually reject. What human mother or father would choose cancer for their daughter in order to tame her pride?... Those preachers and chaplains who try to comfort the sick by telling them to accept their illness as a blessing from God are giving an immediate consolation, but at what an ultimate cost!"*[6]

God wants to heal, because he is compassionate and because it convinces the world that his Gospel is true.

Again, I would quite like to believe that it is presumptuous to assume that God is always willing to heal. That would excuse my many woeful failures. Yet Matthew tells us this story in chapter 17 precisely to quash such muddled theology, just as he did in 8:1–4 when he told us that a leper prayed *"If you are willing, you can..."* and Jesus replied *"I am willing. Be clean!"* The New Testament rudely offends my rational mind, which has been so well leavened by the yeast of the Sadducees. There is simply no avoiding the scope of its promise when it asks *"Is **any** one of you sick?... The prayer offered in faith **will** make the person well; the Lord **will** raise him up."*[7]

---

[4] To clarify, there *is* a clear "theology of suffering" throughout Scripture. But it is significant that Jesus and the apostles were surrounded daily by crowds of sick people but never taught a "theology of sickness".

[5] Philippians 2:25–27; 2 Timothy 4:20; Galatians 4:13–15.

[6] Francis MacNutt, *Healing* (1974).

[7] James 5:14–15. Note that this also reminds us that healing is as much for Christians as for non-Christians. Indeed, Matthew tells us in 15:26 that it is in

Let me nail my colours to the mast. Until recently, I never used to pray for people to be healed. I was too scared of failure, and I had some great Bible verses to tell me that I needn't try. Then God ambushed me. Through the straight-talking challenge of a friend, I grew increasingly convicted that I was peddling a watered-down Gospel out of fear of looking foolish if I preached it in all its glory. When I realized that God's Kingdom came through Jesus looking foolish on the cross, and that it advanced when his early followers looked foolish as well, then I started to see that it could only come through my life if I was willing to look foolish myself.[8]

I've been praying for the sick for a few years now, convinced that it is a non-negotiable part of the Gospel. Only about two in every ten are healed, which on some levels makes me an 80 per cent failure. But when I started out it was only one in ten, and before that of course it was no one at all. I'm learning every day, taking stumbling steps and feeding myself on passages like this one to keep myself going on the journey. Little by little, I'm seeing God heal, as I look foolish so that God can look great. What's more, I've never seen so many people saved as I have since I started preaching the Gospel of healing.[9]

Jesus gives his diagnosis in verse 20 for why we often fail to see people healed: *"It is because you have so little faith."* We can increase our faith *"by prayer and fasting"*,[10] and it only takes a mustard seed of faith to push back Satan's defeated kingdom. Jesus is looking for an army of followers who believe his Kingdom message, preach his Kingdom message, and demonstrate its

---

the first instance *"the children's bread"*.

[8] 1 Corinthians 1:18; 4:9–10; Hebrews 12:2.

[9] I examine practical questions, such as *how* to pray for the sick, in my book *Straight to the Heart of Acts*.

[10] Most older English translations include these words in v. 21, but since not all Greek manuscripts contain them, most newer translations footnote them or leave them out altogether. We do know that Jesus said these words, since they are undisputed in the parallel text of Mark 9:29.

power with miracles of healing. If we preach it as he gave it to us, he promises in verse 21 that *"Nothing will be impossible for you"*.

Act Four:

Kingdom Community

Warning-Beacons (18:1–35)

If he refuses to listen to them, tell it to the church;
and if he refuses to listen even to the church, treat
him as you would a pagan or a tax collector.

(Matthew 18:17)

Thanks to a chain of bonfires, I do not speak Spanish. In the year 1588, centuries before Alexander Graham Bell made the first-ever telephone call, the fate of England hinged upon her ability to communicate urgent news fast. If Spanish ships were sighted in the English Channel, the whole nation had to rise to arms in time to repulse the threat of invasion. Every hour lost might spell disaster, but a simple plan could carry the day.

Finally, after many days, masts were seen and a nervous watchman lit a warning-beacon on the Plymouth hilltop. Several miles away on another vantage point, a second watchman saw the signal and lit a great woodpile of his own. Before dawn, a great network of bonfires burned upon a thousand English hills. The news of invasion spread with breakneck speed, and a nation rose with one accord to defeat the Spanish Armada.

Jesus also has a plan to spread his urgent message around the world. He alerts the nations to the news of his Kingdom invasion through his own network of warning-beacons called the Church. From the moment that he lit the first bonfire in Jerusalem in 30 AD, the flame has spread from city to city and from nation to nation, shining the bright light of his Kingdom Revolution in every dark place on the earth. That's why Matthew devotes Act Four of his gospel to Jesus' teaching on the character of his Kingdom community. With little over six months left before his crucifixion, Jesus prepared the disciples to found the Church which would herald his heavenly invasion.

Jesus may have coined the word *Church*, but he didn't make it up. He deliberately chose the Greek word *ekklēsia*, the equivalent of the Hebrew word *qahal*, which was used in the Old Testament to refer to the *assembly* of Israel, in order to stress the continuity between the Church and ethnic Israel, the nation he chose many years before to be his ancient warning-beacon. The Church would be a holy community which took Israel's mission global. Perhaps that's why Matthew is the only gospel writer to use the word *Church*, stressing three times to his Jewish readers that they needed to be saved into God's new community of Christ-followers.[1] The first beacon was about to be lit in the Jewish capital, and it would spread the hope of Israel all around the world.[2]

Like a bonfire burning in the black of night, the Church's witness depends on her being very different to the cultures in which she dwells. She is a colony of heaven, living the values of God's Kingdom in a world where Satan has his throne. Therefore in chapters 18 to 22 Jesus instructs, rebukes, and fashions his first followers in the way that they must live. If they bowed to his Kingdom teaching in chapter 18, they would not merely perform signs and wonders through his Holy Spirit, they would be signs and wonders which convinced a rebel world that the Gospel of Christ was true.[3]

First, Jesus told them, they must humble themselves

---

[1] Matthew uses the word *ekklēsia* once in 16:18 to refer to the global Church and twice in 18:17 to refer to the local church. Ezra 10:8 shows us that one of the most terrible Jewish curses was for someone to be cut off from the assembly of Israel. Matthew wants his readers to feel the full weight of this threat.

[2] Jesus deliberately stresses in Act Four that the Church is the continuation of bc Israel. One of the clearest verses is 19:28 where Jesus tells the Twelve that *"you who have followed me will sit on twelve thrones, judging [i.e. governing] the twelve tribes of Israel"*.

[3] Isaiah 8:18. See also Deuteronomy 4:5–8; Philippians 1:27–28.

like little children and choose downward-mobility in a world of naked ambition and of greedy lust for fame and honour.[4] They must turn their back on the dog-eat-dog mentality of their culture, and cherish the weakest believer as a dear brother or sister. Because every single Christian has been sought and saved by God,[5] and because guardian angels protect each one of them,[6] those who follow Christ gladly suffer personal loss and injury for each other's sake. Their mutual love far exceeds the sentimental affection of the pagans, for they dare to challenge, confront, and even discipline one another out of a common passion for godliness. They are marked by a radical willingness to forgive, and yet they eject the ungodly from within the Church community because that is the only way to win them back as true brothers or sisters in broken repentance. Local churches of this calibre shine like mighty warning-beacons in every nation, proclaiming brightly through their witness that the message of the Kingdom is true.

Jesus makes bold promises to such churches in 18:18–20. These fiery hotbeds of his Kingdom Revolution speak with an authority which Satan and his demons are powerless to resist. They pray with such authority that the Father will not refuse them. They experience his presence in their meetings such that unbelievers are disarmed and respond to his call.[7] In short,

---

[4] Mark 9:33–37 tells us that Jesus gave the teaching of Matthew 18:1–4 in response to a dispute among the Twelve over which of them was the greatest. Peter may have caused the argument in the wake of 16:18–19.

[5] Jesus tells the Parable of the Lost Sheep once in Luke 15:3–7 with *evangelistic* application, and once in Matthew 18:10–14 with *pastoral* application. The Church is to reflect both of these passions in God's heart.

[6] Matthew 18:10 stands alongside Hebrews 1:14 in teaching that God assigns guardian angels to each believer. Jesus' logic is that we dare not dishonour anyone who is honoured by the Father and his angels.

[7] Paul makes a similar distinction between Christians gathering socially and as a church in 1 Corinthians 5:4; 11:18; 14:19, 28, 34, and 35. We must not devalue the crucial important of meeting *en ekklēsia,* or *as a church*.

Kingdom communities that look like Jesus, live like Jesus, and burn like Jesus, change the world.

Amazingly, through a miracle which only the Day of Pentecost can explain, Jesus built this group of twelve haughty, ambitious, and self-seeking disciples into the mighty warning-beacon Jesus describes in this chapter. Their flame so ignited Jerusalem that James could point to tens of thousands of Jewish converts in the capital. It lit other warning-beacons from Samaria to Antioch, and on to Ephesus, Corinth, and Rome. By the time that Emperor Nero torched hundreds of tar-coated Christians to serve as lanterns in his palace gardens, he was already too late in the game.[8] Jesus had already set fire to communities of Christians all around the world, as mighty warning-beacons which proclaimed his Kingdom invasion.

Athenagoras of Athens gave his own explanation for why Greece and Rome succumbed to the bright allure of the Christian message:

> *Among us you will find uneducated persons and artisans and old women who, if they are unable in words to prove the benefit of our doctrine, even so by their deeds exhibit the benefit which comes from their belief that it is true. They do not rehearse speeches, but exhibit good works.*[9]

The Gospel message is more than an abstract concept, and more than an individual lifestyle. It is the call of the Living God who bids a rebellious world to submit to his rule. However convincing signs and miracles may be, the greatest miracle of all is the lifestyle within the Church. So let the Lord set your church on fire, and become a radical beacon of hope in the town or city where Christ has placed you.

---

[8] Tacitus in his *Annals of Imperial Rome*, 15.44.

[9] Athenagoras of Athens in his *Plea for the Christians*, chapter 11, which he addressed to the emperors Marcus Aurelius and Commodus in c. 180 AD.

Kingdom Forgiveness (18:21–35)

This is how my heavenly Father will treat each of you unless you forgive your brother from your heart.

(Matthew 18:35)

On Sunday 8th November 1987, in the midst of an open-air Remembrance Day service, a sudden explosion tore its way through the crowd of people gathered round the Enniskillen cenotaph. An IRA bomb, the latest in a series of terrorist attacks, claimed the lives of twelve worshippers and shook Northern Ireland to the core.

That same evening, Gordon Wilson gave an emotional interview to the BBC in which he described the final words of his daughter as she died, holding his hand, at the scene. To the amazement of a nation, instead of calling for revenge, the devout Christian simply said: *"I bear no ill will. I bear no grudge. Dirty sort of talk is not going to bring her back to life... She's dead. She's in heaven and we shall meet again. I will pray for these men tonight and every night."* Irish historian Jonathan Bardon pinpoints those words of forgiveness as a major turning point in the history of his nation: *"No words in more than twenty-five years of violence in Northern Ireland had such a powerful, emotional impact."*

Forgiveness is very, very powerful, but it is easier to admire than to copy. The Pharisees liked to receive it, but they didn't know how to give it. Their creed was *"eye for eye, and tooth for tooth"* and they were very quick to pick up stones to punish those

who wronged them.[1] Jesus' revolutionary call is very dif̲̲
and it is this kind of God-empowered forgiveness which ̲̲
the Church such a beacon of hope to the world. Jesus de̲ ̲̲̲
almost half of his teaching on Kingdom community to this
issue of forgiving people from the heart. It's the passage which
inspired a nation-changer like Gordon Wilson, but it's also one
which inspires a multitude of objections.

Isn't this kind of forgiveness *unreal*? I think back to a friend
who came to see me when he discovered that his wife had had
an affair. Is Jesus really suggesting that he should pretend that
her sin doesn't matter?! Well, in a word, *no*. There's nothing in
this parable that seeks to minimize the gravity of human sin. The
servant in the story is owed 100 denarii by his colleague – the
equivalent of five months' wages. There's nothing trivial here
in Jesus' treatment of the wrongs committed against us. He is
simply telling us that unforgiveness lays a path towards torment
and destruction (as my friend found when his marriage was
destroyed, not by his wife's affair, but by his adamant refusal to
forgive her). Jesus does not take Peter up on his offer to forgive
seven times, and nor does he really want us to forgive no more
than *seventy-seven* times.[2] He tells us to forgive freely without
counting, because if we refuse to forgive the wounds of those
who hurt us, we will reap a consequence more deadly still.

Isn't this kind of forgiveness *unjust*? Those who sin deserve
to be punished, so how can Jesus ask us to treat them as they
don't deserve? That's the right question to be asking, because
it is exactly the question which Jesus addresses in the parable.
The first servant is owed 100 denarii, but he himself owes
10,000 talents of silver – over a million times more than he is
owed. He offers to pay off the debt in a series of instalments

---

[1] Matthew 5:38; Acts 7:57–58; John 8:2–7; 8:59; 10:31.

[2] The Greek could also read *seventy times seven* times. Lamech boasted in
Genesis 4:24 that Cain had avenged himself sevenfold but that he would
avenge himself seventy times sevenfold. Jesus is not telling us to forgive 490
times, but to be as full of forgiveness as wicked Lamech was full of revenge.

(a bit like people who hope to atone for their sin by attending church and singing loudly enough to attract God's favour), but the Master knows there is no way that he could ever make a dent on the massive debt that he owes. In a vivid picture of God's grace towards our sin, the Master completely erases the debt and offers total forgiveness in the place of a repayment plan. How is this just? Because *"with the shedding of blood, there is forgiveness"*.[3] God forgives our massive debt of sin because Jesus Christ paid the debt for us when he died in our place on the cross. He died crying out *"Father, forgive them!"*[4] and the Gospel is the wonderful news that he has.

Can you see now why Jesus treats the sin of unforgiveness so seriously? It is a dead giveaway that we have confessed our sin to God but not grasped either its gravity or his grace. Jesus is not saying in verse 35 or in 6:14–15 that people who fail to forgive can lose their salvation.[5] He is saying that people who have truly repented instinctively forgive. If you force others to squirm in the debt that they owe you, it's a sign that you have never truly repented or received true forgiveness for your own debt to God.

But isn't this kind of forgiveness *impossible*? Well, yes and no. You can tell people that you forgive them, but without God's help it is indeed humanly impossible to *"forgive your brother from the heart"*. Sooner or later, we find that bitter feelings and imaginary conversations rear their ugly heads afresh, and that we are back where we started. But through the Gospel of Jesus Christ – the message that Jesus paid our cripplingly large debt through the shedding of his own blood – what is impossible in our own strength becomes possible in his. Jesus did not merely bear our sin; he also bore our pain. He died as a victim of injustice, as one wronged on every side by friend and foe alike,

---

[3] This states positively the same thing as Hebrews 9:22 states negatively.

[4] Luke 23:34 is Jesus' perfect example of forgiveness, as copied by Stephen after him in Acts 7:60.

[5] He specifically denies this possibility in verses such as John 10:28.

and because he bore our *pain* as well as our sin, we need bear it no longer. We can forgive.

Corrie ten Boom suffered terrible injustice at the hands of the Nazis during World War Two, but she learned this lesson when she met one of the guards from her concentration camp after the war. He approached her, held out his hand, and asked her for forgiveness:

> *I tried to smile, I struggled to raise my hand. I could not. I felt nothing, not the slightest spark of warmth or charity. And so again I breathed a silent prayer. Jesus, I cannot forgive him. Give me your forgiveness. As I took his hand the most incredible thing happened. From my shoulder along my arm and through my hand a current seemed to pass from me to him, while into my heart sprang a love for this stranger that almost overwhelmed me. And so I discovered that it is not on our forgiveness any more than on our goodness that the world's healing hinges, but on his. When he tells us to love our enemies, he gives, along with the command, the love itself.*[6]

Jesus does not minimize the wrong that you have suffered, but nor will he let you minimize the sin of unforgiveness. He calls us to pray, and live, the prayer of Matthew 6:12: *Lord, to the degree that I forgive people who sin against me, that's how I know you will forgive me.*

---

[6] Corrie ten Boom, *The Hiding Place* (1971).

Back to the Beginning (19:1–12)

Jesus replied, "Moses permitted you to divorce your wives because your hearts were hard. But it was not this way from the beginning."

(Matthew 19:8)

Anyone who thinks we live in a uniquely sex-mad generation has a rose-tinted view of history. In about AD 23, Herod began an affair with his brother Philip's wife and divorced his own wife to marry her. Not satisfied with this unlawful marriage, he then directed his lust at his new fourteen-year-old stepdaughter.[1] Meanwhile, at his palace on the island of Capri, the Emperor Tiberius amused himself with peep shows, orgies, rape, homosexuality, and gross paedophilia.[2] Even in Palestine, Rabbi Shammai struggled to resist the disciples of the liberal Rabbi Hillel, who wanted to make divorce as easy for the Jews as it was for their Roman masters.[3] None of this background excuses our own generation, but it does set Jesus' teaching in its context.

It was now the beginning of 30 AD, and Jesus was moving south through the mixed-race province of Perea on his way to Jerusalem and Calvary. Herod ruled Perea as well as Galilee, and so the Pharisees asked him a question on divorce in the hope

---

[1] Matthew 14:1–12.

[2] Suetonius, *Life of Tiberius*, chapters 43–45. Don't read his account unless you want to feel sick. It's horrible.

[3] Rabbi Hillel died in about 10 AD and Rabbi Shammai in about 30 AD. Their influence long survived them.

that he might incur the same fate as John the Baptist.[4] Jesus rebuked those Scripture experts with the question *"Haven't you read...?"*, and then leapt at a chance to teach about marriage. In the bright fires of Christian witness, godly marriage shines brightest of all.

The problem with their discussions on divorce, he told them, was that they acted as if marriage were the invention of men. Yet *"at the beginning **the Creator** 'made them male and female', and said, 'For this reason a man will leave his father and mother and be united to his wife, and the two will become one flesh'".* Marriage was God's invention, not ours, and he founded it on a vital creational principle.

God made humankind male and female to reflect something of his own Triune nature – Father, Son, and Holy Spirit. In the words of Genesis 1:27, *"God created man in his own image, in the image of God he created him; male and female he created them."* This means that the endless love-ballads you hear on the radio, and Tom Cruise's famous statement to Renée Zellweger that *"You complete me"*, are at their deepest level theological statements.[5] God made humans to feel incomplete until they find a life-partner with whom they can have children, so that together as a family they can reflect the glory of the Trinity.

As part of this, God gave humankind a wonderful wedding present called sex, which unites them physically and spiritually so that two people become one. This is not just sentimental fancy, but something so real that Paul can argue that *"he who loves his wife loves himself"* and that each person owns their spouse's body as well as their own.[6] God uses sex to unite married couples in body, soul, and spirit, so that they can reflect his three-in-one nature as the pinnacle of his creation.

---

[4] John the Baptist provoked his own execution when he dared to condemn Herod's marriage to his brother's wife in Matthew 14:3–4.

[5] Tom Cruise says this immortal line in the movie *Jerry Maguire* (TriStar Pictures, 1996).

[6] Ephesians 5:28; 1 Corinthians 7:4.

It should therefore not surprise us that Satan hates "holy matrimony" with a bitter venom. He is determined to deface the image of God in humankind by corrupting sex and marriage in a hundred different ways. He promotes the view that illicit sex, premarital sex, and kinky sex are fun, while sex within marriage is boring and monochrome. He persuades people to unite themselves body and soul with prostitutes, girlfriends, boyfriends, and one-night stands, so that they bring a crowd of intruders into their marital bed as a foul mockery of the Triune God.[7] An alternative tactic is same-sex attraction, where Adam-and-Eve becomes Adam-and-Steve in a mixed-up corruption of the God they reflect.[8] Satan loves to corrupt sex and marriage as much as he can – anything except one man and one woman united exclusively for life as a loving reflection of the Trinity.

But Satan has a favourite weapon, and if you've been on the receiving end of its trauma and pain you will know why he loves it so much. Nothing rips, hurts, and devastates like divorce, the unnatural separation of two individuals who have been united by God. Rabbi Hillel and his followers had simply not grasped the depth of that union. The Mosaic Law permitted divorce in a few exceptional cases,[9] but permission to divorce was not permission to remarry.[10] "'I hate divorce,' says the Lord God of Israel" in Malachi 2:16, and that hatred prompted the disciples to exclaim that "It is better not to marry!" Some may

[7] 1 Corinthians 6:16, 18 tells us that sex unites two individuals even outside of marriage. A 2008 survey revealed that the average British bride or groom has ten sexual partners before their wedding night.

[8] Homosexuality was as common in the first-century Roman Empire as it is today, yet Scripture explicitly forbids it in Romans 1:27; 1 Corinthians 6:9; and 1 Timothy 1:10.

[9] Moses did not *command* divorce as the Pharisees claimed. The instructions in Deuteronomy 24:1–4 were aimed at discouraging divorce! It restricted divorce to cases of *'ervah*, or *improper sexual behaviour*, and it forced a husband to write a legal document which renounced all future right to change his mind.

[10] Matthew stresses this by calling Bathsheba literally *"Uriah's wife"* in 1:6 and Herodias *"Philip's wife"* in 14:3.

choose singleness after divorce for the sake of the Kingdom,[11] but those who assume that the law-courts or their culture can grant easy permission to remarry are treading on very dangerous ground.[12]

Does this make Jesus judgmental and unforgiving? No. He extended his grace to prostitutes and adulterers, refusing to condemn them and urging them to leave their lives of sin.[13] He founded a Church which was full of ex-adulterers, ex-prostitutes and ex-homosexuals, all freed from their former way of life by the power of his life-changing cross.[14]

But in a world where marriage is cheap and divorce is quick – in my country 45 per cent of marriages end in divorce[15] – Jesus calls on his followers to reflect the glory of the Trinity by loving their spouse until parted by death. Through the good times, through the bad times, through the pain and disappointments, always trusting, always hoping, and always persevering. Such God-reflecting marriages turn local churches into fiery beacons of hope – extending arms of grace to those hurt by Satan's lies, but proclaiming that there is another way, a better way, a God-given way for men and women to live.

---

[11] Jesus chose not to marry at all, and Paul probably chose not to remarry after he was widowed or divorced. Note that both chose singleness not for its own sake but *for the sake of the Kingdom*, and simply reflected the glory of the Trinity by building the Church, the Bride of Christ, instead. See 1 Corinthians 7:25–35.

[12] I understand v. 9 to mean that people can remarry if their spouse commits adultery against them, but not if they themselves commit adultery or their spouse remains faithful. Some Christians understand v. 9 differently – to his own Master each person stands or falls.

[13] John 8:1–11; Matthew 21:31–32; Luke 7:36–50.

[14] 1 Corinthians 6:9–11. Paul preaches glorious freedom from sexual sin when he states simply, *"that is what some of you were"*.

[15] British Office for National Statistics, March 2008.

Possible with God (19:16–30)

Jesus looked at them and said, "With man this is impossible, but with God all things are possible."

(Matthew 19:26)

When I was a child, my dad used to take me fishing for crabs. We would ask at the fishmonger's for scraps of bait, and then throw our line over the harbour wall. Crabs are not very clever. When they find food, they never let go, even when it is reeled thirty feet up a harbour wall into the waiting hands of a dad and son. The hard part is simply getting them to latch on to the bait in the first place.

One sunny morning, I was given a treat by the fishmonger. She had an off-cut of fresh salmon which was bright pink and very tasty. It would be irresistible to the crabs, she assured me, and she was not wrong. No sooner did the salmon hit the seabed than crabs of all sizes rushed to devour their luxury breakfast. When I reeled in the line, half a dozen crabs clung on greedily. But there was a problem, which I ought to have foreseen. Pink salmon is very eye-catching and very tasty, but it is also very crumbly. As I pulled the line up the harbour wall, great chunks of meat fell away from the bait and all of the crabs plunged back into the sea. Each time I threw out the line it quickly drew a great catch. Each time I reeled it in, the same thing happened.

After a fruitless hour's fishing, I removed the salmon from my line in disgust, threw it to the seagulls, and went back to the fishmonger's to try a different kind of bait. This time I was given an old squid-head – grey, smelly, and incredibly unattractive.

Sure enough, it took a little while for the salmon-gorged crabs to show any interest in my new offering, but eventually I felt a tug on the line. Reeling it in, I saw just one measly crab clinging on to the bait, but he easily made it to the top of the harbour wall. Squid may be unattractive bait, but there's no pulling it apart. It took much longer to attract each crab to the squid-head on my hook, but I didn't lose a single one of them when they did. An hour later, I had forty crabs in my bucket, and had learned an important lesson. Salmon may attract more crabs to the hook, but only squid can land them in the bucket.

I'm telling you this story because it illustrates why Jesus responded to the rich young ruler in such a blunt manner. Here was someone who asked the perfect Gospel question, *"What good thing must I do to get eternal life?"* What better example of a willing new convert? Yet Jesus rebukes him for calling him *teacher,*[1] and orders him to sell all he has and give it to the poor before he tries to apply for salvation. Why on earth does Jesus make such an aggressive demand? Because he fished with squid and not salmon.

It's very tempting to preach a salmon-Gospel. We desperately want people to respond to our message, so we try to make it as attractive as possible. We tone down talk of sin, of hell, and of counting the cost. Instead, we hope to reel people in with a cut-price conversion and to disciple them later along the way. At first it looks to be working, as many people rise to our message, but the problems start when we try reeling them in. Very few of those who are "saved" get added to our churches, because they frankly have better things to do. They responded to the message that Jesus could improve their life, and they can't for the life of them see how giving up their Sunday mornings could be part of that package. We preached to their flesh and persuaded their flesh, yet we shied away from confronting their

---

[1] The parallel verses in Mark 10:17–18 and Luke 18:18–19 make it clear that Jesus told him off for merely calling him teacher when his evident goodness should have convinced the man that he was actually God.

flesh. Salmon-preachers exhaust themselves trying to disciple their converts. It's no wonder, when they are not disciples at all.

Preaching the squid-Gospel requires a lot more patience, but it is far more fruitful. It means partnering with the Holy Spirit, since only his power can quicken dead spirits to bite at such an unattractive message. No one repents, submits, and takes up his cross unless the Lord first works in his heart. That, of course, is the beauty of fishing with squid. Those who get saved get added too. At the moment of conversion they accept Jesus' call to become true disciples, so discipling them afterwards is easy. They sign up for Jesus' mission, which means they go of their own accord to win thirty, sixty, or a hundred more like themselves. Meanwhile, the salmon-converts down the road take up thirty, sixty, or a hundred hours of counselling as they make little progress in their man-made faith.

This is why Jesus spoke so brutally yet so lovingly to the rich young ruler.[2] He attacked his self-righteous conceit by unpacking what *"love your neighbour as yourself"* really meant,[3] attacking the very issue on which he needed to yield. If he left unconverted but convicted, it would be successful evangelism. If he could be converted as well, then better still. But Jesus was determined to preach nothing but the squid-Gospel and to let the Holy Spirit do what he alone can do.

I am learning to preach the squid-Gospel too. Last month a friend came to my house, convicted of sin, and told me she was ready to become a Christian. I spent two hours persuading her that she was not yet ready to pray a prayer of conversion.

---

[2] The parallel verse in Mark 10:21 tells us that *"Jesus looked at him and loved him"* as he said these words. Rich people can enter the Kingdom of God, despite v. 24, since Joseph of Arimathea was a very wealthy man in 27:57–60. The issue was not the man's wallet, but how it had captured his heart.

[3] It is not enough to argue that *"the law convicts of sin"* (Romans 3:20) and to preach the Ten Commandments slavishly. Jesus shows us that we need to unpack what God's law means to bring people to conviction.

She would need to renounce many cherished sins and face up to Christ's many unpalatable commands – was she truly willing to make such a change? Finally, I told her that I was not willing to pray with her that evening, but would be free the following evening if she still wanted to surrender her life to the Lord. She looked at me aghast and exclaimed, *"You're a rubbish church leader!"* She was wrong – I think I used to be, but I'm fishing with squid nowadays. The following evening she came bounding back with news of how God had spoken to her during the day as she mulled over the previous night's conversation. She then prayed a prayer of conversion and immediately set about changing her lifestyle, with very little need for any chasing or cajoling. The Gospel does that to people. The squid-Gospel, that is.

Jesus calls us to follow his lead, just as Paul did as he set out for Rome. Writing to the Colossians, he did not ask them to pray for him to see a record number of responses to the Gospel. He simply asked them to *"Pray for us… that we may proclaim the mystery of Christ… that I may proclaim it clearly, as I should"*.[4]

Away with the salmon-Gospel. Let's preach the squid-Gospel. Nothing less can produce Christian churches which are worthy of the name. *"With man this is impossible, but with God all things are possible."*

---

[4] Colossians 4:3–4.

Ambition (20:20–28)

Whoever wants to become great among you must be your servant, and whoever wants to be first must be your slave.

(Matthew 20:26–27)

In the US sitcom *Friends*, Joey Tribbiani is an out-of-work actor. He is out of work for a reason. He is desperate to be the star of the show, even when he is only cast as an extra. When he takes part in a crowd scene, he improvises lines to bring himself centre-stage. When he plays the part of a corpse, he tries to rise from the dead to steal the show. Even when he finally lands himself a leading role, he is fired when he lies to the press that he, and not his scriptwriters, makes up his best lines. Joey Tribbiani is simply unemployable because he cannot bear to stay out of the limelight.

Peter, James, and John were Joey Tribbianis of the first century. They struggled to play second fiddle to Jesus, let alone to one another. Peter thought to give Jesus strategic advice in 16:22, buoyed by what he hoped was a promise of church leadership a few verses earlier.[1] Later, in 19:27, he reminded Jesus of all he had given up to follow him and tried to negotiate better compensation. James and John were even more like Joey Tribbiani. In what must surely go down as one of the most pitiful moments in the Bible, they send their mum – yes, really – to talk

---

[1] Actually, James and John would not have made their request in 20:20–23 if Jesus had truly awarded supreme leadership to Peter in 16:18–19. To claim he did is to commit the very sin which Jesus rebukes here.

to Jesus and to ask him to make them his right- and left-hand men in the age to come.[2]

It was now only days before Jesus' crucifixion, and these petty bids for power must have broken his heart. He had already told his disciples in 19:14 that the Kingdom belongs to the humble and the guileless. He had warned them in the parable of 20:1–16 that they must not pollute his Church with their selfish ambition.[3] Now, as James and John staked their claim on the best seats in the heavenly throne-room, the ten other disciples were indignant that the brothers had beaten them to it. All twelve of them wanted to be top dog in the Church which Jesus founded. A dozen self-obsessed and self-promoting Joey Tribbianis, only days away from Calvary. So little time left and so much yet to learn.

Jesus responds to his ambitious disciples with perfect patience. He reminds them of his own humility, how he entered the world as Isaiah's Suffering Servant to lay down his life so that others might live. As he told them in 10:24–25, *"A student is not above his teacher, nor a servant above his master. It is enough for the student to be like his teacher, and the servant like his master."* True greatness in the Kingdom of God – pretty obviously – comes from being *more* like Jesus, not less like him, and so Christians are not to walk the path of selfish ambition.

Christians, whether leading in the Church or leading in business, must not do so in the self-serving manner of unbelieving bosses. They must not be ambitious to be stars but to be slaves. Those who have embraced Jesus' Revolution know that the only way up is down and the only way to greatness is smallness. The

---

[2] Since the parallel Mark 10:35 simply tells us that James and John made this request, it appears that they goaded their mother's ambition and not vice versa. They were probably motivated by hearing Jesus' promise of twelve thrones in 19:28.

[3] The meaning of the Parable of the Workers in the Vineyard is found in the repeated phrase which brackets it in 19:30 and 20:16. It is not a model for just employment law, but a rebuke to anyone who demands a reward from God for his sacrifice on behalf of the Kingdom. Salvation alone is enough.

watching world cannot understand his Revolution – Friedrich Nietzsche dismissed it as *"slave morality"* – yet they are drawn in their thousands to its irresistible attraction.

Jesus' rebuke convicted his disciples and worked an amazing transformation in their proud hearts. Less than two months later, at the beginning of Acts, we find Peter stepping up to lead the Church but telling the crowds to turn their eyes away from him and onto the real star, Jesus.[4] James, John, and the other disciples gladly submit to his lead and gather together with one accord for the sake of the Kingdom, even when it means a flogging for John and beheading for James.[5] US President Harry Truman observed that *"It is amazing what you can accomplish if you do not care who gets the credit"*. The disciples learned this lesson powerfully in the sixty days between Matthew 20 and Acts 1.

Peter shed his pride when he tasted bitter failure and denied Jesus three times. James, John, and the other disciples shed their own as they deserted Jesus when he needed them most. When Jesus was stripped bare and nailed to a criminal's cross, when their dreams were left in tatters in the dark hours before the resurrection, when they saw Jesus ascend to heaven and realized with a gulp that the fortunes of the Church now lay upon their shoulders, and when they received power from God on the Day of Pentecost – when they passed through the nightmare training programme which Jesus had mapped out for them – these proud men renounced all claim to hold centre-stage and enrolled as eager extras in the drama which belongs to Jesus alone.

All of this begs an obvious question for those who follow in their footsteps: *Are you a Joey Tribbiani?* If you are, and you long for the limelight in the Kingdom of God, Jesus simply has no

---

[4] He asks the crowd in Acts 3:12 and 16, *"Why do you stare at us as if by our own power or godliness we had made this man walk?... It is Jesus..."*

[5] Peter and John were the first apostles to be flogged in Acts 5:40, and James was the first apostle to be martyred in Acts 12:2.

use for you. John Calvin puts it this way: *"God cannot bear with seeing his glory appropriated by the creature in even the smallest degree, so intolerable to him is the sacrilegious arrogance of those who, by praising themselves, obscure his glory."*[6] Three times Scripture warns us that *"God opposes the proud but gives grace to the humble"*.[7] Do you want to muster the might of heaven to oppose you, resist you, thwart you, and defeat you? Then try to steal centre-stage in your life away from Jesus. Do that and it's guaranteed. Or do you want to receive the power of heaven to build God's Kingdom in the place where he has put you? Then humble yourself to play second fiddle to Jesus, and he will swiftly be drawn to your aid.

Sadly, the Church is full of Joey Tribbianis, who love to be first and who dampen her fiery witness to the world.[8] The Church only burns brightly, distinctively, and successfully when her members follow the lead of their Servant-Master. Let your dreams of greatness die at his nail-pierced feet, and pursue the true greatness of his Kingdom. Whoever wants to be great must become the servant of all.

---

[6] John Calvin's *Commentary on the Psalms*, commenting on Psalm 9:1.

[7] Proverbs 3:34; James 4:6; 1 Peter 5:5.

[8] Like Diotrephes, whom this same John disciplined publicly for his love of being first in 3 John 9.

Ransom (20:28)

The Son of Man did not come to be served, but to serve, and to give his life as a ransom for many.

(Matthew 20:28)

When I was twelve years old, I was kidnapped. There were no news reports or ransom notes – I was merely kidnapped by a gang of boys from a rival school. Before the gang descended, I was a normal, cocksure, self-confident twelve-year-old. By the time they had surrounded me, insulted me, threatened me, and marched me to their secret camp in the woods, I had become very humble. What would happen to me? Would they let me go? Would they do unspeakable things to me? My mind raced as I sat there in the makeshift prison they had made out of branches and cast-off rubbish. Finally, in desperation, I started to cry.

Jesus chose the word *lutron*, or *ransom-price*, in Matthew 20 for a reason. When Peter demanded rewards, and James and John demanded recognition, Jesus chose this word to strip them down to size. There is nothing respectable about the person who needs a ransom. He is a slave, a hostage, a prisoner-of-war, or a convicted criminal. As I discovered in my prison deep in the woods, such captives feel no pride. They simply shout a desperate cry for help and pray that some saviour on the outside might come and deliver them. In my case, I was lucky. One of the gang took pity on me, interceded for my release, and sent me running through the woods, my tear-stained cheeks smiling with relief. Jesus chose the word *ransom* because it casts us in the role of helpless prisoner and him in the role of Saviour and

Redeemer. It reminds us that the only role that we play in our salvation is our humble cry for help.

The word *ransom* is very vivid but it can also be confusing. It confused the disciples and, for different reasons, it can confuse us as well.

The disciples were confused because they knew the Old Testament. They knew that the *Son of Man* was a name for to the Messiah in Daniel 7:13–14,[1] and that he *"was given authority, glory and sovereign power; all peoples, nations and men of every language worshipped him"*. They expected the Son of Man to be the ultimate all-powerful ruler of the world, and that all the earth would grovel before him in worship and servitude.[2] Jesus rocked this expectation by reminding them that Daniel's Son of Man would also be Isaiah's Suffering Servant. The Messiah would indeed be the greatest man in history, but he would also be the least. He would be served by all nations, but only after he had served them himself. The idea of a suffering, dying, ransom-paying Messiah was so at odds with Jewish expectations that Jesus needed to repeat it five times to his disciples to drive the message home.[3] The Messiah had not come to be served, but to serve.

We tend to be confused because we do not know the Old Testament well enough. If Jesus paid a ransom, to whom did he pay it? God the Father? No, that would cast God in the role of wicked kidnapper. Satan? No, that would make the cross the Devil's payment and reward, whereas Scripture tells us it was his ruin and defeat.[4] Some Christians try to sidestep the question, arguing that it stretches the ransom metaphor too far,

---

[1] This was the essence of Jesus' question in Matthew 16:13 *"Who do people say the Son of Man is?"* and of Peter's God-inspired insight that he is the Messiah, the one whom Psalm 2 calls the *Son of God*.

[2] The Aramaic verb *pelach* strictly means *to serve* rather than *to worship*. In the Greek Old Testament it is also translated by the verb *douleuō*, or *to serve*.

[3] Matthew 16:21–23; 17:9, 22–23; 20:17–19, 28.

[4] Colossians 2:15.

but Jesus chose the word "ransom" for a reason, and if we follow its thread through the pages of the Old Testament we will not be disappointed.

Although the word "ransom" speaks generally of slaves, hostages, and prisoners, it spoke specifically to first-century Jews of the great ransom-payment which dominated the history of their nation. Moses told the Hebrews in Exodus 15 that the Lord had not merely freed them from slavery in Egypt, but had *ransomed* and *purchased* them.[5] They were not just freed by might, but by right, as the shed blood of the Passover Lamb purchased their sinful souls from slavery and death.[6] Paul applies this to the cross of Christ, telling us that the Passover Lamb was an Old Testament picture of Jesus and that the waters of the Red Sea, which destroyed Pharaoh and his army, were a picture of Christian baptism.[7] Pharaoh was not rewarded when Yahweh ransomed his 2 million Hebrew slaves – he was destroyed! Similarly, Satan was not rewarded at the cross but destroyed as well. God the Father paid his Son's blood as a ransom-price to his own justice, so that all could be *"justified freely by his grace through the redemption that came by Christ Jesus... He did it to demonstrate his justice at the present time, so as to be just and the one who justifies those who have faith in Jesus".*[8]

This actually makes a tremendous difference to our Christian lives. God could have saved his People by force, but he is so committed to justice that he paid his Son's blood to be just even as he declares the guilty innocent. He refused to ignore the legal authority of Pharaoh or Satan, but purchased his

---

[5] The Hebrew verb *ga'al* in v. 13 means *to redeem* or *to ransom*. The verb *qanah* in v. 16 means *to purchase*.

[6] Since the Lord had promised in Genesis 2:17 that sin always leads to death, the Passover Lamb was necessary to satisfy his justice and enable him to free them from the curse of slavery and the plague of death.

[7] 1 Corinthians 5:7; 10:1–4.

[8] Romans 3:24, 26.

People through a legal transaction which completely satisfied his justice. We are utterly free from Satan's claim on our lives, and utterly secure in our salvation. We can sing the song of the redeemed in Exodus 15 far better than Moses ever could. Like Pharaoh after the Red Sea, Satan can never re-enslave us.

Nothing short of a ransom can explain how proud Peter, James, and John became humble apostles within sixty days. It meant that Jesus' death was far more than an *example* for his followers: it was their one-way ticket to freedom. They were purchased beyond Satan's legal control, and they didn't have to work for him any longer. When pride reared its ugly head, they cried out to their risen Redeemer and asked him to apply his death and resurrection to their lives. They were not religious people who resolved to try harder, but ransomed people who were freed from their prison of sin.[9] They were powerless in their own strength to burn with the radical humility of God's Kingdom community, but they believed that Jesus had paid their ransom, and cried out for him to apply it in their lives.

Only Jesus the Ransom-Payer could turn proud disciples into humble apostles. Nothing less than his ransom-price could ever grant them, or us, true freedom.

---

[9] This is the argument behind Revelation 5:9–10 and 14:3–5, and also behind 1 Corinthians 6:19–20 and 7:22–23.

The King Enters the Capital (21:1–17)

The crowds that went ahead of him and those that
followed shouted, "Hosanna to the Son of David!
Blessed is he who comes in the name of the Lord!
Hosanna in the highest!"

(Matthew 21:9)

In April 46 BC, Julius Caesar entered the city of Rome to celebrate a mighty triumph. He had defeated the Gauls and subdued his Roman enemies, and he was determined to enjoy his victory in style. His chariot was followed by a long chain of captives, and his men toured the city, distributing more than 2,000 of silver and gold to the delighted crowds. The city shook with loud parties and public games, all proclaiming one message in unison: Julius Caesar was at the helm of the Roman state.[1]

The Jews expected their Messiah's triumphal entry into Jerusalem to be no less impressive. After all, even Judas Maccabaeus was feted with palm branches and praised from the Psalms when he recaptured the city in 164 BC.[2] But Jesus had other ideas. He rode not on a mighty charger but on a donkey, not to distribute gold but to pour out his blood, not from the battlefield but to the battlefield,[3] not with a train of captives but

---

[1] Appian of Alexandria in his second-century work, *The History of the Civil Wars*, (2.15.101–102).

[2] 2 Maccabees 10:1–8.

[3] Since Passover was 14th Nisan and Jesus entered Jerusalem four days earlier, he rode into town on 10th Nisan, the day when the Passover lambs were herded into the city ready to be sacrificed. See Exodus 12:3 and marvel at the perfect detail of God's plan of salvation.

to seize one through his cross,[4] to recreate Israel not from the ashes of Rome but through the ashes of repentance. It was a surprising move to say the least, and so Matthew supports it with an Old Testament prophecy from Zechariah 9:9.[5] God had promised that his Messianic King would ride into Jerusalem on a donkey. Daniel's Son of Man would enter his capital as Isaiah's Suffering Servant – a far cry from Julius Caesar, but incontestably greater.

Unlike the triumphal entry of Caesar, who was welcomed by many through gritted teeth, everything about Jesus' entry sent out a call to surrender *voluntarily*. He rode on a borrowed donkey on the cloaks and branches of others.[6] A massive crowd gathered of their own accord, recognizing him as the Messianic Saviour-King of Psalm 118 and shouting *"Hosanna!"* from verse 25, and *"Blessed is he who comes in the name of the Lord!"* from verse 26.[7] Hailing him as the Messianic *Son of David*, they obeyed the instruction of verse 27 to *"join in the festal procession with boughs in hand"*. Even the following day, children still praised him as Messiah, and infuriated the priests in the process. Caesar came with a show of force because he ruled with an iron fist. Jesus came in meekness because he gathers a people who freely choose his rule.

But don't let that lull you into a false sense of security. A

---

[4] Paul uses the Greek verb *thriambeuō* in Colossians 2:15, the same word used to describe a Roman general celebrating a triumph over his foes. Jesus celebrated his triumph on Easter Sunday, not Palm Sunday.

[5] Unlike the other three gospel writers, Matthew mentions that both a colt and its mother were involved in order to fulfil Zechariah's prophecy to the letter.

[6] Throwing down robes and branches hailed a royal visitor, like the robes spread before King Jehu in 2 Kings 9:13 or, more recently, the cloak which Sir Walter Raleigh famously spread before Queen Elizabeth I.

[7] The Greek word *hōsanna* is a transliteration of the Hebrew words in Psalm 118:25 which mean *"O Lord, save!"* Psalm 118 was one of the most clearly Messianic psalms, talking in v. 22 about the Messiah being rejected but vindicated, and in v. 17 about him being raised from the dead. Although the crowd called Jesus a prophet in Matthew 21:11, Matthew wants us to grasp that they also welcomed him as the Messiah.

Day of Judgment is coming when every rebel will be forced to bow before Christ's Second Coming.[8] Even his meek arrival on a donkey was laced with strong hints of judgment if Jerusalem refused her King. As God prophesied in Malachi 3:1–2, *"Suddenly the Lord you are seeking will come to his temple... But who can endure the day of his coming? Who can stand when he appears? For he will be like a refiner's fire."* Most Gentiles read this story as a message of God's grace, but Matthew aims it at his Jewish readers as a warning of God's judgment.

First, Jesus brought judgment upon the leaders of Israel. The chief priests, scribes, and elders failed to see in Jesus what was obvious to little children. Even the blind and the lame, who were barred from God's presence in the Temple,[9] saw Jesus more clearly than the priests. It only took him one well-aimed question in verse 25 to expose them as hypocrites and rebels. This was a time for a make-or-break decision from the leaders of Israel. Within four days they would crucify their Messiah and bring down heavy judgment upon their nation.

Second, Jesus brought judgment upon the Temple of Israel. He had already purged its courtyards two years earlier in John 2:13–16, warning them that they had turned it into a *"market"*, but this time he did so again with a sterner warning that they had made it a *"den of robbers"*. This was a quotation from Jeremiah's great "Temple Sermon" in the years leading up to the Babylonian exile,[10] when the Lord warned Judah that the Temple would not save them if they failed to repent. Jesus warns his hearers that unless they submit to God's plan for his Temple to be *"a house of prayer"* he will destroy them as thoroughly as he did back in 586 BC.[11]

---

[8] Philippians 2:5–11; Romans 14:9–12.

[9] Leviticus 21:18 and probably also 2 Samuel 5:8.

[10] Jeremiah 7:11.

[11] This is a quotation from Isaiah 56:7, which carries on to say *"for all nations"*. The Lord wanted the Temple to be a centre for Gentile mission, but the foreigners who arrived at its courts found it no better than corrupt pagan

Third, he brought judgment upon the nation of Israel, symbolized here by a fig tree.[12] Its great show of leaves promised much but delivered little, so Jesus instantly withered the fruitless tree as a graphic picture of what John the Baptist had threatened would happen to Israel in Matthew 3:7–10. When the fickle crowds turned from shouting *"Hosanna!"* to shouting *"Crucify!"* four days later, God granted forty years' grace – a generation during which to repent – before destroying the leaders, the Temple, and the nation of Israel in the carnage of 70 AD. Jesus arrived in meekness, but his call to submission was more powerful than all of the Caesars put together.

Matthew aims this challenge at his fellow first-century Jews, but his challenge also applies to the Church throughout history. If we try to put God in a box, if we hijack his Church with our own unevangelistic and self-serving agenda, and if we play at being Christians without the fruit of true repentance, we will share the same fate as Jerusalem.

Jesus comes in meekness, calling us to submit voluntarily to his Kingdom Revolution, but don't mistake his meekness for weakness. This Passover Lamb is no pushover. Look at the withered fig tree and quickly bow the knee.

temples. Jesus would establish his New Covenant Temple and destroy the defunct one in Jerusalem.

[12] Perhaps referring back to Micah 7:1 and Jeremiah 24:1–10.

Blessing and Cursing
(21:18–22)

Seeing a fig tree by the road, he went up to it but found nothing on it except leaves. Then he said to it, "May you never bear fruit again!" Immediately the tree withered.

(Matthew 21:19)

When I was in my twenties, I managed to convince myself I was a pretty good negotiator. I represented one of the largest companies in the world, managing a business portfolio worth £200 million, and I had no problems getting my voice heard. *"It's Phil Moore from Procter & Gamble,"* I would say on the phone to my contact at Tesco, the UK's largest retailer. *"We need to talk. What time can you do tomorrow?"* As I arrived at Tesco head office the following morning, I brimmed with self-confidence. When I spoke, people listened. Or so I thought.

God likes to humble the proud, and humble me he did. A year later, I set up my own business, confident that a negotiator like me would quickly establish my new company in the marketplace. I simply needed to start with the small customers and work my way up. *"It's Phil Moore from Gotbetter.com,"* I told the first woman who answered the phone. *"I've got a great product for you. When can we meet?"* When she and twenty more like her fobbed me off with a flimsy collection of excuses, I suddenly grasped a sobering truth. There had never actually been any power in the words *"It's Phil Moore"*. There had only ever been power in the words *"from Procter & Gamble"*. Words can carry great power, but I learned the hard way that their power is entirely dependent upon the one in whose name we speak.

The Old Testament patriarchs understood this lesson very clearly. Jacob was convinced that God would honour any blessing or curse which his prophets spoke in his name. That's why he went to such extraordinary lengths to trick his father into blessing him, and why he wrestled with the angel of the Lord and told him that *"I will not let you go unless you bless me"*. In later life, Scripture tells us that *"By faith Jacob, when he was dying, blessed each of Joseph's sons"*.[1] For all his faults, Jacob had no doubt that one great fact was true: when one of the Lord's servants speaks a blessing or a curse in his name, the whole universe lines up to enforce what they say.

Jesus of Nazareth understood this too. Matthew never tells us that he prayed for anyone to be healed or delivered, but simply that he commanded people to *"Be clean!"* and told demons to *"Go!"* When Jesus spoke the word, sickness and demons were powerless to resist.[2] When Jesus told cripples to *"Get up!"* or *"Stretch out your hand"*, their dysfunctional bodies fell into line.[3] When he invoked a blessing over five loaves and two fish, they jumped to attention and fed the five thousand.[4] No wonder Peter felt confident in 14:28 that if only Jesus said *"Come!"* the laws of physics would submit to his word and permit him to walk on water. When Jesus spoke, all heaven's power rushed to back up what he said.

This is the context for the incident with the fig tree. Jesus is on his way from Bethany to Jerusalem, hungry for some breakfast, and in the distance he spots a fig tree in full leaf like

---

[1] Genesis 27:1–29; Genesis 32:26; Hebrews 11:21

[2] Matthew 8:3; 9:32.

[3] Matthew 9:6; 12:13.

[4] The Greek verb *eulogeō* in Matthew 14:29 means literally *to invoke a blessing upon* something. The normal rules of catering simply could not apply to any food upon which Jesus had invoked a blessing.

those which are laden with fruit.[5] He licks his lips and draws near – only to find that for all its foliage there is not a fig in sight. The tree promises much but delivers nothing, just like the empty religion which he saw the day before at the Temple, and so he curses it as a warning of what God will do to faithless Israel. As the disciples stare, open-mouthed, while the fig tree withers and dies,[6] Jesus promises them that this is nothing compared to what they will do if only they believe the promise which he gave them in 18:18. They will not just be able to wither fig trees; they will be able to relocate the very Mount of Olives by the power of their commands.[7]

If we note that this event towards the end of Act Four is linked to Jesus' teaching at the beginning, we will be spared from misunderstanding his teaching here. He promised literally in 18:18 that *"whatever you bind on earth will have been bound in heaven, and whatever you loose on earth will have been loosed in heaven"*.[8] This means that we are not given carte blanche to abuse Jesus' name by issuing strange commands on a whim. We have been given authority to command God's Kingdom to come on earth as it *already* is in heaven. Jesus has ascended to heaven with all authority and power, and he has commissioned us as his

---

[5] March was not the right season for figs, but it was not the right season for leaves either. Jesus judged the tree for making empty promises of fruitfulness – just like the hypocrites who led the nation of Israel.

[6] Mark 11:12–26 tells us that the disciples commented on the withered fig tree the day *after* Jesus cursed it. Evidently the tree withered immediately and amazed the disciples, but it withered even more throughout the day and provoked Peter to make a second comment which received the same answer.

[7] Jesus speaks specifically in v. 21 about moving *this* mountain. He effectively says to the disciples, *"Are you amazed that this fig tree on the Mount of Olives died? I was barely flexing my faith muscles! When you issue a blessing or a curse in my name, you can make the whole of the Mount of Olives do what you command!"*

[8] These two Greek perfect tenses tell us that we can bind and loose on earth what has already been bound and loosed in heaven. Through our words, we assert the finished victory of Jesus in heaven upon the earth.

agents on earth to speak commands in his name which assert his great victory.[9]

Let me end by grounding this in a couple of concrete examples. Last Sunday as my church gathered to worship, I felt stirred to put into practice what I had been reading in this passage. I stood up in the meeting and simply commanded sickness and pain to leave the room in Jesus' name. Suddenly a middle-aged man leapt up to the microphone and told the church that severe pain and stiffness had instantly disappeared from his shoulder when I spoke the command. Another man testified that he had suffered from chronic back pain for over a decade, but it had completely gone. *"I feel like a completely new man!"* he beamed as he did a little dance.

Then on Friday my wife and I helped a woman to rededicate her life to Christ after years of unforgiveness and backsliding. When she finished her long and heartfelt prayer of repentance, I commanded any demons which had latched on to her bitterness to go in Jesus' name. She looked up and told me that when I issued the command she had felt something horrible leave. Her face looked noticeably different and she shone with a new sense of peace. When those who follow Jesus issue commands in his name, demons have no choice but to flee before them.

I'm excited by baby-steps like these, and you should be excited by them too. Jesus has given us authority to issue blessings and curses in his name, and when we do so he releases his mountain-moving power through us. Jesus wants to use your tongue to advance his Kingdom: *"If you have faith and do not doubt... it will be done!"*

---

[9] Matthew 28:18–19: *"All authority on heaven and on earth has been given to me... Therefore [you] go!"*

Israel's Ultimatum
(21:23 – 22:46)

Therefore I tell you that the kingdom of God will be taken away from you and given to a people who will produce its fruit.

(Matthew 21:43)

God loves the Jewish nation. He loved them before he made the universe. He loved them when he laid hold of an idolater called Abraham in ancient Ur of the Chaldees. He loved them when he led them out of slavery in Egypt, and he loved them when he walked the streets of Jerusalem, seventy-two hours before they nailed him to a cross. That's why he ends Act Four of Matthew's gospel with one last call for the Jewish nation to repent. They were his original Kingdom community, and to them belonged the Messiah, the Gospel, and the promise of eternal life. Jesus reaches out to them, warning them that they are about to reject God's purpose for their lives, and using three great parables to issue an eleventh-hour ultimatum.[1] He tells them that it is not too late for the Jewish nation. They can still turn and receive their Messiah.

The Parable of the Two Sons struck an instant chord with Jesus' Jewish listeners. God's history with Israel was full of occasions when he chose one of their ancestors over his older brother. He chose Shem instead of Japheth. He chose Isaac instead of Ishmael. He chose Jacob instead of Esau. The Jews were the proud descendants of those brothers who had said

---

[1] God is sovereign, but Luke 7:30 nevertheless tells us that *"the Pharisees and experts in the law rejected God's purpose for themselves"*.

"yes" to the purposes of God, and they easily saw their role within Jesus' parable. But there was a twist in the tale. The son who said "yes" would not be the hero of the story unless he did what he promised he would. If the heirs of Shem, Isaac, and Jacob refused the message of the Kingdom of God, then Ham, Ishmael, and Esau would receive it instead. In fact, they had already seen this happening around them, when the outcast tax collectors and prostitutes received John's baptism and they stood on the sidelines and criticized.[2] Jesus shows the Jews in 21:23–27 that they have no excuse for ignoring the message. The first story goes straight to the heart of Israel's history, and leads right into the second.

The Parable of the Tenants also struck a similar chord. The reference to a vineyard with a wall, winepress, and watchtower made an instant link back to the famous prophecy in Isaiah 5:1–7. The Lord had told this story to Judah before the exile, likening the Jewish nation to a beautiful vineyard which was called to bear fruit.[3] In that Old Testament prophecy, he promised to destroy the vineyard and turn it into a wasteland, but this new parable promised that he would instead give it to other nations who would produce the fruit he deserved.[4] Jesus warns the Jews that God will not sit by and let them murder his prophets, one by one. He had sent them his only Son to issue a final ultimatum, and if they killed him too their own words in verse 41 would act as their judge. The words of Psalm 118 would be fulfilled and God would vindicate the Son they crucified,[5] raising him from

---

[2] As a former tax collector himself, Matthew wants to provoke his Jewish readers to jealousy and action.

[3] The Lord also used the *vine* as a picture of the Jewish nation in Psalm 80:8–15, Jeremiah 2:21, Ezekiel 17:5–8 and Hosea 10:1. Verse 45 tells us that Jesus' Jewish hearers were in no doubt that he was talking about them.

[4] This reminds us, importantly, that God has not *replaced* the Jewish nation, but made people from all nations into his true "Jewish nation". Paul explains this in detail in Romans 11.

[5] The quotation of 21:42 is deliberately taken from the very same psalm as the *"Hosannas"* of 21:9 and 15.

the dead and making him King of all nations.[6] But the Gentiles, not Israel, would become the gloriously fruitful vineyard of Isaiah 27, and they would *"bud and blossom and fill all the world with fruit".*[7]

The Parable of the Wedding Banquet struck a third and final chord with Jesus' Jewish listeners. They knew the promise of Isaiah 54 that the Lord would take his People as his Bride, as well as the allegory of Psalm 45 that the Messiah would "marry" God's People. This third parable takes the same ultimatum but intensifies its threat.

The Jews had been invited to take their place at God's great wedding,[8] but they had refused to come. They had murdered God's messengers – from Isaiah to Zechariah to John the Baptist – and if they also murdered the Messiah himself the wrath of God would fall heavily upon their nation. Those who hoped to be saved through their Jewishness but rejected the clothes of Christ's salvation would be thrown outside into hell. The Gentile outsiders – both good and bad – would then be invited to sit in their place. Jesus silences the empty Jewish boast that *"We are God's Chosen People!"*[9] The invitation to the Wedding Banquet belonged first and foremost to the Jews,[10] but their election to privilege was no guarantee of election to salvation. They needed to RSVP with repentance and faith. *"Many are invited, but few are chosen."*

---

[6] Jesus uses a play on words for his Jewish hearers, since the Aramaic words for *son* and *stone* are *ben* and *eben*. To reject the Son of Man is to reject the Stone of Psalm 118. Compare also Daniel 2:34–35 and 7:13–14.

[7] Isaiah 27:6. Note that God gave this prophecy about *"Israel"* but has fulfilled it through the Church.

[8] Jesus refers to those who hear the Gospel as *wedding guests*. We discover later in Ephesians 5:22–33 and Revelation 21:2 that God actually turns those who respond to the Gospel invitation into the *Bride*.

[9] The Lord referred to Israel as his *chosen* People in key verses such as Deuteronomy 7:6, 14:2, 1 Kings 3:8, Psalm 135:4, Isaiah 41:8, and 44:1. Jesus warns them that they need to respond to his choice to be saved.

[10] Paul reiterates this Romans 1:16, but also warns in 2:9–10 that they need to respond to the Gospel invitation.

Matthew brings us to the end of Act Four, and to the end of Jesus' teaching about the brightness of his Kingdom community. These three parables from the heart of Jewish history issued them a final ultimatum to receive him as King and do what he said. Time was running out. They only had seventy-two hours to comply.

Tragically, chapter 22 ends not with repentance but with more petty questioning. The Jewish leaders ignored Jesus' ultimatum and tried to trick him into endorsing their earthbound campaigns. They still wanted him to be a Warrior-Messiah who would rebel against Rome, a Philosopher-Messiah who would side with their logic, or a Pharisee-Messiah who would debate their rules and forsake his own Revolution. Jesus asked them a devastating question of his own in 22:41–46 and then set his face for what must now come to pass.

Matthew makes us spectators of the great Jewish national tragedy because he wants to use it as a warning and ultimatum of his own. As he moves his drama into its fifth and final act, he is about to call the horrors of Kingdom Judgment to take their place upon the stage. Matthew urges us to obey him, yield fruit for him, and respond to his invitation, before it is too late. Whether we are Jews or Gentiles, he tells us that we cannot ignore the Messiah of Israel.

The Greatest Commandment (22:34–40)

Jesus replied: "Love the Lord your God with all your heart and with all your soul and with all your mind... Love your neighbour as yourself. All the Law and the Prophets hang on these two commandments."

(Matthew 22:37–40)

When Jesus of Nazareth was asked to describe the essence of his Revolution, he used a four-letter word: *love*. If someone were to describe the essence of your life, or the essence of your church, would they say the same thing? I hope that if someone spent a day with me or the church I lead, they would say things like *faith* and *worship* and *Bible-teaching* and *prayer* and *evangelism*, but I would be devastated if above all those things they didn't also say *love*. Love isn't just part of the Christian life; it *is* the Christian life.

The Old Testament is a very long book. It has 929 chapters, 23,145 verses, and 593,493 words.[1] So when Jesus tells us that 23,143 of those verses *"hang on"* on only two headline verses, we need to sit up and listen. They are his God-given executive summary of 1,500 years' worth of Scripture, and they help us to check that we haven't missed the heart of his message.[2]

The first and greatest headline verse is from Deuteronomy 6:5: *"Love the Lord your God with all your heart and with all*

---

[1] The actual number of words depends on which English translation we use as our benchmark.

[2] Jesus uses the phrase *"the Law and the Prophets"* as a way of referring to the whole of the Old Testament.

your soul and with all your mind." Love involves feelings, but it also means much more than that. Jesus actually adds the words *"with all your mind"*, even though they are not in Deuteronomy, to remind us that real love for God involves our thinking, our planning and our actions, as well as our emotions.

The second headline verse is from Leviticus 19:18: *"Love your neighbour as yourself."* It's not a separate command, but another one *like* the first. Those who love God will love those around them; those who don't love those around them, don't truly love God. That's why John tells us: *"Love comes from God. Everyone who loves has been born of God and knows God. Whoever does not love does not know God, because God is love... Anyone who does not love his brother, whom he has seen, cannot love God, whom he has not seen."*[3]

These two headline verses which summarize the Old Testament also summarize the 260 chapters, 7,957 verses, and 181,253 words of the New Testament. James calls love *"the Law of the Kingdom"*, and John says that God's New Covenant command is simply *"to believe in the name of his Son, Jesus Christ, and to love one another as he commanded us"*.[4] That's Christianity in a nutshell. That's the Revolution of Jesus Christ. It's that simple.

It's also impossibly difficult. So difficult, in fact, that many churches opt for a slightly less demanding alternative. They excel in teaching or worship or prayer or mission or charismatic gifts or generous giving. At first, they look impressive, but not when we read 1 Corinthians 13:1–3:

> *If I speak in the tongues of men and of angels, but have not love, I am only a resounding gong or a clanging cymbal. If I have the gift of prophecy and can fathom all mysteries and all knowledge, and if I have a faith that*

---

[3] 1 John 4:7, 8, 20.

[4] James 2:8; 1 John 3:23. *The Royal Law* is another way of saying the *Law of the Kingdom*.

*can move mountains, but have not love, I am nothing. If
I give all I possess to the poor and surrender my body to
the flames, but have not love, I gain nothing.*

Love is at the heart of Jesus' Kingdom Revolution. It's not just an important aspect of Christianity. It is the lifeblood of Christianity.

Jesus tells a story in Luke 10 to illustrate this. A man was mugged by robbers as he journeyed from Jerusalem to Jericho. As he lay by the roadside, naked and bleeding to death, a priest came along. Jesus' listeners breathed a sigh of relief, for they knew that the priests were called to represent God to the people. He was bound to help the man. Except he didn't. Jesus shocked his audience by telling them that the priest even crossed the road to avoid him and simply left him to die. He was into *purity* and *prayer* and *teaching*, but not rolling up his sleeves to help the needy. That would make him ceremonially unclean! Getting bloody and dirty for the sake of a stranger would be so – well – ungodly.

But there was a glimmer of hope. A Levite arrived, one of the logistics managers at the Temple. Surely he would stop to help the man. No, yet again Jesus shocked his listeners by telling them that the Levite also crossed the road and left the man to die. He was *busy* with serving on a ministry team. He felt sorry for the man; he said a prayer for the man; he may even have arrived in Jericho and organized an all-night prayer vigil for those in trouble on the roads. But the fact is he left the man to die. He was religious but loveless.

Finally, a Samaritan came along. The Samaritans were doctrinally impure, worshipping God on the wrong mountain and alongside pagan superstitions. The listeners instinctively wrote him off as a loser and a no-hoper... and yet he truly loved the dying stranger. He risked his own life to stoop down and put the man on his donkey. He got his hands and clothes dirty to clean the man's wounds. He emptied his wallet at the next inn to pay for him to recuperate in style. He demonstrated the love that God is looking for. Ahead of our teaching, our worship, our evangelism, and our service, God is looking for a people who love him and those around them as much as they love themselves. That's the heart of the Old and New Testaments. That's the heart of God's Kingdom Revolution. If we don't have Christ's love, we're not really Christians at all.

Jesus doesn't expect us to grit our teeth and manufacture love for him and for others. His revolutionary lifestyle is far too demanding for us to be able to do that. He calls us to love the unlovable[5] and even those who bitterly oppose us,[6] and we can only do that through the love of Christ. It's not just a better version of the world's love that we can manufacture for ourselves, nor is it even something that God manufactures for us. God *is* love, and when we receive the Holy Spirit into our hearts, we find that God himself dwells inside us. We find ourselves filled with the love of Christ so that we naturally love as the world cannot love. This is the great factor which makes the Church so refreshingly different: *"God has poured out his love into our hearts by the Holy Spirit."*[7]

It's no coincidence that Matthew brings Act Four of his gospel to a close with this radical message of selfless, matchless, death-defying love. Act Four has been all about Kingdom community, and how godly character makes the Church a warning-beacon to arouse a dying world. It shouts aloud that God's Kingdom has come, that the Devil has been routed, and that the nations of the earth need to rally and fall in behind King Jesus.

How will the world sit up and take notice of the reign of

---

[5] Paul is able to say in Philippians 1:8 that *"I long for **all of you** with the affection of Christ Jesus"*.

[6] Matthew 5:44; Luke 6:27, 35.

[7] Romans 5:5. See also Galatians 5:22.

Jesus Christ? It's very simple, really. *"By this all men will know that you are my disciples, if you love one another."*[8]

---

[8] John 13:35.

Act Five:

Kingdom Judgment

Hypocrisy (23:1–39)

Woe to you, teachers of the law and Pharisees, you hypocrites! You are like whitewashed tombs, which look beautiful on the outside but on the inside are full of dead men's bones and everything unclean.

(Matthew 23:27)

Let me confess to you my ignorance. When I first read Shakespeare's *Othello*, I didn't know it was a tragedy. I enjoyed the play right up to the last scene, when to my surprise and consternation almost all the main characters were suddenly killed off one by one. Somebody should have told me that *Othello* was a tragedy. Maybe they just assumed that I knew.

Please don't make the same mistake with Matthew. This book is a tragedy and its final act is a crescendo of Kingdom Judgment. There's a warning of judgment for all those who reject God's Messiah, graphically portrayed by the swaying body of Judas Iscariot as he hangs upon a tree. In contrast, there's also bloody judgment borne for our sake by the suffering Messiah as he hangs upon a different tree at Calvary. Either way, Act Five of Matthew's gospel is a story of death and of judgment. The judgment can be our own as we die without Christ, or else it can be Christ's as he dies in our place. Someone will be judged for our sin, and Matthew calls us to choose before the play is over.

The curtain rises on this final act with Jesus calling down a series of woes upon the Pharisees. They represented Israel at its worst, so his woes speak to Israel as a whole. Jesus told the Parable of the Tenants in 21:33–46 using words which deliberately pointed his listeners back to Isaiah 5:1–7, and the seven woes which he speaks over the Pharisees in chapter 23 are also meant to point back to the six woes on the city of Jerusalem in Isaiah 5:8–30. Those earlier woes warned the nation of Judah to repent or be destroyed by foreign armies, and Jesus speaks a fresh series of woes to warn the Jewish nation of his own day that they need to do the same. Matthew hopes to win over his Jewish readers by confronting them with the ugliness of their religion in the lives of its leaders. It is empty and lifeless, and will lead them to hell unless they exchange it for the Gospel of Jesus their Messiah.[1]

The word which dominates Jesus' attack on the Pharisees[2] is *hupokritēs*, from which we get the English word *hypocrite*. Jesus uses the word seven times in this chapter,[3] and it was a word used in the theatre for the *stage actors* who played parts in a play. Jesus' main charge against the Pharisees is that they are pretenders who look like pure whitewashed tombs on the outside but conceal the rotting stench of wickedness on the inside.[4] They were good at telling others what to do but poor at doing it themselves.[5] They were good at acting like rabbis in public but poor at living like disciples in private. They were good at preaching law but poor at practising love. They majored

---

[1] Jesus is very clear with the Jewish leaders in vv. 13, 15, and 33 that they are heading to hell unless they repent.

[2] Jesus addresses the Pharisees *and* the scribes or teachers of the law, but most of these scribes also tended to be Pharisees. See Matthew 5:20; 12:38; 15:1; 22:34–35.

[3] It is actually eight times if we include v. 14, but the most reliable Greek manuscripts omit that verse.

[4] Jesus' reference to *whitewashed tombs* needs some explanation. Any Jew who touched a grave became ceremonially unclean (Numbers 19:16), so tombs and gravestones were whitewashed once a year to warn people to steer clear. Their clean white exterior but rotten interior was a vivid picture of religious hypocrisy.

[5] The Greek of v. 4 could mean either that the Pharisees did not lift a finger to help people to obey their rules, or that they did not lift a finger to obey their own rules. This ambiguity is probably intentional.

on externals as a substitute for internals. Jesus saw behind their masks and warned that God was not fooled.[6]

Although most of us are one step removed from the Pharisees and teachers of the law, Matthew records these words for us as well as for them. It is all too easy for church leaders to puff themselves up with titles[7] and to preach a list of rules and regulations which have no power to help those who listen. It is easy for Christians to turn the Gospel into a list of rules which *"shut the kingdom of heaven in men's faces"*, and to turn its call into something less than Revolution. Passion for purity can all too easily become hypocritical self-righteousness, and debates about doctrine can very quickly replace our radical calling towards *"justice, mercy and faithfulness"*. It is easy to admire the revolutionary Christian zealots of yesteryear and to look down on the established churches which resisted them, but much harder to accept the new revolutionaries of our own day.[8] When I read this chapter of judgment on the Pharisees, I do not find it comfortable reading. I see too much of myself in it, and too much of the Church, to discard it as nothing more than somebody else's mail.

I take God's judgment seriously, and hopefully you do too. In that case, let's use this chapter as a mirror for our hearts and deal with the rottenness it reveals. Let's repent of seeking leadership as a stepping-stone to praise; of letting the

---

[6] Peter stresses this in Acts 15:8, when he calls the Lord the *Kardiognōstēs*, or *The-One-Who-Knows-The-Heart*.

[7] Many Protestants quote vv. 8–12 and criticize Roman Catholic priests for using the title *Father*. They have a point, but they do not take it far enough. Jesus is telling spiritual leaders not to boast in any title which steals glory from God and gives it to themselves. This can be done just as easily with the title *Pastor* as with *Father*.

[8] The Pharisees fooled themselves, even as they plotted to murder the Messiah, that they would have accepted the martyred prophets of old. Francis of Assisi, Wycliffe, Luther, and Wesley were all hated by many in their own day but are honoured by most churches today. Dead radicals are far less threatening than live ones.

trappings of religion smother the Revolution of love; of spiritual play-acting which destroys Christian community; and of the apathetic compromise which resists the alarm-bell sounded by God's prophets. Hypocrisy is hypocrisy, whether in a Pharisee, a Jew, or a Christian. God is no respecter of persons.

We need to gaze into the mirror of this chapter because there is hope for us if we repent of the sin that we see in our hearts. Jesus' ends this chapter of judgment with a passionate plea for Jerusalem to turn back to him and let him gather her to himself like a hen gathering chicks under her wings. He makes this plea to us too, so that he can fill us with his Holy Spirit and work his righteousness in our hearts from the inside out. Jesus sobs over Jerusalem with tears of desperation as he tells his beloved city that *"you were not willing"*. We, the New Jerusalem, must take off own masks and give up our play-acting, once and for all. If we don't, we may discover one day with surprise that the role that we are playing ends in bitter, bitter tragedy.

The King Comes Twice
(24:1–51)

At that time the sign of the Son of Man will appear
in the sky, and all the nations of the earth will mourn.
They will see the Son of Man coming on the clouds
of the sky, with power and great glory.

(Matthew 24:30)

There was a reason why the Jews didn't recognize Jesus as their Messiah. The Old Testament described him in two different guises, and they simply couldn't reconcile the two.

In Psalm 2 he is the mighty King, smashing his enemies to pieces with an iron sceptre and destroying all those who failed to kiss his feet in homage. Turn a few pages to Psalm 22, however, and he is *"a worm and not a man, scorned by men and despised by the people"*. How could this nail-pierced and dying Messiah have anything to do with the King of Psalm 2? So most first-century Jews did what many of us do when we struggle to understand a passage of Scripture; they ignored it and found some easier chapters for their daily devotions.

Or how about the book of Isaiah? In chapter 53 he is the Suffering Servant, *"led like a lamb to the slaughter"* and *"despised and rejected by men"*. Yet turn a few pages to chapter 63, and he is a mighty warrior clad in royal robes and stained with the blood of his enemies. How could one man fit both of these descriptions? How could the Messiah be the King of kings, a mighty warrior, and yet a meek and suffering victim, all in one lifetime? Even the greatest rabbis had no real answer to that question. And so, putting Psalm 22, Isaiah 53, and a host of other passages into a bottom drawer labelled "difficult texts", they concentrated on the Warrior-King passages and ignored all the rest. They made the Messiah into less than he was, then they rejected Jesus for being more than they expected.

Jesus had an answer to their dilemma and he gives it in Matthew 24. What they had failed to understand was that the Messiah would actually come *twice*. He would come the first time as the Suffering Servant, hiding his royal power in the unimpressive body of a manual labourer from Galilee. He would be rejected and crucified so that *"the writings of the prophets might be fulfilled"*.[1] He would still be the Mighty King,[2] proving it to those who would listen through his miracles and his teaching,[3] but he would call for *voluntary* surrender and never force his rule. He refused to resist when the Jewish nation bayed for his blood and fulfilled the very passages which they kept in their bottom drawer. King Jesus looked for willing volunteers the first time he came, and the only bloodstains on his garments were his own.

But he was coming back a second time, in a very different manner from the first. He would come visibly, undisguisedly, and *"on the clouds of the sky, with power and great glory"*. He would not come asking for volunteers, but gathering those who had already volunteered. Then he would unsheathe his sword to deal with all who had not.[4] His Second Coming would mark the harvest-day he described back in 13:40–43, and he would come

---

[1] Matthew 26:56.

[2] To clarify, I am not saying that Jesus was *only* the Suffering Messiah at his first coming and will *only* be the Mighty Messiah at his Second Coming. Revelation 6:16 talks of his Final Judgment as *"the wrath of the Lamb"*. My point is simply that Jesus could say of his first coming that *"I did not come to judge the world, but to save it"* (John 12:47), and that he will not be able to say this at his Second Coming.

[3] In Matthew 11:2–6, John the Baptist began to doubt that Jesus could truly be the promised Warrior-Messiah. Jesus reassured him with a reminder that only the Messiah could bring miracles and teaching like his own.

[4] Matthew 24:26–31.

with such power and glory that the nations of the earth would mourn over their disastrous mistake. Do not be fooled: those who live as if the King will never come back will find themselves on the wrong side of his judgment when he does.[5]

This Final Judgment would be prefigured by the utter destruction of Jerusalem in 70 AD. The Old Testament prophecies against Jerusalem often pointed to another, bigger Judgment to come, and so do these words of Jesus.[6] Prompted by an admiring comment about the size of the stones in the Temple walls,[7] Jesus warns his disciples that the Temple and the city will both be destroyed. In fact, when this happened in 70 AD, only a fraction of Jerusalem's Christians were caught up in the Roman slaughter because they obeyed the command of verse 16 to *"flee to the mountains"*.[8] God would grant Jerusalem a forty-year period of grace, and only after that would their curse of 27:25 – *"Let his blood be on us and on our children!"* – be ratified. Even then, when his wrath was poured out, he would still remember mercy towards the Jewish nation. He promises in verse 34 that it will not be wiped out before he comes again.[9]

Although this chapter begins with talk of Jerusalem, the disciples ask in verse 3 about the events at *"the end of the age"*, and this is the context for most of the chapter. Jesus warns that the long centuries of AD history will be full of wars, famine,

---

[5] Verse 51 does not tell us that we can lose our salvation through unfaithfulness, but that unfaithfulness shows we have never truly responded to the Gospel of the Kingdom. The same is true in v. 13.

[6] We already looked at a classic example in the chapter on "Gehenna". Isaiah 66:24 described the slaughter of Jerusalem in 586 BC, but it also pointed to the far greater torment of hell at the Final Judgment.

[7] Josephus tells us in his *Antiquities of the Jews* (15.11.3) that some of the Temple stones were 11 metres long, 5.5 metres wide, and 3.5 metres high. No wonder the disciples were impressed!

[8] Eusebius of Caesarea notes this in his *Ecclesiastical History* (3.5.3), written just after 300 AD.

[9] The Greek word *genea* simply has to mean *race* and not *generation* in v. 34. There are no Russian Philistines or American Amalekites, yet there are millions of Jews living as a distinct race throughout the nations of the world.

earthquakes, false religion, apathy, backsliding, and trouble.[10] These will not simply mark the end of the age, but will be part of the "labour pains" of more than two millennia of history. In that time, some parts of the Church will grow cool and apathetic, while other parts maintain their beacon-fires and spread their contagious message throughout all nations of the earth. Such churches will be hated and many Christians will be killed, yet nevertheless they will be fruitful and victorious. Jesus warns those who willingly embrace his Kingdom Revolution that they must expect fierce resistance from the former régime. They must simply serve, sow and sacrifice in the face of all opposition, because they know that their King is coming back.

Act Five of Matthew's gospel will go on to describe the Suffering Messiah who dies for the sins of the world, but we must never forget that he is also God's Mighty Warrior-King. Psalm 22 may start with Jesus on the cross, but it does not end with him there. It finishes with an urgent call to worship the risen Christ before it is too late: *"All the ends of the earth will remember and turn to the Lord, and all the families of the nations will bow down before him, for dominion belongs to the Lord and he rules over the nations."*

---

[10] Jesus hints at the length of AD history with a warning in v. 48 that we may think *"My master is staying away a long time."* See also 25:5 and 19.

Parables of Judgment (25:1–46)

Therefore keep watch, because you do not know the day or the hour.

(Matthew 25:13)

If you don't have a problem with some of Jesus' parables, you need to go back and read them more slowly. Take the three parables in Matthew 25, for example. At first glance, they seem to tell us that we are saved through being *ready*, being *active*, and being *generous*. That comes as something of a surprise, since the heart of the Christian Gospel is that we are saved by grace through our faith. So what is Jesus saying here, and what does he want us to do with what he says?

It's tempting to gloss over these questions, eager to dive into the narrative which follows, but we mustn't. They form a vital part of Jesus' teaching on Kingdom Judgment, and they hold an important lesson for every believer.

Sometimes all we have to do to understand the Bible is to read it a little bit more slowly. On closer inspection, this is *not* a chapter which speaks about Christ judging the world and saving his Church. In each of the three parables, Christ judges his *Church* and separates true believers from play-acting phoneys. The ten bridesmaids all look the same until the bridegroom comes and pronounces his judgment. The three servants all look faithful until the master returns and calls them to account. The flock graze together until the shepherd comes and divides the sheep from the goats. Here, the echo of a Messianic prophecy in Ezekiel 34:11–24 confirms that this chapter is about Christ judging his

Church, not the world. The foolish bridesmaids, the lazy servant, and the self-centred goats all name Jesus as their *Lord*,[1] but when the Son of Man returns, their hearts will be exposed.

The bridegroom does not shut the five foolish bridesmaids out of his party because they failed to be ready for his coming. He shuts them out because *"I never knew you"*. They are like churchgoers who try to "borrow" Christian experience through association with others, but no one can borrow relationship with Jesus Christ. Their lack of diligent preparation is the external symptom of an internal problem. They are religious freeloaders whose lack of devotion to Christ stems from a lack of true conversion. They hope to piggyback their way to heaven, and they find the door shut firmly in their faces. They are those whom Jesus described in 7:21–23: *"Not everyone who says to me, 'Lord, Lord,' will enter the kingdom of heaven, but only he who does the will of my Father who is in heaven... Then I will tell them plainly, 'I never knew you. Away from me, you evildoers!'"*

The master does not throw the lazy servant into *"the outer darkness"*[2] because he is lazy. His laziness is another external symptom of the same internal problem. The servant has a false view of his master, which he uses to justify his lack of devotion. He has many excuses for not using his talent,[3] but his master sees through them all. Those who truly know the Lord work hard for him, and they receive his reward as *"good and faithful servants"*. Those who refuse his commission simply reveal that they do not really know him at all.[4]

Nor does the Son of Man throw the goats into hell because

---

[1] They all use the word *kurios*, or *Lord*, in 25:11, 24, and 44, but there is a world of difference between calling Jesus Lord and truly surrendering to his Lordship.

[2] Matthew 22:13 tells us that this is another metaphor for hell.

[3] The word *talent* has been taken from this parable in the English language to mean *gifting*, but at the time Jesus told the parable it simply referred to a measure of silver which weighed 45 kg.

[4] Jesus gives stern advice to those in the Church who feel inadequate to serve him. He tells them in v. 15 that their task is no bigger than their gifting, and in

they failed to help those in need. The issue at stake here is not simply how they treated the *poor*, but specifically how they treated the *brothers*.[5] Jesus insists that those who profess love for him should prove it by loving his People in the context of a local church.[6] He gives short shrift to those who try to reduce the Christian faith to nothing more than Jesus-and-me, or to the self-centred life of a churchless nomad. True believers, he warns, show their love for their Shepherd by feeding his sheep. They share their homes, their tables, and their wardrobes with each other, and they commit themselves to one another in sickness and in health, in persecution and in peacetime.[7]

When we love our Christian brothers and sisters, Jesus treats it as loving him personally, and when we neglect them in their need he treats is as neglecting him personally.[8] Jesus leaves us in no doubt as to how important this is: those who fail to love their brothers reveal a more basic failure to respond to his Kingdom Revolution. They cannot enter heaven because they are not truly saved. They belong with the play-acting hypocrites he condemned in chapter 23. They belong with the Devil and his demons and with everyone else who hates God's People.[9]

---

v. 27 that those who lack initiative can at least give themselves willingly to the initiatives of others.

[5] The key word in v. 40 is *adelphoi*, or *brothers*. The New Testament consistently uses this word to refer to Christians rather than to non-Christians, although note that Jesus does also call himself a *xenos* – a *stranger* or *outsider* – in v. 35. We must welcome strangers as well, and turn them into brothers.

[6] John 21:15–17; 1 John 4:20–21; 2 Corinthians 8:5.

[7] Prison-visiting is a wonderful expression of the Gospel, but in this context Jesus is talking specifically about visiting believers who are in prison for their faith. Associating with such believers meant risking one's own life. Onesiphorus did this for Paul in 2 Timothy 1:15–18, even when Paul's other friends abandoned him.

[8] Jesus also taught this to Saul of Tarsus in Acts 9:4. Mistreating his Church is to mistreat *him* personally.

[9] In the midst of this sobering parable is the teaching of v. 41 that Jesus originally created hell for Satan and his demons, not for humankind. We belong in heaven, not in hell, but first we need to surrender to the Gospel.

Those who rush over the difficult questions of Matthew 25, and make a beeline for the narrative of Matthew 26, usually do so because they assume that these are parables aimed at the Jews, at non-Christians or at somebody other than themselves. It is sobering to realize that they are not. Jesus told these three parables to his twelve disciples on their own,[10] not as a warning for Jews who reject the Messiah, but as a warning for churchgoers who only pretend to accept him. There are only two destinations for humankind – heaven or hell – and Jesus says that play-actors will share the same fate as out-and-out rebels. God's Kingdom Judgment is not just for those outside of the Church. It is for all those who join her community but resist her radical calling.

If you are a church leader, consider that some of your flock may be "goats" and that you must address them as Jesus did here in a last-minute challenge to Judas Iscariot. If you are a believer, examine your life and repent of any external symptoms which may be the sign of an internal problem.

But if you examine yourself and find that you are a wise bridesmaid, a faithful servant, and a sheep in the flock, then rejoice. Jesus promises you in verse 34 that the Kingdom was prepared for *you* from the very creation of the world.

---

[10] This chapter continues directly on from 24:3, where the disciples came to Jesus *privately*.

Worship Leader (26:1–16)

I tell you the truth, wherever this gospel is preached throughout the world, what she has done will also be told, in memory of her.

(Matthew 26:13)

Act Five of Matthew's gospel is dark and grim. Its message of Kingdom Judgment is so stark and horrific that, at the end of the act, even the sun stops shining and the earth shakes at the feet of the crucified Son of God. These chapters are gloomy as well as glorious, which is why Matthew decides to start the narrative of Act Five with a bright and beautiful love story.

He's been saving it for this moment, to sandwich it between the plotting of the bloodthirsty priests and the betrayal of the money-hungry Judas. It actually took place on the night before the Triumphal Entry, but Matthew tells the story several days later to use this woman's worship as a powerful example of the unabashed devotion which these chapters should stir in our hearts.[1] So much so, that Jesus issues an astonishing ruling that this love-story must form part of his Gospel message wherever it is preached around the world. This is the kind of devotion Jesus wants from his People, and he calls those who worship him to follow her lead.

The woman – John tells us it was Mary of Bethany – worships Jesus as her undisputed King. The Jewish leaders may reject him, Judas Iscariot may sell him, and the disciples may

---

[1] Mark tells the story in the same order as Matthew, but John 12:1–11 tells us plainly that this event took place on the night before Jesus rode into Jerusalem on a donkey. Luke 21:37 agrees, telling us that Jesus slept the night in the Garden of Gethsemane after giving the teaching of Matthew 23–25.

desert him, but she will not falter. She anoints his head with perfume like Samuel anointed David with oil when he recognized him as the true king of Israel.[2] Mark 14:3 and John 12:3 both stress this point still further by telling us that the perfume she used was *nard*, which was imported from far-off India and was normally found in a palace. The beloved bride in Song of Songs expresses her love for King Solomon by telling her friends: *"While the king was at his table, my nard spread its fragrance."*[3] Mary, either consciously or unconsciously, re-enacts this verse from Solomon's Song to worship Jesus as Israel's undisputed King. He is David's greater Son, Solomon's true heir, and the one who deserves to be anointed with nothing but the very best from the royal perfumeries. Even as Israel rejects him as their King, Mary mimics the royal bride of Solomon and adores him as the promised Messiah.

Mary also worships Jesus as her unrivalled Lord. The disciples complain that she is "wasting" her perfume since it could have been sold on behalf of the poor, but Mary is not for persuading.[4] She had *"chosen what is better"*, a few months earlier, and she was determined to do so again.[5] This is often referred to as Mary's *extravagant* act of devotion, but the whole point of the story is that, for all its cost, such sacrifice was not extravagant at all. The nard cost 300 denarii, the equivalent of one year's salary,[6] but this was nothing more than a reasonable response to the Lord of the universe as he poured out his life

229

---

[2] 1 Samuel 16:1–13.

[3] Some translations of Song of Songs 1:12 simply render the Hebrew word *nayrd* as *perfume*, but it is the same word that is translated as *nard* in Song of Songs 4:13 and 14.

[4] Most of the disciples may have been sincere, but John 12:6 tells us that Judas only said this because he wanted to steal some of the money before it ever got to the poor.

[5] Luke 10:38–42. Some Christians try to use Jesus' words here as an excuse not to help the poor, but Jesus will not let us. He tells us that true Christian churches will always have the poor among them. Does yours?

[6] John 12:5.

for our own. Paul says that if we give him the whole of our lives, it is simply our *logical* response to his mercy.[7] The needs of the world will never go away, but our worship leader Mary reminds us that, first and foremost, the Lord Jesus deserves our everything.

Matthew also saved this love story until now because Mary worships Jesus as something more than her Lord and her King. She also worships him as her Saviour, the Suffering Servant whom God had sent to die. While Peter straps on his sword in the hope of defending his Master, and while the other disciples resolve to stand shoulder-to-shoulder to resist his arrest, Mary humbly accepts his message of the cross and begins a wave of worship which will ripple across the world. This was the woman who treasured Jesus' friendship so highly that she left her sister Martha to do the cooking back in Luke 10:38–42, so that she could simply sit at Jesus' feet.[8] Now, while her sister is once more serving dinner, she ignores the scowls of the others at the table to pour out her love for her Saviour. The corpses of the dead were perfumed before burial, but Mary knows that her beloved Jesus will be denied such care when he is taken down from the cross. So she "wastes" her most precious possession to prepare his body ahead of his death – a final act of devotion from the woman who knew that *"only one thing is needed"*.[9]

This love-story is placed here for a reason, and Matthew wants us to slow down to digest what it means. The next two chapters will see Jesus betrayed by Judas, denied by Peter, abandoned by the other disciples, rejected by the Jewish nation, condemned by the Sanhedrin, crucified by the Romans, taunted by passers-by, insulted by criminals, and even abandoned by

---

[7] Romans 12:1. The Greek word *logikos* means literally a *logical* or *reasonable* act of worship.

[8] Actually, John 12:2 tells us she was at it again here. Martha, who appears to have been the wife or widow of Simon the Leper, was serving Jesus dinner as her sister poured perfume on his body.

[9] Luke 10:41–42.

God the Father. And yet out of the gloom shines a glimmer of light. Mary recognizes him for who he really is. She hails him as King, as Lord, as Saviour, and as Friend, and she expresses her devotion through a lavish, but logical, act of worship.

Do you see now why Jesus wants this love story to form part of his Gospel message to the world? Mary's nard travelled all the way from India, but what she did with it must travel to every nation of the earth. She sets an example for how Jesus' followers must pour out their lives in his service.

Nothing less than this is worthy of him. Nothing less than this is logical. In the words of the English hymn-writer, Isaac Watts:

Were the whole realm of nature mine,
That were an offering far too small.
Love so amazing, so divine,
Demands my soul, my life, my all.[10]

---

[10] This is the last verse of his hymn "When I Survey the Wondrous Cross", which he wrote in 1707.

Bread and Wine (26:17–30)

While they were eating, Jesus took bread, gave thanks and broke it, and gave it to his disciples, saying, "Take and eat; this is my body."

(Matthew 26:26)

The British novelist George Orwell wrote in 1939 that *"The restatement of the obvious is the first duty of intelligent men."*[1] Jesus of Nazareth certainly agreed. On the final evening before his crucifixion, he taught his followers to share bread and wine together as a restatement of the message of his cross. He wanted each succeeding generation to do the same as a graphic, regular reminder of the centrality of his death and resurrection.

It's been successful, but only up to a point. Eating bread and drinking wine is not enough in itself to keep the Gospel at the centre of Church life. Don Carson writes that

> *I fear that the cross, without ever being disowned, is constantly in danger of being dismissed from the central place it must enjoy, by relatively peripheral insights that take on far too much weight. Whenever the periphery is in danger of displacing the centre, we are not far removed from idolatry.*[2]

We need to do more than share bread and wine together in our churches in Jesus' name. We also need to keep reminding ourselves of why he asked us to do so.

---

[1] Orwell wrote this in his review of Bertrand Russell's book *Power* in the magazine *The New Adelphi*.

[2] D.A. Carson, *The Cross and Christian Ministry* (2004).

The Lord's Supper[3] is at its heart a radical expression of humility. You might not have guessed that from the way people have fought over it, but it's true.[4] Each time we eat it, we confess to Jesus that we can only be saved through complete dependence upon his work on the cross. When his listeners were offended by the idea of eating his flesh and drinking his blood in John 6:53, Jesus refused to back-pedal or explain that it was simply a clever metaphor. He chose this deliberately offensive spiritual meal so that he could drive away everyone save those who truly admit they have no other hope but him. The Lord's Supper is a polarizing event, and it's meant to be. It's a moment for each worshipper to restate their faith in salvation through God's grace alone.

I'm not interested in whether you are a Roman Catholic or a Protestant. I'm simply interested in whether or not you eat and drink the Lord's Supper in this way. When Protestants talk of communion simply as an act of symbolic remembrance, they can undervalue the life-changing power which is released each time that we bow before Jesus and eat afresh of his body and his blood. When Catholics take Mass in the hope of earning favour with God, they turn an act of humble dependence into a work of human endeavour.[5] The Lord's Supper is not superstition, but nor is it mere symbolism. It is a regular, outward confession to Jesus that we draw our life from his death alone.

The Lord's Supper is also at its heart an expression of victory. Jesus tells us in verses 28 and 29 that it speaks of

---

[3] Luke calls it *"breaking bread"* in Acts 2:42, 46, and 21:7, and Paul calls it *"the Lord's Supper"* in 1 Corinthians 11:20. Other terms such as *communion*, the *Mass*, or the *Eucharist* may be helpful, but they are not in the Bible.

[4] For example, Luther and Zwingli both opposed the Roman Catholic view of the Mass, but then fell out with each other at the Colloquy of Marburg over what they believed instead. William Booth, the founder of the Salvation Army, felt it caused so much division that he banned it altogether in his churches.

[5] Near my house is a medieval chantry built by a medieval nobleman so that priests could say masses on his behalf and speed his soul to heaven. It is still possible to take the Mass with that same spirit of superstition.

his New Covenant, of his coming Kingdom and of complete forgiveness for sin. Paul adds in 1 Corinthians 11:26 that it is a proclamation that Jesus has won the victory through his cross and that we are waiting for his return in glorious triumph. The Catholic danger is to view the Mass as an event in which the bread and wine are literally turned into Christ's flesh and blood so that his body can be sacrificed afresh for our sins. This very literal view of what *"this **is** my body"* might mean[6] undermines the once-for-all nature of his victory at Calvary, turning what should be a celebration of complete victory into a continuation of the battle.[7] The Protestant danger, on the other hand, is to treat communion as an introspective guilt-fest which focuses more on how we have let Jesus down than on how he has lifted us up. Jesus did not intend breaking bread to be as sombre as funeral but as joyful as winning the Superbowl. Acts 2:46 tells us that the early believers *"broke bread in their homes and ate together with **glad** and sincere hearts"*, and so should we. Jesus has won complete victory over our enemies, and we get to eat the fruit.

The Lord's Supper is also at its heart an expression of family. Jesus hands the disciples one cup and tells them to *"Drink of it, all of you"*. His blood would be shed for them all so that each of them could enter the Kingdom of God. Paul also stresses the family aspect of breaking bread in 1 Corinthians 10:17, telling us that *"We, who are many, are one body, for we all partake of the one loaf"*. Whatever our background, we must not treat the Lord's Supper simply as an expression of how Jesus has saved us as individuals, but as a meal shared with brothers- and sisters-in-Christ from all around the world. Paul warns

---

[6] The same literalism would mean that Jesus *is* a tree (John 15:1), *is* made of wood (John 10:9), and that the New Covenant *is* a small goblet in Jerusalem (Luke 22:20).

[7] Hebrews 9:26–28 and 10:12 are very clear that Jesus' death on the cross was a *once-for-all* sacrifice for sin. He has completely won the victory, and does not need to "top it up" today.

us most severely of the consequences when we ignore this corporate bond with the wider Body of Christ: *"For anyone who eats and drinks without recognizing the body of the Lord eats and drinks judgment on himself."*[8] Jesus gave us this spiritual meal not just to humble us before him, but also to humble us next to one another. We all eat the same bread and drink the same wine, levelled as fellow-diners at the foot of the cross.

So eat and drink the Lord's Supper as often as you can. Enjoy it in your large Sunday meetings and, like the church in Acts 2:46, enjoy it regularly and informally with others in your home. Jesus turned the Old Covenant Passover meal into the New Covenant Lord's Supper to provide you with a potent reminder of the message of his cross.[9] Feast often and deeply, remembering its threefold meaning: we are graciously saved through Christ's work alone, we are completely victorious through Christ's work alone, and we are united as brothers and sisters through Christ's work alone.

> *For whenever you eat this bread and drink this cup, you proclaim the Lord's death until he comes.*[10]

---

[8] 1 Corinthians 11:29.

[9] Jesus was able to celebrate the Passover Meal in Matthew 26:17–30 but still die at the same time as the Passover lambs were slaughtered the following afternoon because the rabbis disagreed over the times Moses set for the Passover meal. Modern imams disagree in a similar way over the exact dates of Ramadan.

[10] 1 Corinthians 11:26.

The Only Way (26:36–54)

*Going a little farther, he fell with his face to the
ground and prayed, "My Father, if it is possible, may
this cup be taken from me. Yet not as I will, but as
you will."*

(Matthew 26:39)

Many people struggle with the idea that the Christian Gospel
is the only way that people can be saved. They readily consent
that Jesus is a way to God, and even the best way to God, but
they dare not claim he is the *only* way to God. That just sounds
too arrogant and intolerant in our multi-faith society.[1] If you
struggle with this question personally, I have some very good
news for you. So did Jesus. He grappled with the question three
times in the Garden of Gethsemane, and he got up from his
knees with the answer.

One of the main reasons we shy away from the exclusive
claims of the Christian Gospel is that we don't want to come
across as arrogant Westerners. We assume that our affection
for Jesus must be tied to the fact that he is the most important
figure in Western civilization, and that if we had been born in
Bahrain, Bhutan, or Borneo we would think very differently. We
don't want to be short-sighted, so we try our best to be inclusive
of all religions. In doing so, we walk into the very trap that we
seek to avoid.

---

[1] When the BBC recently produced a documentary series called *Around the
World in Eighty Faiths*, there was no suggestion that one of the eighty might
be right and the others wrong. Our culture celebrates religious diversity and
tolerates any belief except the intolerant belief that there is only one way to
God.

Let me demonstrate this with a story which one of my schoolteachers told me as an eight-year-old. There were once four blind men who stumbled across an elephant. The first one felt its leg and declared, *"I know what an elephant is like; it is a strong, immoveable tree."* The second blind man laid hold of its trunk. *"You are mistaken, my friend,"* he replied. *"It is strong and wriggling, like a python."* The third man stroked its tusk and the fourth held its tail. *"It is smooth and sharp,"* said one. *"No, it is like a piece of old rope,"* said the other. My teacher then explained the moral of the story: *"Every religion claims to be right, but they are all blind men touching an elephant. All of the world religions hold part of the truth; they just approach God in a different way."*[2]

Such humility was attractive, and most of the class nodded in agreement. I couldn't put my finger on why it didn't ring true. It was only twenty-five years later that I remembered the story and suddenly spotted the gaping flaw in its logic: it assumes that the narrator can see! The religious people of the world are all cast as blind men, but – thank God (if there is one) – we sophisticated Westerners can see!

This is the parable which undergirds our pluralist doctrine that all religions lead to God. It sounds like a humble creed, yet it masks a breathtaking arrogance. It presupposes that all the world's religions are essentially *wrong* about sin, judgment, and the need to make peace with God or the gods before it is too late. Instead, armed with Alexander Pope's pithy observation that *"to err is human, to forgive divine"*,[3] it argues that God will gladly overlook any sin on our part, and will usher us into heaven where we Westerners belong. This is the rival "gospel" which makes Christians too embarrassed to proclaim their message that Jesus alone can save. But we cannot be persuaded to own such a creed. We cannot be so arrogant.

---

[2] This story originated in India, but was popularized by in West by a poem in 1873 by John Godfrey Saxe.

[3] The English poet Alexander Pope wrote this line in his 1711 poem *An Essay on Criticism.*

Instead, we turn our eyes to Jesus Christ and let *him* be the narrator as we admit our blindness. We meet him in Gethsemane and hear a very different moral to the story. Jesus doesn't declare that every major world religion is wrong – in fact, just the opposite. He tells us that they are all absolutely *right* in their diagnosis of the problem. They are right that we have sinned against God, right that we need to be forgiven and reconciled to him, and right that those who die unforgiven will be punished for their wickedness.[4]

It is because the religions of the world are *right* in this diagnosis that Jesus struggled in Gethsemane and asked if any other way might be found to pay the penalty for human sin. As he felt the deadweight of sin crushing down on his shoulders, he told his disciples in verse 38 that *"My soul is overwhelmed with sorrow to the point of death."* He withdrew to pray, pleading that the Father might find a way to save humankind without his having to drink the bitter cup of judgment for them on the cross.[5] If Judaism, Hinduism, Buddhism, Mithraism, paganism, or any other man-made religion could save mankind, then please would the Father do it that way and spare his Son from the next few hours of torture and death? Once he asks; twice he asks; three times he asks. Then he stands up, understanding the message of Scripture that *"without the shedding of blood there is no forgiveness"*.[6] He tells Judas to get on with it, Peter to stop opposing it, and friend and foe alike that *"it must happen this way"*. Jesus Christ has issued his verdict to a world full of blind men. There is only one way to God, and it is through the blood of God's own Son.

---

[4] I'm talking here particularly about the main religions of the world. In Islam and Judaism sin leads to hell instead of heaven, and in Hinduism and Buddhism sin leads to a bad rather than good reincarnation. Most other religions contain a rough a variation of this same theme – unlike Western universalism.

[5] The Old Testament often spoke of the *cup* of God's judgment. See, for example, Isaiah 51:17, 22; Jeremiah 25:15–17; Ezekiel 23:31–34. For another example in Matthew's gospel, see 20:17–23.

[6] Hebrews 9:22.

You can cling to the view that other religions lead to God, but you must recognize that to do so you must argue that Christianity does not. If people can be saved without the cross of Jesus, the Christian God is so nasty or foolish that he asked his Son to die in pain simply to offer the world an extra choice in their catalogue of options for salvation. It means he did so while knowing all along that they could be saved without his Son's death, simply through the moralism of Islam, the legalism of Judaism, the moksha of Hinduism, or the detachment of Buddhism.

But if you believe the verdict of the narrator Jesus Christ, that there is no forgiveness and no salvation outside of his own self-sacrifice on the cross, you need to work through the implications of what he says. Where is the crucified Christ in Islam or Judaism? Specifically denied. Where is the crucified Christ in Hinduism or Buddhism? Not even offered a walk-on part in the play. Where is the crucified Christ in self-righteous and self-confident Western spirituality? Sidelined as an embarrassment, both offensive and unnecessary. Where is the crucified Christ in the Christian Gospel? He's there, in full view, marching willingly to his death and crying out *"Father, forgive them, for they do not know what they are doing."* He is declaring from the cross, *"It is finished!"* – the penalty for sin paid in full.[7]

Jesus' death and resurrection is not just one of many ways of salvation. It is the *only way* through which all people of the earth must be saved. As Peter grasped in the days which followed the resurrection and ascension of the vindicated Jesus: *"Salvation is found in no one else, for there is no other name under heaven given to men by which we must be saved."*[8]

---

[7] Luke 23:34; John 19:30.
[8] Acts 4:12. See also John 14:6.

The Revolution on Trial
(26:57–68; 27:11–31)

The high priest said to him, "I charge you under oath by the living God: Tell us if you are the Christ, the Son of God."

(Matthew 26:63)

Every revolution has its moment of truth. For the Revolution of Jesus Christ, it was now. All through that long night and into the morning, his Revolution was, literally, put on trial by those who resisted its call. One by one, they pitted their might against the Messiah, determined to extinguish his Kingdom message for good. But it was a colossal miscalculation. The trials of Jesus did not destroy his Revolution; they merely sounded its triumph.

The Jewish leaders made no attempt to conceal their excitement. Thirty pieces of silver had been a very small price to pay to have Jesus finally in their grasp. Their own law dictated that prisoners must be tried in public and by daylight, but such legal details could not contain their lust for his blood. By the time that the sun rose over Jerusalem, they were already beginning Jesus' third hearing.[1] Amazingly, with three long years to prepare their case, they had neither truth nor lies upon which to convict him, until at last High Priest Caiaphas found a chink in his armour.[2] Jesus had claimed to be Israel's true King,

---

[1] Matthew 26:57–68 and 27:1 gives the account of Jesus' second and third trials before the Sanhedrin. John 18:12–23 tells us that before this he was also tried by the high priest Annas.

[2] The fact that even Jesus' enemies could not find any sin he had committed, other than claiming to be God, is great proof that Jesus truly was and is the Son of God. Follow me round for three hours and you will find plenty of grounds

the promised Messiah who was known as *"the Son of God"*.[3] If he could be forced under oath to do so again, they would easily convict him of sedition against Caesar. Jesus obliged willingly, quoting from Psalms 110:1 and Daniel 7:13 to confess freely that he was the same *"Son of Man"* whom Daniel had seen destroy and outlast the mighty Roman Empire. The faces of the Jewish leaders brightened. Such revolutionary talk was all that they needed to carry out their plan. They blindfolded him, beat him, taunted him with his claim to be *"Christ"*, and then led him to be tried by Caesar's man in Palestine.[4]

Governor Pilate was hoping for a quiet Passover Feast until the arrival of his early-morning prisoner. *"Are you the king of the Jews?"* he asked Jesus, struggling to reconcile the appearance of his bound and bleeding captive with the outlandish claim that he made. *"Yes, it is as you say,"* replied Jesus, unashamed of his message as he stood before Rome. Pilate knew he was innocent,[5] but he could not overlook such open defiance against his emperor.[6] Forced to choose between Rome and Revolution, he cravenly chose to do neither. He washed his hands in a feeble abdication of his legal responsibility, and passed the decision to the lynch mob which was gathering at his door. If they wanted their Messiah to die, his soldiers would see it was done. They would dress Jesus with a mock crown, robe and sceptre, and show him exactly what they thought of his claim to be King.

to accuse me, but they followed round Jesus for three years and found no grounds at all.

[3] The phrase *"Son of God"* was also a key Old Testament description for the Messiah in passages such as 2 Samuel 7:14, Psalm 2:7 and 89:26. This is what the Sanhedrin meant when they asked Jesus in Matthew 26:63 to *"Tell us if you are the Christ, the Son of God"*. See also Matthew 16:16; John 1:49; 11:27; 20:31.

[4] They commanded Jesus to *"Prophesy!"* because Deuteronomy 18:15–19 called the Messiah *"the Prophet"*. Even as they called him *"Christ"* and asked him to prophesy, the Jewish leaders were sealing their own guilt.

[5] Matthew shames his Jewish readers in 27:19 by telling them even a pagan could see what they failed to see.

[6] John 19:12.

Then they would nail him to a cross under a placard bearing his crime: *"This is Jesus, the King of the Jews."*

Ultimately, those who passed judgment on Jesus' life were the crowd which gathered round Pilate's courtroom like a pack of hyenas tracking their bleeding prey. They willingly assumed the role which Pilate dared not play, and with all the sober judgment of a lynch mob cried out *"Crucify!"* Jesus had healed their children, fed their families, and told them his message of hope, but they preferred to release the murderer Barabbas than accept the Messiah who came in peace. *"Let his blood be on us and on our children!"* they cried, thinking little about their unthinkable curse. As he died, they mocked him, taunting him again and again with his claim to be the Messiah, *"the Son of God"*.[7] Jesus' Revolution had been put on trial and rejected by a unanimous jury. Six hours later, the man who claimed to be King of kings would be dead.

Yet, astonishingly, the trials which might have destroyed the radical message of Jesus were the very trials which proved it to be true. He only stood before his judges because he chose not to resist them,[8] and he kept silent in the knowledge that just one well-aimed reply was all it would take for him to walk free.[9] His judges could not destroy his Revolution; they merely demonstrated its power to the world. As they blindfolded and beat him, he turned the other cheek in a silent but powerful sermon of love. As they flogged him and offered him mock worship, he forgave his enemies and prayed for those who persecuted him.[10] As they nailed him to a cross and hoisted him up before the crowd, stripped of all covering except his

---

[7] Note how their insults in vv. 40, 42, and 43 are all around him being *"the Son of God"* or *"the King of Israel"*.

[8] Matthew 26:52–56; John 19:10–11.

[9] Jesus remained silent in Matthew 26:63 and 27:12–14 because he knew the effect of his words in 21:23–27 and 22:46. This fulfilled the prophecy about the Messiah's trial in Isaiah 53:7.

[10] Jesus practised what he preached in Matthew 5:39 and 44. Peter explores this further in 1 Peter 2:19–23.

own blood, still he loved, still he forgave, still he demonstrated another way of life. The crucifixion did not destroy King Jesus and his Kingdom Revolution. The cross became a pulpit from which Jesus the Messiah preached once and for all to the world that God's love is greater than humanity's sin, and that neither pain nor injustice nor torture nor even death could ever exhaust the compassion of God towards the ugly rebels who dwell on Planet Earth. Jesus of Nazareth cried out and died, but his radical message had never shone brighter.

This did not go unnoticed, even at the time. As the earth shook with Jesus' death, the Roman centurion and some of his men stopped their mocking and suddenly confessed that *"Surely he was the Son of God!"* As his corpse was taken down from the cross, one of the Jewish Sanhedrin turned his back on his colleagues and came out publicly as a disciple of Jesus the Messiah. For they had seen in Jesus' death the radical truth and death-defying power of the message he had preached. The leaders of the Jewish religion had been exposed as envious hypocrites who cared nothing for justice but only for self. The Roman Empire had been exposed as a spineless false saviour which lusted for power but lacked the character to use it when the world needed it most. But King Jesus had been exposed as the one who loved, forgave, and endured unto death, validating his Revolution with a signature written with his own blood.

The Revolution had been put on trial, and the crushed and crucified King who was laid in Joseph's tomb had won.

Remorse and Repentance
(26:69 – 27:10)

When Judas, who had betrayed him, saw that Jesus
was condemned, he was seized with remorse... Then
he went away and hanged himself.

(Matthew 27:3, 5)

Two men. Two friends. Two betrayals and yet two very different destinies. Simon Peter and Judas Iscariot both renounced their Master on the night before his crucifixion. Judas was convicted and filled with remorse, but only Peter turned remorse into repentance.

In many ways, Judas was the most promising of all the disciples. For a start, he was the only pure Judean among eleven second-rate Jews from *"Galilee of the Gentiles"*.[1] He was also a fine administrator, chosen even over the former tax collector Matthew to look after the disciples' finances. When he slipped out of the upper room partway through the Last Supper, the other disciples did not assume that he was the betrayer whom Jesus had warned was in their midst.[2] He had been too active in healing the sick, driving out demons, raising the dead, and feeding the five thousand for anyone to think him anything less than a wholehearted disciple of Jesus. His credentials were so impeccable that they assumed he had gone on a late-night

---

[1] Isaiah 9:1 and Matthew 4:15 call it this because it was under Gentile rule for over 500 years from 732 BC and then became an international trade route. It was so influenced by the Greek language and culture that Judeans regarded it as an "impure" region. Judas came from Kerioth, a town in the "pure" region of Judea.

[2] John 6:70–71; 13:10–11; Matthew 26:20–25.

errand of mercy.[3] When the Twelve argued on the road over which of them was the greatest, Judas had looked like a strong contender.

But his godly persona was an elaborate façade. Judas' heart had been slowly enveloped by a creeping disappointment with the meek and humble Messiah for whom he had given up everything. On one occasion he stole some of the money which he managed for Jesus and his team – after all, he reasoned, he had personally become one of the deserving poor through his sacrifice for the Gospel – and this one-off act soon turned into habitual theft. When Jesus stubbornly sided with Mary of Bethany's decision to waste a good bottle of imported nard, Judas could bear it no longer and paid a secret visit to the chief priests at the Temple. Enough of this petty siphoning of Jesus' purse! He would betray him once and for all for a lump sum of thirty pieces of silver, the value accorded in Exodus 21:32 to the life of a slave.[4] When Jesus dipped his bread in the Passover dish and offered it to Judas, he gave him a graphic warning that he was like Pharaoh, hardening his heart and choosing a terrible fate. Judas ignored the warning, took the bread, and *"Satan entered him"*.[5] He led the troops to the Garden of Gethsemane, kissed Jesus as a poignant act of treachery, and then watched as they led him away to his death.

Unlike the chief priests, Judas quickly regretted his evil deed. Matthew tells us that *"He was seized with remorse and returned the thirty silver coins to the chief priests and the elders.*

---

[3] John 12:5–6; 13:27–29.

[4] Matthew 26:15. Judas did not realize it, but this also fulfilled Exodus 30:11–16, which allowed the Hebrews to ransom a person's life by paying silver coins as atonement money.

[5] John 13:26–27. Matthew and Mark only tell us that Judas dipped his bread in the bowl with Jesus, but John tells us that Jesus switched Judas' bread with his own in fulfilment of Psalm 41:9. The Passover bowl contained bitter sauce, which represented slavery in Egypt – a graphic picture of the choice which lay before Judas.

'I have sinned,' he said, 'for I have betrayed innocent blood.'"[6] His regret was genuine, and he flung his money down on the Temple floor as a dramatic expression of remorse. He confessed his sin to the priests and sought atonement at the Temple, but he dared not look for forgiveness in the one place he could find it. He refused to take his sin to God himself, and in torment he rushed out and hanged himself.[7]

He reminds me of a man I once met at the theatre. Since he was on his own, my wife and I struck up a conversation with him, and at the end of the evening I gave him a Gospel tract with my phone number on it. Several months later, on New Year's Eve, the phone rang and it was him. He remembered our conversation and told me he had rung because he knew I was a Christian. *"What happens to wicked people when they die?"* he asked me, before confessing a catalogue of vice which weighed heavily on his conscience. *"Is there any hope for a person like me?"* I explained the Gospel down the phone, and a few days later spent an evening at his flat, sharing with him the good news about a dying Messiah and a God who does not treat the wicked as they deserve. After several hours of discussion, he ended the evening with an agonized exclamation that, *"What you say makes sense, but I just can't believe that God would forgive someone like me!"* He was deeply convicted of sin, but refused to combine it with faith.

That was the great difference between Judas Iscariot and his fellow turncoat, Peter. For all his tormented conviction of sin, Matthew tells us that Judas was seized by *remorse* but not *repentance*.[8] He bitterly regretted his love of Mammon and his

---

[6] Matthew 27:9–10 quotes a freestyle mixture of Zechariah 11:12–13 and Jeremiah 19:1–3 and 32:6–9 to show us that this fulfilled Old Testament prophecy. He only names Jeremiah, as the greater prophet of the two.

[7] Acts 1:18–19 adds the detail that his body later fell from the rope with such force that his stomach burst open and his intestines spilled out.

[8] The Greek word *metameleia* means literally *care-after-the-event*, and therefore means *regret* or *remorse*. It is quite different from the word *metanoia*, which means literally *change-of-mind* or *repentance*.

willingness to sell out his Master, but he lacked the faith to take his regret to the Lord and find forgiveness and restoration. He ran away from God instead of to God, wishing he could change his past but unwilling to believe for the future. He had watched Jesus stoop to embrace and save prostitutes, tax collectors, lepers, and the demonized, and yet he refused to believe that God would forgive and save him by that same grace in spite of his sin. He had heard Jesus' promise in 20:28 that he would pay a ransom-price for sin at the cost of his own blood, but he chose to find solace in hanging himself from a tree even as the Messiah hung on the tree of Calvary in his place.

Dr Martyn Lloyd-Jones puts it this way: *"That is the difference between remorse and repentance. The man who has not repented, but who is only experiencing remorse, when he realises he has done something against God, avoids God... tries to get away from God, to avoid him at all costs."*[9] Judas ran away from Jesus instead of to Jesus, and chose remorse instead of repentance. He refused to believe that the Messiah he had betrayed might return his kiss of betrayal with a loving kiss of forgiveness. He refused the way of grace and paved his own way to hell.[10]

But we are not like Judas, or the man I met at the theatre. We are like Peter, who turned bitter tears of regret into tears of repentance and faith. He who cursed himself with hellfire dared to believe that Christ's blood-bought forgiveness could yet atone for his foul sin.[11] He ran to Jesus' empty tomb, he jumped eagerly into Lake Galilee and swam towards him, and he ate a shared breakfast with him in faith that through God's grace he might yet be restored and forgiven and cleansed.[12]

---

[9] This quote comes from one of Lloyd-Jones's sermons in 1949 on David's prayer of repentance in Psalm 51.

[10] Matthew 26:24 and John 17:12 both make it clear that Judas went to hell.

[11] The word *katanathematizō* in Matthew 26:74 refers the most serious of Jewish oaths (see also Acts 23:14). Peter's third denial of Jesus literally *cursed himself with being cut off from the People of God and going to hell.*

[12] John 20:1–8; 21:7–19.

It is not enough for a person to feel convicted of sin. Even Judas Iscariot felt that. We must combine conviction with faith in the love of Christ, the power of his cross, and the all-encompassing reach of his Gospel. Only this faith can change regret and remorse into saving repentance. Peter and Judas were both friends and betrayers, but only one of them had faith: *"Godly sorrow brings repentance that leads to salvation and leaves no regret, but worldly sorrow brings death."*[13]

---

[13] 2 Corinthians 7:10.

Perspective (27:46)

About the ninth hour Jesus cried out in a loud voice, "Eloi, Eloi, lama sabachthani?" – which means "My God, my God, why have you forsaken me?"

(Matthew 27:46)

If you ever doubt that reading the Bible makes a difference, then learn from Jesus. As he buckled under the weight of the world's sin, he drew strength from the Scriptures he had learned. No one can know the depths of pain and torment which Jesus endured on the cross, but Matthew at least wants us to know how he did so. It was the Word of God which gave him perspective to see glorious victory in the face of defeat, and blessed assurance in the face of abandonment.

Jesus had been reading the Psalms in the run-up to his crucifixion. He quoted from them four times in the previous four days.[1] They gave him strength when the Jewish leaders rejected him, and they upheld his claim to be the Messiah in the face of opposition and doubt. But it was his fifth quotation from the Psalms – an agonized cry from the cross – which gave strength when he needed it most. As blood ran from the thorns in his forehead and into his eyes, blurring his natural vision, Jesus saw the true perspective of Scripture and cried out with triumphant faith: *"Eloi, Eloi, lama sabachthani?"*

You might be confused by that statement. How can the Aramaic words for *"My God, my God, why have you forsaken me?"* be an exclamation of faith? How can they be anything other than

---

[1] Psalm 8:2 in 21:16, Psalm 118:22–23 in 21:42, Psalm 110:1 in 22:44, and Psalm 118:26 in 23:39.

a cry of despair? Jesus spoke twenty-one recorded prayers in the gospels, and in all but this one he calls God his intimate *"Father"*. Surely this prayer which addresses him merely as *"God"* is an accusation that he deserted him when he needed him most? How can this be a prayer of faith and of triumph? It's all to do with the divine perspective which God's People must draw from the pages of Scripture. Let me backtrack a little.

Although Jesus spoke those words in Aramaic, they are a translation of the first line of Psalm 22. Remember that this is David's clearest Psalm about the Suffering Messiah, and you will begin to see what Jesus is doing here. He is meditating on the promises of that Psalm as his only companion in his lonely and terrible ordeal.

He was thirsty, so he remembered verse 15: *"My tongue sticks to the roof of my mouth."* He was stripped naked, and the soldiers drew lots for his clothes, so he remembered verses 17 to 18: *"I can count all my bones; people stare and gloat over me. They divide my garments among them and cast lots for my clothing."*[2] He was nailed to the cross and hoisted up to hang there in excruciating pain, so he remembered verses 14 and 16: *"All my bones are out of joint... A band of evil men has encircled me, they have pierced my hands and feet."* Any normal man would have surrendered to the pain, given up his Revolution, and succumbed to despair, but not Jesus. He was no ordinary man. And with the perspective of Scripture to strengthen his resolve, he saw each fresh attack as the fulfilment of David's 1,000-year-old prophecy. He knew that his Father's plan was working. The cross would not be the end of the story.

When the crowds insulted him, he remembered verses 6 and 7: *"But I am a worm and not a man, scorned by men and despised by the people. All who see me mock me; they hurl insults,*

---

[2] A few late manuscripts make a specific link back to Psalm 22:18, but this is almost certainly a copyist's addition based on John 19:24. Matthew expects the quotation in v. 46 to be enough to point his Jewish readers back to the whole of Psalm 22.

shaking their heads." When the Jewish leaders mocked him, he could hardly believe his ears. They had unwittingly quoted the words of verse 8: *"He trusts in the Lord; let the Lord rescue him. Let him deliver him, since he delights in him"*! They meant to break his spirit and gloat over his death, but they encouraged him more than the words of a friend. His Father's plan was working so well that even his enemies were dancing to his tune! If verse 8 had been fulfilled, then so too would verses 4, 30, and 31: *"In you our fathers put their trust; they trusted and you delivered them... Posterity will serve him; future generations will be told about the Lord. They will proclaim his vindication to a people yet unborn."*[3]

Without these Scriptures, Jesus' physical, emotional, and spiritual torment would have been unbearable. Yet through these Scriptures, Jesus saw his Father's perspective and rejoiced with hope as he drew his final breaths. For the first time in his life, he felt the Father withdraw his presence from him and lost the sense of love and approval which had echoed forth in 3:17 and 17:5. As he became the sponge which soaked up all the sin and filth of the human race,[4] Jesus felt the horror which pervades hell, the place of *"outer darkness"*. He cried out *"My God, my God, why did you forsake me?"*[5] but even as he did so, his cry of horror was filled with hope. The Father is still *"my God"* and not someone else's, since he who had fulfilled verse 1 would also fulfil verse 24: *"He has not despised or disdained the suffering of the afflicted one; he has not hidden his face from him but has listened to his cry for help."* He had forsaken him, but only to redeem the nations of the world through the ransom-price

---

[3] The Hebrew word *tsedaqah* means either *righteousness* or *vindication*. As Jesus died a criminal's death as the unjust victim of a lynch mob, *vindication* was especially on his mind.

[4] 2 Corinthians 5:21; Galatians 3:13.

[5] The Greek word *enkatelipes* is an aorist rather than perfect tense, and therefore refers to a sudden sense of separation from the Father. It probably means literally *"why did you?"* rather than *"why have you?"*

of his dear Son's blood. In the words of verses 27 and 28: *"All the ends of the earth will remember and turn to the Lord and all the families of nations will bow down before him, for dominion belongs to the Lord and he rules over the nations."*

Matthew does not tell us what Jesus shouted in verse 50 as he gave up his spirit, but John 19:30 fills in the blank. John tells us that Jesus lifted up his head in triumph and, even as he died, raised the victory-cry of Psalm 22:31: *"He has done it!"* or *"It is finished!"*[6] So do you see now why the cry of Matthew 27:46 was a cry of victory and not defeat? Do you see why Jesus' knowledge of Scripture gave him true perspective in his suffering and transformed his grief into glory, his tears into triumph and his death into deliverance?

And do you also see how important it is for you and me to study Scripture, to learn Scripture, to meditate on Scripture, and gain true perspective from what we read? Jesus led the way for us, showing us that through the Word of God we can overcome in the midst of the darkest hour. Let's follow his lead and prepare our perspective for the trials which lie ahead.

---

[6] The last two words of Psalm 22 in Hebrew are *kiy asah*, which means literally *"Because it is done!"*

The Curtain (27:51)

At that moment the curtain of the temple was torn in two from top to bottom.

(Matthew 27:51)

God is very good at painting pictures. You've probably guessed that from every sunset, night sky, and creature that you've seen. But he also loves to paint Gospel pictures which reinforce the message of his Kingdom. He is the God of the Word and the God of illustration, and as his bleeding Son died he painted a beautiful picture of salvation.

He began painting it in the desert sands around Mount Sinai nearly 1,500 years beforehand. For forty days and nights, alone on top of the mountain, Moses listened to God's description of the picture he wanted to paint through him. A man-made tent called a Tabernacle, in which the living God would camp among his People. The Tabernacle's inner room would be his dwelling-place and throne-room, his permanent address and command-centre on the earth. Five hundred years later, God told Solomon to upgrade the portable Tabernacle into a magnificent Temple, but the same glorious picture remained: God had set a place where people could find him and bring their requests to his Throne.

God painted his Tabernacle and Temple with a brush labelled *presence*, but he also used another one labelled *holiness*. He dwelt in the midst of his People, but he would not let them think he was like them. The inner room, or Most Holy Place, was shut off by a finely embroidered four-inch-thick curtain.[1] It was

---

[1] The Jewish Mishnah tells us in Shekalim 8:4–5 that the curtain was a handbreadth thick.

out of bounds to all but the high priest, and even he could only enter it on one day of the year. The outer room, or Holy Place, was also shut off by another four-inch-thick curtain, and was out of bounds to all but a select group of priests.[2] Even the inner courtyard around the Temple building was barred to all but the Jews. God was present in power, but too holy to receive his People at close quarters. A series of barriers between them and God reminded them of the fatal result if a sinful person dared enter the presence of the holy God.

The colours of *presence* and *holiness* sat awkwardly together on the canvas, which is why God used a third colour between them with a brush labelled *blood sacrifice*. As Jesus confirmed in the Garden of Gethsemane, there can be no forgiveness for sin without the shedding of innocent blood in our place.[3] Therefore a massive bronze altar dominated the courtyard in front of the Tabernacle and Temple, and no one could enter without shedding sacrificial blood en route. Morning and evening, the altar ran red with blood, and on the Day of Atonement – the one day of the year when the high priest could enter the Most Holy Place – this blood was needed more than ever.[4] Three brushes – *presence*, *holiness*, and *blood sacrifice* – together formed the tricolour picture of Old Covenant grace. Then on the day that Jesus died, God changed the picture forever.

Gentiles tend to read verse 51 and express amazement that a mighty earthquake should tear rocks apart. Jewish readers are more shocked by the first half of the verse than the second.[5] At the exact moment that Jesus gave up his spirit, the Temple

---

[2] Matthew is not very clear which of these two curtains was split in 27:51. The New Testament normally talks about them as if they were one single "veil" between God and man.

[3] See Hebrews 9:22.

[4] Leviticus 16; 23:26–32; Numbers 29:7–11.

[5] Matthew uses the Greek word *schizō* to describe both the *splitting* of the rocks and the *splitting* of the curtain in order to emphasize that each was as miraculous as the other.

curtain which protected God's dwelling-place and throne-room from unholy eyes was torn apart in one dramatic gesture. It was not torn from bottom to top, as if the human race had paved a way into God's presence, but from top to bottom as a downward brush-stroke which spoke of God paving a way on our behalf. It was not just torn slightly to be stitched up later, but all the way down as a permanent statement of grace. Jesus Christ had painted all over God's Old Covenant picture with a paintbrush dipped in his own blood.

The writer to the Hebrews explains this picture for the benefit of his Jewish readers:

> *Christ is the mediator of a new covenant... now that he has died to set them free from the sins committed under the first covenant... Therefore, brothers, since we have confidence to enter the Most Holy Place by the blood of Jesus, by a new and living way opened for us through the curtain, that is his body... let us draw near to God with a sincere heart in full assurance of faith, having our hearts sprinkled to cleanse us from a guilty conscience.*[6]

They say that a picture speaks a thousand words, and God's finished New Covenant picture certainly does. It speaks powerfully of a God who is so holy that nothing but the blood of his Son could ever bridge the gulf between our sin, guilt, and filth on the one side of the curtain and his pure and sinless presence on the other side. It speaks of a perfect once-for-all blood sacrifice, which grants us total forgiveness, complete acceptance, and unbroken access to his dwelling-place and throne-room. It speaks of his death-defying longing to dwell closely and intimately with the people he created.

It speaks of something more too. The curtain was not just torn in two to let us *in* to God, but to let him *out* to us. Because of

---

[6] Hebrews 9:15; 10:19–22.

Jesus, the *"new and living way"*, we can not only step into God's presence, but also receive his promise to pour his presence into us! Paul writes to the Corinthians that, *"We are the Most Holy Place of the living God. As God has said: 'I will live with them and walk among them, and I will be their God and they will be my people.'"[7]* When Jesus ascended to heaven, he received the promised Holy Spirit from the Father as a blood-bought gift for his People, which would turn them into God's new dwelling-places and throne-rooms on the earth. No more curtains, no more blood-sacrifices, and no more barriers between us. Just God dwelling with us and us dwelling with God.

Act Five of Matthew's gospel therefore ends not with the falling of a curtain, but with the tearing of one. These five chapters of Kingdom Judgment come to a close with God's powerful picture of Kingdom mercy. He will judge those who reject his New Covenant – as the rubble of Jerusalem's Temple would very soon proclaim – but he will also lavish grace upon all who receive it by faith. He will permit them to dwell in the glory of his presence, and he himself will dwell in them as his New Covenant Temple, all over the world.

Stand back and enjoy God's great masterpiece. It's a picture he painted for you.

---

[7] 2 Corinthians 6:16. The Greek word *naos* refers not just to the *Temple* in general but specifically to the *Most Holy Place*.

Epilogue:

The Proclamation of the Kingdom

Alive (28:1–15)

The angel said to the women, "Do not be afraid, for I know that you are looking for Jesus, who was crucified. He is not here; he has risen, just as he said."

(Matthew 28:5–6)

This is the part in the story where Matthew wants you to doubt. In fact, he gives you permission to do so. As he draws his five-act drama to a close with a short concluding chapter, he wants your wholehearted faith or your considered refusal. What he doesn't want is the dithering discipleship which so many mistake for genuine Christianity. That's why he tells us in verse 17 that some of the disciples *"doubted"* Jesus after his resurrection. He wants to make it easy for us to search our own hearts and to count the cost of his message, because Jesus is after our everything. It was not wrong for some of the Eleven to doubt him when he gave them the Great Commission, because Jesus' call to lay down our lives for his Kingdom Revolution deserves weighty consideration.

Some Christians feel uncomfortable with the idea of doubting their faith, but that's the very reason why so much second-rate obedience and bargain-basement discipleship masquerades as conversion to Christ. The message of the Kingdom demands our complete surrender or none at all, and only those who have grappled with this truth are ready to pour out their lives in its cause. The empty tomb meant that the lives of the Jews, the Romans, the women, and the disciples could never be the same again. They needed to stop and doubt and consider and decide, because the resurrection was not a private affair. It was the public declaration that Jesus Christ is supreme King of the universe and that we need to lay down our lives in his service.

Non-Christian readers tend to assume that they do not live by faith at all, but Matthew shows us that unbelievers are never *non*-believers. The Jews and the Romans did not try to suppress the message of the empty tomb because they had no beliefs, but because they were so blinkered in their beliefs that they refused to doubt them even in the face of incontrovertible evidence. I find Tim Keller very helpful on this point:

> *All doubts, however sceptical and cynical they may seem, are really a set of alternate beliefs. You cannot doubt Belief A except from a position of faith in Belief B. For example, if you doubt Christianity because "There can't be just **one** true religion", you must recognise that this statement is itself an act of belief. If you went to the Middle East and said, "There can't be just one true religion," nearly everyone would say, "Why not?" The reasons you doubt Christianity's Belief A is because you hold unprovable Belief B. Every doubt, therefore, is based on a leap of faith.*[1]

Matthew urges his readers to doubt their doubts as much as their beliefs, because *doubt* can save us from *unbelief*.

The Romans tried to *ignore* the empty tomb, but doubt quickly exposes their story as unbelief. If the soldiers had been asleep on their watch, Roman law demanded that they pay for it with their lives. But the governor let them walk free.[2]

The Jews tried to *deny* the resurrection, but doubt very quickly exposes their unbelief too. How could the disciples

---

[1] Timothy Keller, *The Reason for God* (2008).
[2] Acts 12:18–19. This law was also the reason the Roman guards acted as they did in Acts 16:27 and 27:42.

have stolen the body from a sealed tomb under Roman guard?[3] Even if they did, why would they concoct a story like Matthew 28, which reports that two women were the first eyewitnesses to the resurrection, even though the testimony of women was considered suspect in first-century law courts? Matthew must have been tempted to change his story to gloss over this unpalatable fact, but he didn't. The only logical reason for him to tell the story this way is that it's how it really happened.

Doubt also exposes the (relatively modern) speculation that the tomb was never empty at all. The Jews and the Romans did not even try to deny that Jesus' body was missing, because they knew it was gone. When Peter preached in Jerusalem seven weeks later on the day of Pentecost that Jesus had been raised from the dead, no one replied, *"Jesus risen? Are you mad?! His corpse is still there in the tomb!"* Instead, 3,000 believed and were baptized, and by the time Matthew wrote his gospel there were over 50,000 Christians in Jerusalem.[4] Even outside of Jerusalem, Paul could challenge his hearers to believe in the resurrection of Jesus because *"It was not done in a corner"*.[5] Doubt is a friend, not a foe, when considering the challenge of God's Kingdom Revolution.

But if, after all our doubting, we keep coming back to the powerful conclusion that Jesus did indeed come back to life, our lives can never be the same again. Some people refuse point blank to believe in the resurrection, but this is not doubt but stubborn unbelief. It is like Herod in Oscar Wilde's play *Salome*, when he hears that Jesus is going round raising the dead. *"I do not wish him to do that,"* he complains. *"I forbid him to do that. I allow no man to raise the dead. This man must be found and*

---

[3] Matthew 27:62–66.

[4] James, the half-brother of Jesus, was a sceptic who was converted when he saw him after his resurrection (John 7:5; 1 Corinthians 15:7). He says in Acts 21:20 that many *muriades*, or *tens of thousands*, of Jews had been saved in Jerusalem.

[5] Acts 26:26.

told that I forbid him to raise the dead."[6] We all have a little Herod inside of us, warring against the idea of resurrection and refusing to consider the implications it would bring. But the facts will simply not yield to our petty protestations. Jesus Christ has been raised from the dead and is now vindicated, glorified, and enthroned as Lord of the universe.

The word Matthew uses for *doubting* in verse 17 is *distazō*, the same word he used in 14:31 to describe Peter *wavering between two opinions* and sinking underwater. Matthew has encouraged you to doubt in this chapter because he wants you to put his gospel down with only one opinion left, not two. Will you live by the story circulated by the Romans and Jews? Will you live by the stubborn unbelief of the God-hating Western world? Or will you live by the thrilling conclusion which caused Matthew and friends to live, work, and die for the sake of their risen King?

Paul told the Romans that *"His unique identity as Son of God was shown by the Spirit when Jesus was raised from the dead, setting him apart as the Messiah, our Master."*[7]

The risen Lord Jesus deserves our everything – beyond a shadow of a doubt.

---

[6] Herod is reacting to news that Jesus has raised Jairus' daughter to life, but we can react the same way to his own resurrection.

[7] Romans 1:4, paraphrased in *The Message*.

The Great Commission (28:16–20)

THE PROCLAMATION OF THE KINGDOM

*Then Jesus came to them and said, "All authority in
heaven and on earth has been given to me. Therefore
go and make disciples of all nations."*

(Matthew 28:18–19)

If all Matthew's gospel makes you want to do is worship, you
haven't understood his gospel at all. Don't misunderstand me:
We mustn't do less than worship Jesus – verses 9 and 17 remind
us of that – but worshipping him is just not enough. That's
why Matthew mentions only two of Jesus' ten resurrection
appearances and completely fails to mention his ascension.
He doesn't want us to finish his gospel and think that worship
is a substitute for obedience. Instead, he closes abruptly with
the verses which have since become known as the Great
Commission. As the curtain falls on Matthew's Gospel drama,
he twists the final spotlight on to the role which we must play.

Matthew has the same heart as the great missionary James
Hudson Taylor. On Sunday morning, 25th June 1865, Taylor found
himself in church in the English seaside resort of Brighton.

> *As the full congregation rose to sing the last hymn, Taylor
> looked around. Pew upon pew of prosperous, bearded
> merchants, shopkeepers, visitors; demure wives in
> bonnets and crinolines, scrubbed children trained to hide
> their impatience; the atmosphere of smug piety sickened
> him. He seized his hat and left. "Unable to bear the
> sight of a congregation of a thousand or more Christian*

262

people rejoicing in their own security, while millions were perishing for lack of knowledge, I wandered out on the sands alone, in great spiritual agony."[1]

Jesus loves it when we worship him, but he loves it even more when we obey him.[2] He has an important task for us to do. He tells his worshipping disciples that his death and resurrection have completely defeated every pretender to his throne, and that now it is time to assert his Kingdom victory across the earth. Reminding them yet again of Daniel's famous vision of the "one-like-a-Son-of-Man", he tells them that what Daniel saw in the future has now finally taken place: *"All authority in heaven and on earth has been given to me."*[3] On the cross he wore a mocking crown of thorns, but nobody is laughing any more. The vindicated Son of God has been crowned with all authority, and now *the nations are his inheritance, the ends of the earth his possession.*[4]

It is easy as Christians to reduce the scope of the Gospel to our own lives instead of to the world. But think about it. If Jesus is truly King of kings and Lord of lords, this affects every nation on the earth. Romans and Russians, Carthaginians and Canadians, Armenians and Americans all need to bow at his feet. If he is truly the only sacrifice for sin and the only way of salvation, this is as important news on the streets of Riyadh and Hanoi as it is on the streets of Jerusalem or Rome or New York. Matthew stresses this by ending his gospel not with a Jewish genealogy like the one with which he began, but with a commission to go to all nations. In fact, the commission is not

---

[1] John Pollock in his biography *Hudson Taylor and Maria* (1962). I'm not too sure why Taylor refers to the *sands* of Brighton beach. I go there often and, nowadays at least, the beach is pebbly, not sandy.

[2] 1 Samuel 15:22.

[3] Note that *edothē* is an aorist tense and means literally that all authority *has been given* to Jesus as a definitive one-off act. He is not just describing who he is, but what his work on the cross has achieved.

[4] Psalm 2:8.

just to <u>make disciples *in* all nations, but to make</u> disciples *of* all nations. Jesus Christ is the victorious Messiah, and no corner of any nation is exempt from the call to submit to his Kingdom.

If the Great Commission had finished there, it would have been very exciting for the disciples. Their Lord and Master the sovereign ruler of all nations. The Messiah whom they abandoned in death was now raised to sit on the Throne of the universe. He had fulfilled the Old Testament prophecies and had given them fuel for a lifetime of worship. But the commission didn't finish there. Jesus calls us to *obey* as well as worship: *"All authority in heaven and on earth has been given to me. Therefore [you] go!"*

Christ's Kingdom would not come on the earth through the trumpet fanfare of angels, but through the diligent proclamation of his Gospel message through his ragged and unspectacular group of devoted disciples. If you're not sure how daunting this felt to eleven Galileans in the comfort of their own backyard, note how Matthew describes the 64-square-mile Sea of Galilee. The cosmopolitan Luke calls it a mere *lake*, but for Matthew and his untravelled friends it was a *sea*.[5] The Great Commission was terrifying for Jesus' disciples. It's terrifying for us all.

As Hudson Taylor walked along the beach at Brighton, he was tormented by the size of the Great Commission alongside the limits of his own strength. What if he led a band of willing volunteers to inland China and *"in the midst of the dangers, difficulties and trials which would necessarily be connected with such a work, some who were comparatively inexperienced Christians might break down, and bitterly reproach me for having encouraged them to undertake an enterprise for which they are not equal"*? And yet, *"A million a month were dying in that land, dying without God. This was burned into my very soul. For two or three months the conflict was intense. I scarcely slept*

---

[5] Contrast Matthew 4:18 and 15:29 with Luke 5:1 and 8:26. The commission to go into all the world was terrifying for this group of untravelled Galileans. In John 20:19 they even locked their doors in Jerusalem!

night or day more than an hour at a time, and feared I should lose my reason." Finally, on the beach, he remembered the passage of Scripture which he had heard before leaving the church in disgust: *"Why, if we are obeying the Lord, the responsibility rests* **with him**, *not with us!* **Thou**, *Lord!* **Thou** *shalt have the burden. All the responsibility lies on Thee, Lord Jesus! I surrender. The consequences rest with Thee".*[6] Hudson Taylor had learned the lesson of Jesus' light and easy yoke, and he returned to China with a team of missionaries who would win a nation for Christ.

Jesus ends his Great Commission with a promise to us that he really will bear the burden of extending his rule through no-hopers like us. He does not split his disciples up into "evangelists" or "pastors", but simply tells them all to go because *"Surely I am with you always, to the very end of the age".*[7] Evangelism is not difficult, it is impossible, and our success relies not on our own power but on his. *All* authority belongs to Jesus, which means that Caesar, sin, and Satan himself have no grounds to resist the power of his Gospel in the hands of his messengers. Satan will resist us with all his might, but only as the desperate last stand of a disarmed fighter and defeated foe. Jesus *will* see people saved into the Kingdom of God from every nation, tribe, and language, as his People turn their worship into radical obedience to his Great Commission.[8]

I was catapulted into my own part in Christ's mission by hearing the words of an old Keith Green song:

> *Jesus commands us to go, but we go the other way.*
> *So He carries the burden alone, while His children are*
> *busy at play,*
> *Feeling so called to stay.*

---

[6] Taken from Pollock and also from Howard Taylor's *Hudson Taylor and the China Inland Mission* (1918).

[7] He literally speaks of the *consummation* of the age, referring to the fullness of the Kingdom at the end of this age. The final words of Matthew's gospel therefore remind us to proclaim the Gospel with that Day in mind.

[8] Revelation 7:9.

Oh, how God grieves and believes that the world can't be
saved,
Unless the ones he's appointed obey
His command and his stand for the world, that he loved
more than life.
Oh he died, and he cries out tonight.

Jesus commands us to go. It should be the exception if
we stay.
It's no wonder we're moving so slow, when God's
children refuse to obey,
Feeling so called to stay.[9]

Do not get distracted: the Revolution has begun, and you have a role to play.

---

[9] Keith Green "Jesus Commands Us To Go!" on Pretty Good Records, (1984).

Conclusion:
The Revolution Has Begun

As Jesus went on from there, he saw a man named Matthew sitting at the tax collector's booth. "Follow me," he told him, and Matthew got up and followed him.

(Matthew 9:9)

You wouldn't have liked Levi, the weaselly little tax collector who manned the tollbooth on the Capernaum road. Levi was the lowest of the low. He was a collector of custom duties on the busy trade route from Damascus to Egypt, a member of that notorious clique of state-sanctioned highwaymen who topped up Caesar's taxes with inflated surcharges of their own.[1] It wasn't enough that Levi and his friends were a treacherous cog in the voracious Roman tax machine. They had become parasites in their own right, feeding on the blood and sweat of their hard-working neighbours. One day, when the Messiah came and broke the yoke of Roman oppression, people like Levi would get what was coming to them. And no one would be sorry.

The Jewish leaders made no attempt to hide their hatred of him. To them he was no better than a common murderer or thief. They barred him from their synagogues and refused to take his money in their offerings.[2] As far as the rabbis were concerned, he had sold his soul to Caesar and to silver, and had placed himself beyond the reach of God's redemption.

---

[1] Income taxes tended to be fixed, but customs duties tended to be arbitrary and offered great scope for abuse.

[2] Nedarim 3:4; Bava Kamma 10:1, both in the Jewish Mishnah.

Except for one rabbi, that is. Jesus of Nazareth was a different kind of rabbi, more interested in exposing the sins of the teachers of the law than he was in picking on the tax collectors. When Jesus spoke, Levi listened, and the more he listened the more he dared to dream. This miracle-working rabbi seemed more at home with the prostitutes than with the priests, and he was fast gaining a reputation for consorting with drunkards, cheats, low-lifes, and tax collectors like him. The locust-eating hermit, John the Baptist – the only man in Israel whom the Pharisees seemed to hate even more than Levi and his cronies – had hailed Jesus as the long-awaited Messiah. Could this man truly be the promised Jewish King who would outshine and outlast Caesar? If so, would he really extend mercy to a sinner like Levi? The traitor from Capernaum allowed himself to dream and hope and believe.

One day, Levi's dreams came true. The rabbi came calling at his tollbooth. He bent across the table and, across the stacks of Roman coins, looked Levi in the eye and said: *"Follow me."* Levi returned the rabbi's gaze. His eyes shifted from the coins to the carpenter, from the face of Caesar to the face of the Saviour. Jesus was asking him to join his Revolution, to leave behind the Empire and enter into his Kingdom. Levi leaped to his feet and left his money-laden table behind. He was working for a new King now. The Revolution had begun.

The first thing Levi did was to throw a party.[3] He filled his house with tax collectors and introduced them to the rabbi who had given him a new start. Levi told them that he had a new name now – *Matthew*, meaning *Gift-of-the-Lord* – as a mark of the lavish grace which God had poured upon his life. Matthew had joined the Revolution, and his new name spoke of a new life to come.[4]

Matthew would be flogged, imprisoned, and eventually

---

[3] Matthew 9:9–13.

[4] Mark 2:13–17 and Luke 5:27–32 call him *Levi*, but Matthew 9:9–13 calls him *Matthew*. It is therefore not unreasonable to assume that Jesus gave Levi a

martyred because he sided with King Jesus on that fateful day on the Capernaum road. He would give his life to proclaim the message of the Kingdom in the pagan lands of Persia, Parthia, and modern-day Georgia.[5] But, before he died, he would write a Gospel account of the life of Jesus. He would write it as a revolutionary pamphlet which called many others to leave everything, just as he did, to follow the Servant King from Galilee.

Millions of people across the past 2,000 years have read Matthew's gospel and laid down their lives for the Revolution of Jesus Christ, but I want to end this book by telling you about just one of them.

C.T. Studd was one of the greatest sportsmen of his generation. He played for the England cricket team at The Oval in August 1882 in the infamous match which gave birth to the Ashes.[6] He was a Cambridge-educated sporting legend and fabulously wealthy, until one day he read a portion of Matthew's gospel. The words of 16:26 sank deep into his heart: *"What good will it be for a man if he gains the whole world, yet forfeits his soul?"* Studd was undone: *"Either I had to be a thief and keep what wasn't mine, or else I had to give up everything to God. When I came to see that Jesus Christ had died for me, it didn't seem hard to give up all for him."* He gave away his fortune and told Hudson Taylor that he would be one of the men he had prayed for on Brighton beach. He would lay down English fame and fortune to preach the Gospel throughout inland China. His

---

new name by grace when he became his disciple, just as he did Simon Peter in John 1:42.

[5] He probably died in a town called Ethiopia in the Caucasus – not to be confused with the African nation.

[6] For non-cricket fans, this was the match where Australia beat England for the first time on English soil. A mock obituary in *The Sporting Times* stated that English cricket had died and *"the body will be cremated and the ashes taken to Australia"*. The English and Australian cricket teams have played each other for the Ashes ever since. C.T. Studd was the last English batsman left at the crease.

decision shocked and challenged a nation, but he laughed at their surprise that he gave up everything for the Kingdom of God: *"I knew that cricket would not last, and honour would not last, and nothing in this world would last, but it was worthwhile living for the world to come... If Jesus Christ be God and died for me, then no sacrifice can be too great for me to make for him."*[7]

This is what it means to be a Christian – living as an all-in, sold-out, gloves-off radical in Christ's Kingdom army. Make no mistake: Jesus of Nazareth sparked the greatest Revolution the world has ever seen, and he deserves nothing less than your total devotion. He comes to you as you finish this book, and gazes into your eyes across the table of your piled-high hopes and dreams. He invites you to play your part in his Kingdom by giving you the same invitation which he gave to Matthew so many years ago: *"Follow me."*

This is King Jesus. This is the long-awaited Messiah. This is the only true Lord of your life. So come. Leave behind your excuses, your compromises, and your half-hearted religion. Jesus the Messiah is calling you. The Revolution has begun.

---

[7] Norman Grubb in his biography *C.T. Studd: Cricketer and Pioneer* (1933).

OTHER BOOKS IN THE
STRAIGHT TO THE HEART SERIES:

ISBN 978 1 85424 989 0

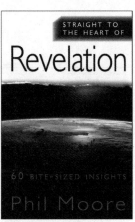

ISBN 978 1 85424 990 6

For more information please go to **www.philmoorebooks.com** or
www.lionhudson.com.